PSAI

foi

EVERYᴜɴʟ

PART 1

OLD TESTAMENT FOR EVERYONE
John Goldingay

Genesis for Everyone, Part 1
Genesis for Everyone, Part 2
Exodus and Leviticus for Everyone
Numbers and Deuteronomy for Everyone
Joshua, Judges, and Ruth for Everyone
1 and 2 Samuel for Everyone
1 and 2 Kings for Everyone
1 and 2 Chronicles for Everyone
Ezra, Nehemiah, and Esther for Everyone
Job for Everyone
Psalms for Everyone, Part 1

PSALMS

for

EVERYONE

PART 1
PSALMS 1–72

JOHN
GOLDINGAY

WESTMINSTER
JOHN KNOX PRESS
LOUISVILLE • KENTUCKY

© 2013 John Goldingay

First published in the United States of America in 2013 by
Westminster John Knox Press
100 Witherspoon Street
Louisville, KY 40202

First published in Great Britain in 2013 by
Society for Promoting Christian Knowledge
36 Causton Street
London SW1P 4ST

13 14 15 16 17 18 19 20 21 22—10 9 8 7 6 5 4 3 2 1

Unless otherwise indicated, Scripture quotations are the author's own translation.

Cover design by Lisa Buckley
Cover illustration: ©istockphoto.com

Library of Congress Cataloging-in-Publication Data

Goldingay, John.
   Psalms for everyone / John Goldingay.
      volumes cm. — (Old testament for everyone)
   ISBN 978-0-664-23383-9 (pbk.)
   1. Bible. Psalms—Commentaries.   I. Title.
   BS1430.53.G655   2013
   223'.2077—dc23

                              2013003067

Most Westminster John Knox Press books are available at special quantity
discounts when purchased in bulk by corporations, organizations, and special-
interest groups. For more information, please e-mail SpecialSales@wjkbooks.com.

CONTENTS

CONTENTS

ACKNOWLEDGMENTS

The translation at the beginning of each chapter (and in other biblical quotations) is my own. I have already translated the Psalms in an earlier commentary (*Psalms*, three volumes, published by Baker Academic in 2006–2008); although I started from scratch for this book, sometimes I have adapted phrases from that commentary. I have stuck closer to the Hebrew than modern translations often do when they are designed for reading in church so that you can see more precisely what the text says. Thus although I prefer to use gender-inclusive language, I have let the translation stay gendered if inclusivizing it would obscure whether the text was using singular or plural—in other words, the translation often uses "he" where in my own writing I would say "they" or "he or she." Sometimes I have added words to make the meaning clear, and I have put these words in square brackets. At the end of the book is a glossary of some terms that recur in the text, such as geographical, historical, and theological expressions. In each chapter (though not in the introduction or in the Scripture selections) these terms are highlighted in **bold** the first time they occur.

The stories that follow the translation often concern my friends or my family. While none are made up, they are sometimes heavily disguised in order to be fair to people. Sometimes I have disguised them so well that when I came to read the stories again, I was not sure at first whom I was describing. My first wife, Ann, appears in a number of them. Two years before I started writing this book, she died after negotiating with multiple sclerosis for forty-three years. Our shared dealings with her illness and disability over these years contribute significantly to what I write in ways that you may be able to see in the context of my commentary and also in ways that are less obvious.

ACKNOWLEDGMENTS

Not long before I started writing this book, I fell in love with and married Kathleen Scott, and I am grateful for my new life with her and for her insightful comments on the manuscript. Her insights have been so carefully articulated and are so illuminating that she practically deserves to be credited as coauthor. I am also grateful to Matt Sousa for reading through the manuscript and pointing out things I needed to correct or clarify, and to Tom Bennett for checking the proofs.

INTRODUCTION

As far as Jesus and the New Testament writers were concerned, the Jewish Scriptures that Christians call the "Old Testament" *were* the Scriptures. In saying that, I cut corners a bit, as the New Testament never gives us a list of these Scriptures, but the body of writings that the Jewish people accept is as near as we can get to identifying the collection that Jesus and the New Testament writers would have worked. The church also came to accept some extra books, such as Maccabees and Ecclesiasticus, that were traditionally called the "Apocrypha," the books that were "hidden away"—a name that came to imply "spurious." They are now often known as the "Deuterocanonical Writings," which is more cumbersome but less pejorative; it simply indicates that these books have less authority than the Torah, the Prophets, and the Writings. The precise list of them varies among different churches. For the purposes of this series that seeks to expound the "Old Testament for Everyone," by the "Old Testament" we mean the Scriptures accepted by the Jewish community, though in the Jewish Bible they come in a different order, as the Torah, the Prophets, and the Writings.

They were not "old" in the sense of antiquated or out-of-date; I sometimes like to refer to them as the First Testament rather than the Old Testament to make that point. For Jesus and the New Testament writers, they were a living resource for understanding God, God's ways in the world, and God's ways with us. They were "useful for teaching, for reproof, for correction, and for training in righteousness, so that the person who belongs to God can be proficient, equipped for every good work" (2 Timothy 3:16–17). They were for everyone, in fact. So it's strange that Christians don't read them very much. My aim in these volumes is to help you do that.

My hesitation is that you may read me instead of the Scriptures. Don't fall into that trap. I like the fact that this series includes much of the biblical text. Don't skip over it. In the end, that's the bit that matters.

An Outline of the Old Testament

The Christian Old Testament puts the books in the Jewish Bible in a distinctive order:

> Genesis to Kings: A story that runs from the creation of the world to the exile of Judahites to Babylon
>
> Chronicles to Esther: A second version of this story, continuing it into the years after the exile
>
> Job, Psalms, Proverbs, Ecclesiastes, Song of Songs: Some poetic books
>
> Isaiah to Malachi: The teaching of some prophets

Here is an outline of the history that lies at the background of the books (I give no dates for events in Genesis, which involves too much guesswork).

1200s	Moses, the exodus, Joshua
1100s	The "judges"
1000s	King Saul, King David
900s	King Solomon; the nation splits into two, Ephraim and Judah
800s	Elijah, Elisha
700s	Amos, Hosea, Isaiah, Micah; Assyria the superpower; the fall of Ephraim
600s	Jeremiah, King Josiah; Babylon the superpower
500s	Ezekiel; the fall of Judah; Persia the superpower; Judahites free to return home
400s	Ezra, Nehemiah
300s	Greece the superpower
200s	Syria and Egypt, the regional powers pulling Judah one way or the other
100s	Judah's rebellion against Syrian power and gain of independence
000s	Rome the superpower

Psalms 1–72

The book of Psalms includes about 135 examples of things you can say to God. They offer many varied examples of about four ways of speaking to God that also correspond to ways human beings speak to one another.

First, we say to God (and to one another), "You are great." Psalm 8 is a convenient example. It begins, "Yahweh, our God, how mighty is your name in all the earth." While the technical English word for the book of Psalms is *Psalter*, the Hebrew title for the book is *Tehillim*, which means *Praises* (it is related to the word *hallelujah*). In praise psalms, we are acknowledging God's power and faithfulness—not in the way these truths apply to us but as facts about God that are truths whatever may be our current feelings or experience. They also relate to the great things that God has done in creation, in freeing Israel from servitude in Egypt, and in bringing Israel to a land of its own. Christians join in such praise and add praise of God for what he did in Christ. One can imagine that these Israelite praise songs would be in regular use in the worship of the temple to the accompaniment of the temple sacrifices.

Second, we say to God (and to one another), "Help!" Psalm 3 thus begins, "Yahweh, how many are the people that trouble me, how many people are rising up against me! Many people are saying of me, 'There is no deliverance in God for him!'" Stories elsewhere in the Old Testament suggest that sometimes prayers like these would be prayed by the king and the community as a whole in the temple when there was some national crisis. Sometimes they would be prayed by ordinary individuals in need, ideally with a group of family and friends, either in the temple or in the village where one lived. Thus the people praying these psalms would not all be people who were themselves in need; they were identifying with people in need. These psalms are intercession (praying for others) as well as supplication (praying for oneself).

Sometimes we may feel less desperate, whether or not the situation actually is less desperate. Thus a third way of speaking to God (and to one another) is to say, "I trust you." Psalm 23 is an example. Such a psalm belongs to the kind of context in life when one is walking through a canyon characterized by deathly shadow and when one is surrounded by enemies. But it expresses a confidence that God will protect and deliver.

Finally, we may have the experience of God (or the other person) taking action to deal with our situation. Then naturally we say to God and to one another, "Thank you." Psalm 30 is an example. It begins, "I will extol you, Yahweh, because you put me down, but you did not let my enemies rejoice over me. Yahweh my God, I cried for help to you, and you healed me." Thanksgiving is a subset of praise, but there is an important difference between the two. Praise psalms honor God for who God always is and for the great things God did to redeem God's people. Thanksgiving psalms relate to what God has done for us ourselves just now, as individuals or as a people. Characteristically they work by telling the story of what God has done just now. Once more, one can imagine the community or the individual with his or her friends gathering in the temple to offer thanksgiving sacrifices in gratitude for what God has done for them and accompanying these sacrifices with the testimony expressed in a thanksgiving psalm.

These four types of psalm are all words spoken to God rather than by God. About fifteen psalms are dominated by God's speaking or by a priest or a prophet speaking—these psalms speak *to* us. Indeed, the Psalter begins in this way. Psalm 1 declares a blessing on people who meditate on Yahweh's teaching. Psalm 2 relates a promise to the Israelite king that God will use him as his agent in ruling the nations—who therefore will be wise to submit to him.

We do not know who wrote the Psalms. Many have introductions describing them as "David's," but these introductions can describe the same psalms as "the leader's" (which seems to denote the worship leader). This suggests that these are not terms for authorship. While the Old Testament does say that David played the equivalent of a guitar, it gives much more prominence to his role as patron and promoter of the worship of the temple, and designating particular psalms as "David's" may tell us that these psalms belong to a collection of psalms that David ultimately commissioned. They could then also (for instance) be "the leader's" in the sense that they belonged to a collection that the worship leader maintained. The book of Psalms likely came into being when various collections of psalms were brought together, a process not unlike the one whereby our hymnbooks come into being. The nature of that process explains why Psalm 72, the last psalm we consider in this book, closes with the statement that the prayers of David, son of Jesse, have come to an end. In the Psalter as we have it, there are more David psalms to follow.

It's best to assume that we know more or less nothing about the authorship and date of the Psalms. Paradoxically, this helps rather than hinders our appreciating them and using them. While they arose in concrete contexts and often reflect concrete experiences of suffering and of God's deliverance, they don't tell us the precise nature of these experiences because they are designed for us to use in connection with what happens to us. Similarly, we don't usually know when hymns and prayers were written, but this doesn't stop us from using them as means of worship and of expressing our own relationship with God. So it is with the Psalms.

The end of Psalm 72 has another feature. It includes a shout of blessing to God followed by "Amen, amen," which doesn't seem to have much to do with Psalm 72 itself. There are similar notes at the ends of Psalms 41, 89, and 106. These notes divide the Psalter into five parts. If we think of David as the patron of the Psalms, there are thus five David books to parallel the five Moses books with which the Old Testament begins (they parallel them in this general sense—not that Book One of the Psalms parallels Genesis, and so on). The five Moses books teach people how to live; the five David books teach them how to pray and praise. In the New Testament, Ephesians 5 and 6 bid people to be filled with the Spirit and to speak to one another with psalms, hymns, and songs from the Spirit; to sing and make music from the heart; to give thanks to God; to pray in the Spirit with all kinds of prayers and requests; and to pray for other people. How do we do so? The Psalter is present in Scripture to teach us.

Someone who read the draft version of this book commented that I make more references to Jesus than I did in previous volumes and wondered why this was so. I wasn't conscious of this fact, but one reason might be that the Psalms are a part of the Old Testament to which Jesus often refers. Another reason might be that some aspects of the Psalms trouble Christians because they think they are in tension with Jesus and the New Testament. I like to point out that these parts are sometimes ones that the New Testament explicitly affirms. If we have a problem with the Psalms, Jesus didn't.

PSALM 1

You Have a Choice

1 The blessings of people
    who have not walked by the strategy of the faithless,
  or stood in the path of offenders,
    or lived in the company of disdainers!
2 Rather, their delight is in Yahweh's teaching,
    and they talk about his teaching day and night.
3 They are like a tree planted by channels of water,
    which gives its fruit in its season,
  and its foliage does not fade;
    all that they do succeeds.

4 The faithless are not like that,
    but rather are like the chaff that the wind blows away.
5 Therefore the faithless do not stand at the judgment,
    nor offenders in the assembly of the faithful.
6 Because Yahweh acknowledges the way of the faithful,
    but the way of the faithless perishes.

It's Independence Day today in the United States, and our visiting preacher on Sunday more than once referred to our freedom to make choices as a reason for rejoicing. I imagine that as well as the freedom not to have one's destiny shaped by guys the other side of the Atlantic, she was referring to our freedom to choose where to live, where to send our children to school, when to retire, where to go for health care, or what treatment to have when we go to our health-care providers. Of course the other side of this freedom is the burden of responsibility. The more choices you have, the more chances you have to make a bad choice. People are more likely to buy jam when there are three kinds on the supermarket shelf than if there are thirty. Making choices can be confusing.

Psalm 1 believes in the importance of choice, believes that the key choice we have to make is enormously important, but also believes that it is straightforward. There are two ways that open up before us as individuals; Jesus takes up the idea in Matthew 7 when he speaks of the broad and narrow way. We are like people on a journey who face a split in the

7

path and have to decide which way to take. One of these ways involves "walking by" **Yahweh's torah;** the image suggests a way to walk that is well signposted. It's a bit like having GPS or SatNav.

Walking this way is both easy and difficult. The kind of thing that the Torah says is "Bow down only to Yahweh; don't make any images; keep the Sabbath; don't commit adultery; tell the truth in court; don't fancy other people's belongings." It's not rocket science; God doesn't expect anything very complicated of us. Yet the Torah's expectations also constitute a narrow way; they go against human instincts. We like to hedge our bets about what we bow down to; we like to worship in ways that are helpful or convenient; we treat the whole week as though it belongs to us; and if another man or woman attracts us—can it be wrong to love and be loved? The psalm calls that the way of the **faithless,** of the offenders, the people who are prepared to take no notice of what the Torah says.

If you want to avoid that way and stick with the company of the **faithful,** you need to watch who you walk with, where you stand around, and who your friends are. Further, you need positively to make Yahweh's teaching what you delight in and talk about. The Hebrew word for "talk about" suggests meditation but not a meditation that happens simply inside our heads— God's teaching is on our lips. And if you need encouragement to delight in Yahweh's teaching, then one encouragement is the promise that the route with those signposts that could seem so limiting (don't you ever get annoyed when GPS keeps telling you what to do?) is the route that leads to blessing. Jesus again takes up the psalm's perspective when he comments on the blessing that comes to people who hear God's word and keep it (Luke 11:28). In contrast, the route that looks like the open road with lots of freedom and good company is actually a route that leads nowhere that you would really want to go.

As the **parallelism** suggests, the "judgment" the psalm refers to is not a final judgment at the end of time. The Old Testament focuses more on the way God's purpose is worked out in our everyday lives. Any local community has an "assembly of the faithful," a meeting of its elders that is charged with resolving matters of conflict in the community, with making a judgment or a **decision** about things that happen. The psalm has a touching faith in the community's civil processes and invites people who pray the Psalms to trust them for themselves. God will see that life works out fairly. God will thus acknowledge the faithful.

The fact that the Psalter begins with this psalm reminds us that the life of worship and prayer on which the Psalter focuses cannot be separated from living life in light of the Torah; you can't expect to worship or pray if you are not living by that teaching. Many psalms that constitute a plea for help include a declaration that we have lived a life of faithfulness. They thus declare that our being in a mess does not result from our own faithlessness, but that you can't pray in that way unless you have lived in light of Psalm 1. If you have lived according to the Torah's teaching, then your being in a mess implies that God has not fulfilled the promises in Psalm 1. In such circumstances, the Psalter invites you to live with the tension between Psalm 1 and the mess you are in. You don't deny the mess, but you don't stop believing in Psalm 1. Indeed, it informs your prayer because when you are in a mess you are in a position to say to God, "Excuse me. What about what you said in Psalm 1?"

PSALM 2

God Laughs on His People's Behalf

¹ Why have nations crowded together,
      why do peoples talk about something that is futile,
² why do the earth's kings take a stand,
      why have leaders made plans together,
      against Yahweh and against his anointed?—
³ "We'll break off their restraints,
      we'll throw off their ropes from us."

⁴ The one who sits in the heavens is amused;
      the Lord laughs at them.
⁵ Then he speaks to them in his anger,
      terrifies them with his rage.
⁶ "But I myself installed my king
      on Zion, my holy mountain!"

⁷ [The king says] "I shall tell of Yahweh's decree:
  he said to me, 'You are my son;
    today I father you.
⁸ Ask of me and I will make nations your very own,
    earth's ends your estate.
⁹ You will smash them with an iron club,
    shatter them like an object made by a potter.'"

¹⁰ So now, be sensible, you kings,
    accept discipline, you leaders of the earth.
¹¹ Serve Yahweh with awe,
    rejoice with trembling, surrender sincerely,
¹² so that he does not get angry and you perish
      as regards the path,
    because his anger will soon flare.
  The blessings of all who rely on him!

We watched Independence Day fireworks last night, and I recalled how people sometimes ask me, "Do you celebrate Independence Day in Britain?" I say, "Yes, of course: parents are glad when their kids grow up and take control of their own lives so that the parents are free of responsibility for them." Living in Britain, I was hardly aware of the fact that the United States had once been a British colony. Only through living in the United States have I come to appreciate the significance of the successful rebellion by the ragtag colonial militias against the British authorities. For the citizens of the one superpower in the twenty-first century, it may also be difficult to imagine the nature of that achievement.

Old Testament Israel had something more like the power of the United States in the eighteenth century than in the twenty-first; for nearly all of its history it was an underdog. An FBI antiterrorism chief is said to have called the U.S.-Pakistani force searching for people behind the first World Trade Center bombing "a small ragtag army of racketeers, bandits, and murderers"; you could have described David's army in the same terms. Yet God told David and his successors that they were going to control the nations. **Yahweh** has become David's father. He has adopted him as his son. David is going to be the means of Yahweh's sovereignty operating in the world.

10

One would have expected God to commandeer the forces of a superpower, but working through a ragtag army fits God's regular way of acting, turning human expectations on their head.

There was a short period in David's lifetime when the king of Israel did rule a small empire, but generally nations such as **Egypt, Assyria, Babylon, Persia,** and **Greece** could indeed have laughed at the idea that Yahweh was going to control their destinies by means of the king he anointed. Usually the nations were invading, besieging, defeating, killing, transporting, taxing, and generally making life unpleasant for Israel. It's easy to picture Israel's praying century after century the psalms about invasion and defeat that will follow in the Psalter. Thus we can see the link between Psalms 1 and 2 at the beginning of the Psalter. What Psalm 1 does for the individual, Psalm 2 does for the nation. It invites Israel to acknowledge the toughness of its life over the centuries but not to assume that this reality will have the last word. As the individual's life stands under the promise expressed in Psalm 1, Israel's life stands under the promise expressed in Psalm 2. To churches living under the autocratic sovereignty of another superpower, the risen Jesus promises that they will exercise the kind of forceful rule of which God here speaks (e.g., see Revelation 2:26–27). Of course neither the psalm nor Jesus' promise is for people who themselves belong to a superpower. In this psalm, Western readers are the nations, not Israel. But reading the psalm as if we are little Israel can help us put ourselves in the position of the little nations that are under our domination.

When a superpower such as Assyria controlled the destiny of little peoples like **Ephraim, Judah,** Syria, **Philistia,** Moab, and Edom, from time to time the little peoples would band together to try to throw off the Assyrian yoke and gain their independence (this usually issued in disaster). The opening of the psalm imagines the shoe on the other foot, with the nations that form the superpower coming into conclave to throw off the sovereignty that Yahweh intends to exercise through the Davidic king. Israel often heard the scornful laugh of a superpower mocking its trust in Yahweh (the story in 2 Kings 18–19 is a great example). Psalm 2 reminds us of another laugh that resounds around a higher court. This laugh, too, has an edge to it. If the nations persist in rebelling against Yahweh's sovereignty, they will find themselves on the receiving end of Yahweh's anger. As Jesus puts it more chillingly in Matthew 25, the nations at the King's left hand are cursed and will depart into eternal fire. But ideally, the nations will all have a place at the King's right hand. In the psalm's terms, they will experience the blessings of people who rely on him (Psalm 2 thus ends with a similar promise to the one that opens Psalm 1). While they need to submit and tremble before Yahweh to surrender to his authority, and to mean it when they do so, paradoxically they can do so with rejoicing, like Israel itself.

As individuals have a choice, so nations have a choice. As individuals can be blessed when they submit to walking Yahweh's way, so nations can be blessed when they submit to walking Yahweh's way.

PSALM 3

You Are Not Alone

A composition. For David when he fled from his son Absalom.

¹ Yahweh, how many are the people that trouble me,
   how many people are rising up against me.
² Many people are saying of me,
   "There is no deliverance in God for him!"   (*Rise*)

³ But you are Yahweh, a shield about me,
   my honor, the one who lifts my head high.
⁴ With my voice I would call to Yahweh,
   and he has answered me from his holy mountain. (*Rise*)

⁵ I myself have laid down and slept;
   I have woken up, because Yahweh sustains me.
⁶ I am not afraid of a company of myriads
   that has taken its stand against me all around.

⁷ Rise up, Yahweh,
   deliver me, my God,
because you have struck all my enemies on the jaw,
   you have smashed the teeth of the faithless.

⁸ Deliverance belongs to Yahweh,
  your blessing is on your people.   (*Rise*)

When I watch a thriller such as one from The Bourne Identity trilogy, I wonder what it would be like to have everyone against me and not be able to trust anyone. Then I come out of the story at the end and realize that it's just a story. But last night we watched a movie called *Fair Game*, about a CIA agent and her ex-ambassador husband who accidentally got involved in exposing the untruths about the intelligence concerning weapons of mass destruction on which our invasion of Iraq was based. Once again someone has everyone against her: people in the White House, her former colleagues in the CIA, the reporters camped on her doorstep, the people who send her death threats, the friends who thought they knew her but to whom she can't explain things, and the husband from whom she splits for a while. This time the movie was "based on true events" rather than being pure fiction. Admittedly a story said to be inspired by true events is not pure history (*Fair Game* was made by the director of The Bourne Identity!), so you can't press the story's details. But being paranoid doesn't rule out the possibility that in real life everyone is against you.

Psalm 3 is designed for that experience. You may find it puzzling to think of David's praying this way on the occasion when Absalom had brought about his coup d'état (2 Samuel 15), but there are overlaps with that story that make it possible to see how one might learn something from putting the story and the psalm together even though they were not originally connected (see **David's story**). Other Davidic kings went through the experience that the psalm describes. In connection with Psalm 2 we noted the story of the **Assyrian** invasion of **Judah** (2 Kings 18–19). On that occasion the Assyrians threw at him exactly the taunt that appears in Psalm 3: "Don't kid yourself that **Yahweh** is going to **deliver** you." The Assyrian king had a huge army. He had all the intelligence on his side. He had won numerous victories. He had taken numerous Judahite cities. Further, if the "many people" who were saying that there was no way he could escape defeat and death included his own subjects, you couldn't blame them for thinking that way.

How do you keep going in those circumstances? First, you face facts; even more, you face God with the facts. There are all sorts of reasons for not facing facts; the British and U.S. conviction that we must put Saddam Hussein down led to hiding from some facts. Facts can be inconvenient or frightening. But if God is part of the picture, facts can be faced, and if we are to lay hold on God in connection with the dangers that threaten us, facts must be faced.

Second, you remind yourself and God and anyone else who is listening of the truths about God that can slip out of mind in a crisis. The psalm mentions two truths about God. One is that whereas people may say that I am hopelessly vulnerable, actually I have a shield all around me. God is not one of those silly little shields that you hold in your hand but that leave much of you exposed. God is one of those giant curved shields that stand on the ground and fold their way around you so that there is no way an enemy missile can reach you. The other is that God is the one who sees that I am honored and that my head can thus be held high. Once again, Psalm 2 has suggested the basis for that conviction about God. For no reason that David or the Davidic king could imagine, God had decided to make him the means of ruling the world. The aim was not to bring him honor, but it was bound to be the result.

Yet suppose you were tempted to wonder whether such convictions are simply fancies that a king invented. Is there any basis for them? Third, you remind yourself of your past experience. It's easy for a crisis to make us forget everything that has gone before, but the psalm knows the importance of being mindful of what God has done with you before. Those are also facts to be kept in mind. The king has been through crises before (David certainly knew all about it when he was on the run from Saul). He has known what it is like to call out to God and to have God respond from where God deigned to live in the temple on Mount **Zion**, where God had installed the king (see Psalm 2 again). He has known what it is like to go to bed not knowing whether you might get killed in the night, but then to wake up in the morning alive and well (unlike Sennacherib's army in that story in 2 Kings 18–19). He has not had to smash his enemies on the jaws; he has been able to watch

14

God do so (yet again, it is what happens in that story about Hezekiah). He can turn the other cheek.

Those considerations mean that you are free to sleep and not to be afraid. What God did before, God will do again, because it was not a random act of deliverance but an act that related to a long-term strategy. Further, David is praying not just for his own sake but for his people's sake. It is their blessing that can come about through God's acting to deliver their leader.

All this means he can pray for God's deliverance with confidence (*deliverance* and *deliver* are key words in this short prayer).

PSALM 4

Who Can I Turn To?

The leader's. With strings. A composition. David's.

¹ When I call, answer me,
    my faithful God!
   In straits you gave me room—
    be gracious to me and listen to my plea!

² You people, how long will the one I honor be for shaming,
     [how long] will you give yourself to something that is futile,
     [how long] will you inquire of something false?   (*Rise*)
³ But acknowledge that Yahweh has set apart the committed
      person for himself;
    Yahweh is the one who listens when I call to him.
⁴ Tremble and do not offend;
    say it inside on your bed and shut up.   (*Rise*)
⁵ Offer faithful sacrifices
    and put your reliance on Yahweh.

⁶ Increasing numbers of people are saying, "Who will enable
     us to see good things?—
    the light of your face has fled from upon us, Yahweh."
⁷ You have put joy inside me
    from the time when their grain and wine has increased.
⁸ In well-being all at once I will lie down and sleep,
    because you alone are Yahweh;
    you enable me to live in security.

We were at the farmer's market (in Britain one would call it a street market). I really wanted new potatoes, which the *New York Times* had assured me should be available, but I was not surprised that East Coast information on such matters does not necessarily hold for California. All I could buy were small potatoes, which are by no means the same thing as new potatoes. We admired the tomatoes, strawberries, cauliflower, and peaches, but noted that they were twice as expensive as the ones in our local Hispanic store, and we came home empty-handed. We had been in a position to take a casual, touristy interest in the produce. We didn't have to buy it—we could get it somewhere else. My wife was more interested in the idea of painting pictures of it.

The Israelites who pray Psalm 4 have a quite different relationship with food. There is no Hispanic store where they can drop by and no big supermarket with mountains of melons. There might be some bartering within the village (e.g., "I'll swap some of my grapes for some of your figs"), but money has not been invented, and mostly people eat what they grow; no grow, no eat. Growing your food depends on putting in the hard work to do so and on knowing how to get things to grow. But you can be the most hard-working, green-fingered farmer in the world yet fail if you don't get rain in the right quantities at the right moment or if you get a locust epidemic at the wrong moment. And Israel often experienced the rains failing or the locusts showing up.

Therein lies the psalm's background. More and more people in the community are asking who will enable them to see good things—to get a decent harvest of grain, figs, olives, and grapes, the necessities of life. The blessing that priests pronounced over the people promised that the light of **Yahweh's** face would shine on them (see Numbers 6). When someone smiles, and the light shines out of his or her face, it means this person will want the best for you, will want to shower you with blessing. But the light of Yahweh's face has disappeared. It doesn't work to look to Yahweh for the good things that you need to keep life going. So people are looking in different directions. Their **Canaanite** neighbors look to other gods to help them with their harvest, and Israelites are giving in to the temptation to

16

look in the same direction. They have stopped honoring the one they were supposed to honor, and they are shaming him by looking elsewhere.

The psalmist knows that the gods they are looking to and praying to have no real power. They are futile. They are false. But when you are under pressure, when you don't know if your family can survive another year of poor harvest, you may well feel that you have nothing to lose by turning to them. If Yahweh doesn't deliver the goods anyway, what have you got to lose? The psalmist is aware of the temptation to join them. He too has a family to feed. But his description of the dilemma the community faces is bracketed or interwoven with plea, recollection, exhortation, and a statement of confidence.

First, the psalm starts with a prayer to the **faithful** God to be gracious, but it doesn't make any concrete request apart from appealing to God to listen and respond; that will be an expression of faithfulness and grace. If the psalmist can just get God's attention, surely God won't be able to resist the inclination to do something. Second, interwoven in the plea is a recollection: "I've been in straits before, and you've brought me out into somewhere with space; so I know you do that kind of thing, and you know it, too; you couldn't say that you never go in for intervening." But third, the psalm spends more time talking to other people than talking to God (compare the exhortation in Ephesians 5 to talk to one another with psalms). The psalmist wants to embolden other members of the community to be faithful to Yahweh, in keeping with their being a people Yahweh set apart for himself. They need to take seriously who Yahweh is and to maintain their **commitment** both in the privacy of their bedrooms and of their hearts and in the costly worship that they offer.

Fourth, the psalm concludes with a statement of confidence and hope. The people who have given up on Yahweh because he didn't produce the goods and have turned to the gods whom the psalmist says are futile have found that it worked. The increase in their grain and wine will have increased the pressure on people who insist on maintaining their commitment to Yahweh. Paradoxically, what the psalmist knows about God and has experienced from God in the past not only issues in

17

maintaining commitment. It issues in joy, based on the assurance that God will come through for his people. It issues in a confidence about enjoying **well-being** and about being able to sleep at night without worrying about the future.

PSALM 5

On Pleading with the King

The leader's. To flutes. A composition. David's.

¹ Give ear to my words, Yahweh,
  consider my call.
² Heed the sound of my cry for help,
  my King and my God,
  because it is with you I plead.
³ Yahweh, at morning may you listen to my voice,
  at morning I lay it out and wait.
⁴ Because you are not a God who delights in faithlessness;
  evil cannot stay with you.
⁵ Wild people cannot take their stand before your eyes;
  you oppose all who do harm.
⁶ You destroy those who speak falsehood;
  people who shed blood and act fraudulently,
  Yahweh abhors.
⁷ But I myself will come to your house
  through the abundance of your commitment;
  I will bow low to your holy palace
  in awe of you.
⁸ Yahweh, lead me in your faithfulness
  in connection with the people who are watching for me;
  make your way direct before me.

⁹ Because there is no truth in their mouth;
  their inner being is destruction.
  Their throat is an open grave,
  they are slippery with their tongue.
¹⁰ Make them pay, God;
  they should fall by means of their own plans.
  Because of the number of their rebellions drive them out,
  because they have defied you.

18

¹¹ But may all the people who rely on you rejoice,
   may they resound forever.
   As you protect them,
       may the people who give themselves to your name
       exult in you.
¹² Because you yourself bless the faithful person, Yahweh;
       you surround him with favor like a body shield.

Tomorrow, South Sudan becomes a separate country, independent of northern Sudan. No one knows what the future will bring for it, but if you belong to South Sudan, you hope that it means an end to the conflict between the south and the north and to what you see as the oppression of the south by the north. While it is an oversimplification to think of the north as Muslim and the south as Christian (many people in the south adhere to traditional African religions), one can picture the Christians in the south and their leaders praying in the way Psalm 5 does. The president of (northern) Sudan has already been (in the words of the *New York Times* [July 8, 2011]) "author of the murderous war in Darfur," the eastern part of Sudan. If readers of the Psalms in other parts of the world do not need to pray for themselves in the manner of Psalm 5, then such a psalm becomes the way we identify with our brothers and sisters who have the experience the psalm describes. We pray it on their behalf, not praying for "them" but thinking of them as "us."

We then pray to God as king. It would make sense if the person who prayed this psalm was himself a king or a leader like Nehemiah, assailed by enemies and familiar with the experience of people watching for him. So in praying the psalm, we can think of the leaders of vulnerable peoples like the South Sudanese, vulnerable to being taken out by the agents of rival nations or by rivals within their own people who would like to be in power or who think their leaders are not aggressive enough in the way they stand up for their country.

Being a leader or king means occupying a frighteningly responsible and frequently dangerous position. At the same time, as king you are used to people coming to you when they are victims of unfair treatment. There might be a line of them when you get to your office, queuing to present their case to you and to **cry out** for help, pleading with you to act as judge on their behalf. It is your responsibility to see that they get justice. You are expected to embody God's **commitment** and God's justice and not to tolerate wild outlaws who will commit perjury to rob people of their land and their lives, schemers whose throats are thus open graves (that is, their words could bring about someone's death); their inner being, their thinking and planning, focuses only on people's destruction. You do not let them parade themselves before you or "stay" with you (the Hebrew verb signifies lodging for the night). They are wise to hide. (The story of Naboth in 1 Kings 21 illustrates the way such people worked, though with terrible irony on that occasion because it is the palace that is involved in corruption and bloodshed.) But at least the experience of that responsibility brings with it the possibility of looking to God to embody the justice that one is expected to implement.

As ordinary people, we can do so on our own behalf if necessary and on behalf of the victims of oppressors whom we are helpless to protect. We can show up first thing in the morning at God's palace on the basis of God's commitment and of God's identification with **faithfulness** rather than **faithlessness**. We can plead with God to note how people are watching for a way to get to us or to others and urge God to come straight to our protection or theirs. We can remind God that those people are not merely rebelling against us but rebelling against God and defying God. They would be doing so if the psalm were prayed by the Davidic king, God's anointed agent, to whom the other peoples are supposed to submit. But the psalm does not make that connection and rather implies that they are rebelling against God simply in being murderous plotters.

Westerners often disapprove of wanting the plotters to be caught by their own devices, though Old and New Testaments consistently assume that people should pay for their wrongdoing in such ways. Further, people who are praying in this way are not taking it into their own hands to implement God's justice. If you are confident about referring things to God as the one to whom redress belongs, it liberates you from having to seek redress for yourself. Indeed, it is for God's sake that the psalm pleads for action—it is because people should not get away with rebellion against God. It would be possible to mask a personal desire for vengeance as a desire for God's **name** to be honored. For us what then matters is to be careful of what is in our own hearts as we pray the psalm.

PSALM 6
The Way Prayer Makes a Difference

The leader's. With strings. On the eighth [tone]. A composition. David's.

1   Yahweh, do not reprove me in your anger,
      do not correct me with your fury.
2   Be gracious to me, Yahweh, because I am faint;
      heal me, Yahweh, because my bones shake in distress.
3   My whole being shakes in great distress,
      but you, Yahweh—how long?
4   Turn, Yahweh, save my life,
      deliver me for the sake of your commitment!
5   Because there is no mention of you in death;
      in Sheol who confesses you?
6   I am tired of my groaning,
      I make my bed swim every night,
      I melt my mattress with my tears.
7   My eye has wasted away through aggression,
      grown old because of all the people watching for me.

8   Go away from me, all you who do harm,
      because Yahweh has heard the sound of my weeping.
9   Yahweh has heard my prayer for grace;
      Yahweh accepts my plea.
10 All my enemies will be shamed and will greatly shake
      in distress;
      they will turn and be shamed instantly.

Two of my friends are celebrating their golden wedding anniversary, and I have been asked to contribute to the greetings book that will be presented to them at the celebratory party. So I wrote that my first wife, Ann, sat up in her cot in the hotel room where she is sleeping under the caring eye of Jesus

(John 14:2), declared "How marvelous!" and then went back to sleep until resurrection day. It is an imaginary fancy, but it depends on the reality of the way the New Testament describes our situation when we die, and it is not more fanciful than the accounts the Bible gives of Samuel waking up to give Saul one last dressing down or of people leaving their tombs to go walk about after Jesus dies (1 Samuel 28; Matthew 27). The underlying idea that death means resting in **Sheol** is one that runs through the Bible—the difference between Old and New Testaments is precisely that Jesus' death and resurrection change the situation by establishing that our stay in the lodging house will be temporary. In the meantime, however, all you do there is doze, with Jesus keeping an eye on you.

The trouble is (Psalm 6 says) that you can't praise God in Sheol. One reason is that praising God essentially involves shouting, standing, bowing down, dancing, and waving your arms. You can't do any of those things when you are dead. The other is that praising God essentially involves talking about what God has done for you this day or this week, or at least this month. It involves what the psalm calls confession. Hebrew uses the same words for confessing what you have done as it does for confessing what God has done because they both involve telling a story. The problem is that God doesn't do anything for people in Sheol; they are just sleeping. Nothing happens there to praise God for.

The psalm thus uses a wily argument to get God to **deliver** us when we are in trouble: "Deliver me; you get praise. Let me die; you get nothing." Children use the sneakiest arguments to get their parents to do what they want, and sometimes the parents grin and let themselves be persuaded. The Psalms operate as if our relationship with God in prayer is like that of children with their parents (what a surprise!). Any argument is fair game to get your heavenly father to do what you want or need.

The psalm also presupposes a more solemn aspect to God's parent-child relationship with us. It is the job of parents to reprove and correct their children. Sometimes they do it in anger, which is not in itself wrong (anger in itself is not a sin) but can be scary for the child because the parent is so much bigger and more powerful, and the anger could issue in a harsh

22

correction. So the psalm begins with an appeal to God not to be that kind of parent. It looks as if the psalmist feels that the correction has gotten out of hand. The psalm speaks of being faint and distressed, of needing healing and deliverance. Typically, the prayer's wording makes it impossible to tell what the psalmist's problem was; it is therefore more useful to other people when they pray because its application is not limited to one set of needs. It speaks in hyperbolic terms: as if there have been so many tears that they have turned the bed into a swimming pool, as if eyes have been looking for so long to see **Yahweh's** act of deliverance that they have worn out. Part of the toughness of the experience is that it has been going on for a long time, but this does not stop the psalmist from praying. In a culture that has a hard time waiting for a few minutes, let alone a few weeks, it may be hard to appreciate the implications of continuing to plead with God for something month in and month out. But the psalm does continue to appeal for grace and for the expression of God's **commitment**, for God to turn instead of walking the other way (it's the verb that would be translated "repent" if it were applied to a human being), and for God to save and deliver.

Then an astonishing change comes in the last three verses. In the Psalms, there can be two stages to answers to prayer. Stage one is when God listens to the prayer and makes a commitment to deal with the matter the prayer raised. Stage two is when God then acts. In between stages one and two you live in suspense and by faith. The psalmist has not yet seen stage two, but evidently stage one has happened. In between verses 7 and 8, did someone minister to the person praying and give assurance that God had heard and would act? Or did the person praying simply know that when a child comes to his or her father, the appeal would be heard? We don't know the answer to that question, and it need not be the same every time the psalm was used. What is clear is the assumption that prayer makes a difference, not because it changes the person praying but because God listens and makes a commitment to act. Listening thus changes the person who prays and makes it possible to face the issues that the prayer raised with a new attitude and confidence, and maybe even sleep when one could not otherwise do so. It

23

doesn't mean the person who prays will not come back tomorrow, though, if stage two has not yet come about.

PSALM 7

The Judge Is on Your Side

Lament. David's, which he sang for Yahweh concerning the words of Sudan. The Benjaminite.

¹ Yahweh my God, on you I rely—
    deliver me from all the people who are pursuing me,
      save me,
² or one will tear me apart like a lion,
    ripping me to pieces when there is no one to save.
³ Yahweh my God, if I did this,
    if there is wrongdoing in my hands,
⁴ if I have repaid evil to my ally
    but released the person watching for me without reason,
⁵ may the enemy pursue me and overtake me,
    may he trample my life to the ground,
    lay my honor in the dirt.   (*Rise*)

⁶ Rise up, Yahweh, in your anger;
    lift yourself up at the great fury of the people watching
      for me.
  Awake, my God, you must order a decision;
⁷   the assembly of the nations should come around you.
  Take your seat over it on high;
⁸   Yahweh must rule the peoples.
  Decide for me, Yahweh, in accordance with my faithfulness
    and with my integrity over me.
⁹ The evil of wicked people really must come to an end,
    and you must establish the faithful person.
  The faithful God
    tests minds and hearts.
¹⁰ God is my shield on high,
    one who delivers the people who are upright in mind.
¹¹ God decides for the faithful person;
    God expresses indignation each day.
¹² If someone does not turn, he whets his sword,
    he has directed his bow and fixed it.

¹³ He has fixed deadly weapons for himself,
    he makes his arrows into flames.
¹⁴ There: someone twists with harm,
    he is pregnant with troublemaking,
    he gives birth to falsehood.
¹⁵ He has dug a pit and made it deep,
    but he has fallen into the hole he makes.
¹⁶ His troublemaking returns onto his own head,
    his violence comes down on his own skull.

¹⁷ I will confess Yahweh in accordance with his faithfulness
    and make music to the name of Yahweh, the One on High.

If you are an Orthodox Jew in Brooklyn and are accused of some wrongdoing, you can hire an Orthodox private eye who wears a black frock coat and a fedora—though when he goes undercover, he confines himself to a skullcap and fringed prayer shawl that can be worn underneath a stocking cap and Yankee jersey. According to the *New York Times* (July 8, 2011), one of his high-profile cases concerned a child molestation that had led to a man's imprisonment. The private eye uncovered evidence that one of the witnesses in the case had been bribed and was thus able to bring about the man's release. "When I wake up in the morning," the private eye says, "I pray to God and I want to believe that there are good people in the world. But when I go to work every day and I see what I see, it's a very big challenge for me."

He works in the world with which Psalm 7 is familiar. It speaks for someone accused of having wrongdoing in his hands or on his hands; the expression recalls the phrase in Isaiah 1 about hands full of blood. There were people with whom he had entered into some kind of committed relationship. They were allies, people with whom he had a relationship of **peace** or who thought they had that kind of relationship but who say he has wronged them. Conversely, he is accused of failing to take seriously the wrongdoing of other people; it is as if he has been relating to wrongdoers in the opposite way to the one set forth in Psalm 1, which urges us to dissociate ourselves from such people. (Second Samuel 16–20 provides the background that could have suggested the links with **David's story** of which the psalm's introduction speaks.)

Such are the accusations. As far as we know, there were no sleuths in Jerusalem whom he could employ in order to clear his name, but the psalm provides him with a way of calling on God to do so. It is a reasonable ploy because God is, after all, a judge with **authority**. A judge is a shield for people. One assumption here is that whereas Western custom separates the making of legal decisions (the business of the court) from law enforcement (the business of the police), in the Old Testament the judge is a leader who both makes the decision and takes the action that follows.

So the first part of the psalm appeals to God to stand up and get angry and thus be energized to take action to **deliver**. It then speaks in specific terms about enacting judgment. God must order a **decision** (the Hebrew word is often translated "judgment"). There needs to be the appropriate assembly. God should issue a ruling about the case in question and decide for the suppliant in accordance with the facts of the case, which are that the accusations are false. The accused person is someone of uprightness or integrity and **faithfulness**—another expression that recurs in the context of talk of making quasi-legal decisions; it suggests being in the right because one has acted rightly toward other people. Boldly he says, "If I have done wrong, may I be punished," because he knows he has not.

The second half of the psalm links with that conviction. It constitutes simply a statement of faith in God as judge. You would hardly dare utter such a statement if your claim to integrity, uprightness, and faithfulness was false, not least because God does test minds and hearts—those of your accusers but also your own. Here it declares the confidence with which the person praying this prayer will approach today, tomorrow, and the next day, waiting for vindication. You have prayed, and you know that prayer makes all the difference; that God's indignation, like God's anger, works in your favor; and that God does not just sit doing nothing but takes decisive action against wrongdoers. God is prepared to exercise force to put them down and rescue their victims. And one of the ways God likes to do so is by making the world a place where people get caught in the traps they have laid for others.

26

Our earthly legal system doesn't always work that way; neither does God's way of administering things in the world. But the occasions when it doesn't work don't hold people back from praying that it should do so. Indeed, they make people pray more fervently.

PSALM 8

Thus Far and No Further

The leader's. On the Gittite [perhaps a tune]. A composition. David's.

¹ Yahweh our God,
    how mighty is your name in all the earth,
  you who put your majesty above the heavens
²   by the mouth of babies and sucklings.
  You established a barricade to deal with your watchful foes,
    to stop the enemy and the person taking redress.
³ When I see the heavens, the work of your fingers,
    the moon and the stars that you established,
⁴ what are people that you are mindful of them,
    human beings that you pay attention to them?
⁵ But you made them fall short of God by a little,
    and crowned them with splendor and honor.
⁶ You let them rule over the works of your hands;
    you put everything under their feet—
⁷ sheep and oxen, all of them,
    and all the animals of the countryside,
⁸ the birds of the heavens, the fish of the sea,
    what passes over the paths in the seas.
⁹ Yahweh our God,
    how mighty is your name in all the earth!

The crying of babies and sucklings is hard to listen to yet hard to avoid. In the area that is now South Sudan, one in seven children dies before his or her fifth birthday. In Darfur, countless young girls have been raped and abducted. The media report that the rebellion of southern Sudan against the north led to the enslaving of children in the south; internecine strife also involved the impaling of children on fence posts. If boys did get the chance to grow beyond infancy, many ended up as boy soldiers. Elsewhere in Africa, girls were captured and drafted into rebel armies where they were also raped. In the United States, it is said that a case of child abuse is reported every ten seconds and that four or five children die each day because of abuse. Then there are the babies that are conceived but do not get as far as birth; in the United States, it is said that over three thousand abortions are performed every day.

When the Old Testament talks about babes and sucklings, it is usually as victims of oppression, war, and death; they are crying out in pain or need. Their cry sounds loudly in the book of Lamentations, a series of psalmlike prayers from the time after the fall of Jerusalem to the Babylonians. The city's siege had meant there is nothing for them to eat and drink, and its fall brought little relief. Lamentations 2 expresses the torment of watching babies and sucklings get weak and fade away in the city in their mothers' arms. Jesus' birth brings the death of the entire population of boys under two in Bethlehem.

Might the abuse of children become all-pervasive in the world? Jesus speaks of wars becoming a pervasive reality in his followers' experience. His declarations might seem more accurate now than in any other time in history. Could the planet be enveloped by a global conflict that destroys humanity? Could some Herod do for the world what the historical Herod did for Bethlehem?

The psalm proclaims that God has set limits to humanity's capacity to destroy itself. In effect, God has said, "Thus far and no further." In the Bible, the sea with its tumultuous power is an image for destructive forces that could have the capacity to frustrate God's purpose, but Job 38 declares that God said as much to the seas when establishing the boundary between sea and land. Job 40–41 puts the point another way: these harmful forces have the energy of a fearsome monster, but it is a monster that God keeps on a leash. It can be destructive, but God has placed limits on its destructiveness.

The psalm's way of making the point is to speak of God's establishing a barricade to restrain people and forces that oppose God's purpose in the world, like the barricade shepherds build to protect their goats and sheep from wolves and bobcats. Human beings have an instinct to lash back when someone acts in a way that harms us or harms our interests; we want to "get our own back," and we speak of it in terms of "justice," which makes revenge sound more acceptable. It's a harmful enough process when it simply involves individuals, but nations work that way too, and the results can be cataclysmic. Thank God, then, that God has set a limit to our capacity to wreak our own justice.

The psalm thus constitutes a sigh of relief that God's **name** is mighty in all the earth—that is, that God himself is mighty. It is a sigh of relief that God has established his majesty in the heavens, indeed above the heavens. The Scriptures recognize how rebellion against God and resistance to God's ways are not merely earthly phenomena. They have a supernatural aspect. But neither earthly willfulness nor heavenly willfulness can get totally out of hand. It is as if even before creation, God anticipated the cry of babes and sucklings, the most wretched victims of that willfulness, and heeded that cry by declaring, "thus far and no further."

The crying of babies and sucklings might make it seem the more extraordinary that God paid attention to humanity and gave us a power in the world that is almost Godlike. God might even seem to have been rather irresponsible in giving humanity a role to play in the created world. Yet it is a consistent pattern of God's work in the world that God takes risks in delegating responsibility and power to people who are supposed to work as his agents but are inclined to abuse their power. Certainly a result of God's giving humanity authority in relation to the animal world has led to our abusing it in a way that is now more far-reaching than it has ever been before. Yet the psalm implies that God's majesty and might will finally have their way. God takes risks but is committed to taking creation to its destiny.

PSALM 9:1–18

Praise and Thanksgiving as a Key to Prayer—I

The leader's. Secrets [perhaps a tune]. The son's. A composition. David's.

1 I will confess you, Yahweh, with all my being,
   I will tell of all your wonders.

29

2 I will celebrate and exult in you,
    I will commemorate your name, the One on High.

3 When my enemies turn back,
    they fall and perish before you,
4 because you gave a decision and a judgment for me;
    you sat on your throne as one who makes decisions
      in faithfulness.
5 You blasted the nations, you destroyed the faithless person,
    you eliminated their name for ever and ever.
6 The enemy is finished, ruins forever;
    you uprooted cities, their memory perished.

7 Them! But Yahweh sits [enthroned] forever;
    he established his throne for taking decisions.
8 He is the one who makes decisions for the world
      with faithfulness,
    he rules the peoples with uprightness.

9 Yahweh has become a tower for the downtrodden person,
    a tower for times of trouble,
10 so that people who acknowledge your name will trust you
    because you have not abandoned people who inquire
      of you, Yahweh.
11 Make music to Yahweh who sits [enthroned] in Zion,
    tell among the peoples about his deeds,
12 because the one who looks for bloodshed has been mindful
      of them,
    he has not ignored the cry of the lowly.

13 Be gracious to me, Yahweh,
    see my affliction at the hand of the people who are
      against me,
    you who lift me up from the gates of death
14 so that I might tell of all your praiseworthy acts;
    in the gates of Ms. Zion
    I will rejoice in your deliverance.

15 Nations plunged into the pit they made;
    in the net that they hid, their foot caught itself.

16 Yahweh caused himself to be acknowledged;
    he has made a decision;
    by the act of his own hands the faithless person
        snared himself. *(Recitation. Rise)*
17 Faithless people should turn to Sheol—
    all the nations that ignore Yahweh,
18 because the needy person will not be ignored without end
    or the hope of the lowly perish forever.

Yesterday a pastor in Florida invited me to look at his blog, where he had written about God's renewing the church. When God renewed the church (as happened with the emergence of Pentecostalism a century ago, for instance), he emphasized, there were always people praying and repenting. God's act of renewal was a response to their repentance and prayer. I commented that we need to be wary of formulating rules about how God acts and of giving the final word to our reaching out to God rather than to God's reaching out to us, but I also told him about how encouraging his piece was. When you live in a context where the church is in a diminishing or diminished state as we do in the West, you need reminders about what God has done in the past (as well as reminders about what God is doing in the present in other parts of the world, but that's another story). Our knowledge of God's acts in the past stokes our conviction about what God might do again. It thus encourages us to pray along the lines that his blog was encouraging.

The same assumption underlies this psalm. That fact is clearer when you realize that Psalms 9 and 10 are one psalm that has been divided into two, maybe so that they could be used separately in Israelite worship. Psalm 10 thus has no introduction, and the two are one psalm in the old Greek translation of the Psalms. The internal evidence that they belong together is that they are an alphabetical psalm: that is, the successive verses of Psalm 9 begin with the first ten letters in the Hebrew alphabet (on average, two verses per letter), and the verses of Psalm 10 begin with nine more letters. Like the forms that poets use in other languages, this "artificial" structure helps the poet's creativity. There are actually twenty-two letters in the alphabet, so three do not appear; further, some of the letters come in a slightly unusual order (perhaps the order of the alphabet wasn't quite settled). This particular poetic form encourages a prayer that works from *A* to *Z* and says all that needs to be said; yet omitting some of the letters also has the effect of mirroring the way life is not working out as it should if it worked by rules such as "Repentance is the key to the renewal of the church."

In content, this psalm works by giving great prominence to God's past acts. For most of the first eighteen verses, you could think it is simply a praise psalm, more specifically a thanksgiving psalm confessing what God has done for the psalmist personally, inviting those who are praying to talk about the way God has rescued them from people's attacks in the past. Like Psalm 7, it pictures God as a person in authority who can make **decisions** and implement them to put down people who unfairly attack others. This psalm speaks more directly about nations and communities that attack other nations and communities. It affirms that God is sovereign in history and in politics. God's sovereignty is not merely a doctrine but a reality that the people praying have experienced. So like that blogger, the psalm invites people who are praying to lift their eyes from their present pressures and remember occasions when God has acted in situations like the one they are in, which means they can trust God for the future.

God does not ignore the **cry** of the oppressed. It's just not God's nature. God "looks for bloodshed"—maybe that means that when people shed blood, God does not let them get away with it, or maybe it makes the stronger point that God is prepared to shed the blood of people who shed the blood of others. Once again that fact means human beings do not need to take matters into their own hands in order to see that justice is done. They can trust God for that action.

Just one line in the first half of this double psalm makes explicit that the psalm is essentially a prayer. The rest focuses on encouraging the faith of the people who pray and encouraging God to act again in accordance with what we know is true of God.

PSALM 9:19–10:18

The Wretched of the Earth

¹⁹ Rise up, Yahweh, a human being should not triumph,
    nations should have decisions made in your presence.
²⁰ Appoint something fearful for them, Yahweh;
    nations should acknowledge that they are human
      beings.   (*Rise*)

¹⁰:¹ Why do you stand far off, Yahweh,
    why do you hide in times of trouble?
² In his position of eminence the faithless person hounds
    the lowly—
    they should catch themselves by the schemes that they
    have thought up.
³ Because the faithless person has praised the desire
    of his heart
    and has blessed the greedy person.
⁴ The faithless person has disdained Yahweh,
    in accordance with the exaltedness of his attitude:
  "God does not inquire, he is not here";
⁵   in all his schemes his ways are profane.
  All the time your decisions are on high, away
    from him;
    all the people watching for him—he snorts at them.
⁶ He has said to himself, "I shall not tumble, ever";
    he has sworn that "I shall not be in adversity."

⁷ His mouth is full of fraud and oppression;
    under his tongue are troublemaking and wickedness.
⁸ He lives in hiding places in the villages
    so that in complete secret he can slay the innocent.
  His eyes watch for the wretched person;
⁹   he waits in secret like a lion in its lair.
  He waits to catch the lowly;
    he catches the lowly by dragging him in his net.
¹⁰ Collapsing, he sinks down;
    the wretched fall because of his strength.
¹¹ He has said to himself, "God has ignored it,
    he has hidden his face, he has never looked."

33

¹² Rise up, Yahweh; God, lift your hand—
   do not ignore the lowly.
¹³ Why has the faithless disdained God?—
   he has said to himself, "He does not inquire."
¹⁴ You looked, because you yourself
   take note of troublemaking and vexation.
   Giving it into your hand, the wretched leaves it to you;
   the orphan—you are the one who has been helper.
¹⁵ Break the arm of the faithless and evil person
   so that when you inquire after his faithlessness,
      you will not find it.
¹⁶ Yahweh will be king for ever and ever;
   the nations will have perished from his country.
¹⁷ When you have heard the longing of the lowly, Yahweh,
   you establish their heart you incline your ear,
¹⁸ to decide for orphan and downtrodden;
   a human being from the country will not ever again terrify.

My stepdaughter and her husband spend their lives seeking to make known the plight of Darfuri refugees in Chad; they make dangerous visits there from time to time. They tell horrifying stories about the way the Sudanese government treated the Darfuri people when they were still in Sudan. In this connection the Sudan president, Omar Hassan al-Bashir, has been indicted by the International Criminal Court (ICC) for war crimes, crimes against humanity, and genocide. The ICC's chief prosecutor in effect accused Bashir of running a four-year genocide campaign against the Darfuri people in western Sudan, killing tens of thousands and driving millions to flee their homes. What can one do for such people and against such an oppressor? Our family involvement with the question led my wife and me to start praying the Psalms on behalf of the Darfuri and against Bashir.

Psalms 9–10 almost seem to be designed for such praying. The second half of the double psalm first challenges God to action. Mere human beings should not be allowed to do what they like in the world. It is an important conviction for people who are oppressed, though it contrasts with the Western conviction that being free to do as you wish is rather important. The Hebrew word for "human being," which comes three times at the beginning and end of this psalm passage, denotes humans in their relative feebleness and insignificance. The psalm asks God, "How can such creatures be allowed to behave as if they are much more significant than they are?" The word for humanity in its insignificance contrasts with the talk of "eminence" and "exaltedness." The psalm is talking about people in positions of importance, and when you are important, it is easy to forget that you are a mere limited human being. But it is also talking about the nations whom these eminent people lead. Nations have to accept responsibility for the actions of their leaders; it is all the more so in a democracy. We also have to accept responsibility for the ways some people are hurt through actions that benefit other people, maybe the majority.

The other side of the coin is that God has the capacity to take action when such people misuse their positions. God ought to be making some **decisions** about these people. Instead, God is doing nothing, letting events take their course. God has the power to intervene in the world but does not do so very often. In one sense, the "Why" question has an answer. God has delegated responsibility for the world to humanity (Psalms 9–10 neatly follow Psalm 8, which makes that point). Parents do not intervene every time their children have an argument; they know that children need to learn to sort things out for themselves. But sometimes a situation reaches a point when parents have to intervene. Similarly, it would compromise God's purpose in making the world if God intervened in every conflict, but the psalm implies that it is quite in order for us to say to God, "CAN'T YOU SEE THIS IS ONE THAT REQUIRES YOUR INTERVENTION?" The "Why" of the Psalms is not a request for information but a challenge to action. God may be exercising sovereignty up there in heaven, but decisions God makes up there aren't making any difference down here, so the **faithless** can ignore God's sovereignty and be indifferent to what any human opponents think.

The psalm shows that it is fine to challenge God to take action to punish people for their wrongdoing, as the New Testament also assumes (see God's reaction to the plea of the martyrs in Revelation 6). Once again the Psalms assume that taking redress is God's business, not ours, but that we are free to urge

God to act; turning the other cheek does not mean passivity in relation to God. Confronted by the wickedness of human oppressors and their unwillingness to acknowledge God as God and to acknowledge fellow human beings as fellow human beings, it is weird if we can shrug our shoulders and not press God to put evil down. And you cannot blame ordinary, lowly, powerless people from coming to the same conclusion as their powerful oppressors—God simply does not take any notice of or interest in what happens in the world. God, you have to do something about it!

The double psalm ends where it began, yet the renewed declaration of praise has a different significance in the new context. Psalm 9 began with praise on the basis of what God has done. Psalm 10 closes with praise that ignores what God is not doing and gives praise for what God is going to do, despite the fact that it has no grounds for assuming that God will make this a moment when he does intervene. It is almost playing chicken with God, daring God not to act and thus forfeit any right to the closing line's description of God.

PSALM 11

Flee or Stay?

The leader's. David's.

¹ On Yahweh I rely;
 how can you say,
"Flit to your mountains, bird,
² because there—the faithless direct their bow,
they have set their arrows on their strings,
  to shoot from the shadow at the people who are upright
  in heart.
³ When the foundations collapse,
 the faithful—what can they do?"

⁴ Yahweh in his holy palace;
 Yahweh whose throne is in the heavens—
his eyes see,
 his gaze examines human beings.

⁵ Yahweh examines the faithful person, and the faithless;
  and the ones who give themselves to violence—
  his whole being opposes them.
⁶ He rains coals of fire and sulfur on the faithless people;
  a scorching wind is the portion in their cup.
⁷ Because Yahweh is faithful, he gives himself to faithful deeds;
  the upright person—his face sees him.

In this first week after South Sudan declared its independence, the president of northern Sudan has spoken before the national assembly as his reduced country starts a new phase of its life. He has described it as the "second republic" that will affirm the rule of law, the extension of justice, the guarantee of the rights of citizens, integrity in public spending, and accountability. A professor at Khartoum University has pooh-poohed the speech as mere tactics designed to get people to believe that things are going to change so that the administration will not be vulnerable to the revolutionary spirit that has gripped Tunisia and Egypt. He spoke bravely, for if he was right and if there is any truth in the International Criminal Court's accusations, someone speaking out in this way is vulnerable to the administration. Such dissident voices have often assumed it was wise to get out of the country.

One can imagine the professor's friends therefore urging him to flit like a bird. They know that the administration is **faithless** and will be directing something more powerful than arrows in his direction. For a bird, its mountains are a safe place; it can fly up to a ridge out of the range of a hunter's weapons. In a human society, it is a sign that the foundations of the social order have collapsed when the faithless are in control and have the people of integrity in their gun sights. Things have been turned upside down. What can a **faithful** person do?

Evidently that professor's answer is that he should stick it out; he has not applied for asylum in the United States and taken a job in a secure place such as Southern California. I don't know if he is a man of faith and whether that faith has encouraged him to take his brave stand. In the psalm, that consideration is the ruling one. Admittedly the psalmist might interrupt to say that talk about being a man of faith puts it the wrong way. The point isn't the faith but rather the one in whom one has faith. The psalm talks about

37

facts, not faith. In effect the psalmist rebukes the friends who are giving him advice by reminding them of some facts about God. **Yahweh** is in his holy palace. In other contexts we might assume this means the Jerusalem temple, which the Old Testament often calls Yahweh's palace. But here the **parallelism** shows that the psalm is referring to God's palace in the heavens, the seat of government on high where Yahweh's court sits.

Like Psalm 5, this psalm contrasts a threatening earthly administration with a much more impressive heavenly administration. The fact that you can't see it doesn't make it any less real and powerful. Second Kings 6 tells of an occasion when an army comes to arrest the prophet Elisha. His aide is naturally scared stiff, but Elisha, unperturbed, asks God to open his eyes to the existence of an army of fiery horses and chariots surrounding them and protecting them. The psalmist's friends resemble Elisha's aide; the psalmist can see things they cannot see.

God's being in the heavens might suggest that he is unaware of events in this world, but the psalm works the logic the opposite way. In a city like Jerusalem the palace lay at its highest point, but it did not mean that the king was isolated from ordinary people. It meant that the king was in a position to know what was happening and to take action to protect the weak and the needy; sound travels better uphill than downhill. Yahweh likewise peers over the walls of the heavenly city, sees what is happening in the world below, and takes action on behalf of the faithful and against the faithless.

God doesn't always do so, and it can be tempting to think God never does so. The psalm invites people not to give into that temptation and invites us to pray for people like that professor, urging God to make its declarations come true.

PSALM 12

Sometimes God Speaks

The leader's. On the eighth [tone]. A composition. David's.

¹ Yahweh, deliver, because the committed people are gone,
  because the people who are true have vanished from
  among humankind.

² Individuals speak emptiness to their neighbors;
   with smooth lip out of a double mind they speak.
³ Yahweh should cut off all the smooth lips,
   the tongue that talks big,
⁴ the people who have said, "With our tongues we will prevail:
   our lips will be with us—who will be lord over us?"

⁵ "Because of the destruction of the lowly,
   because of the cry of the needy,
now I will rise up," Yahweh says.
   "I will take my stand as deliverer," he testifies to him.

⁶ Yahweh's words are pure words,
   silver purified in a furnace on the ground,
   refined seven times.
⁷ Yahweh, you will keep them;
   you will protect us from the generation that lasts forever—
⁸ all around, the faithless walk about,
   as worthlessness stands high for humankind.

Before coming to the United States to resume being an ordinary professor, I was principal of a theological college in
England, a position that is a cross between being president,
provost, and dean of a U.S. seminary, but on a much smaller
scale. I had become the principal at a time when my first wife's
multiple sclerosis was affecting her more than it did when we
were younger, and as I began the job, I was concerned about
how I would cope with the combination of responsibility for
the seminary and for Ann—as, I suspect, were some of my colleagues and members of the board. So I was praying about that
issue, as I think they probably were. Then at the service when
I was installed, one of my friends received this word from God
to give to me: "I will make the north wind your warmth, the
snow your purity, the frost your brightness, and the night sky
of winter your illumination." It was more than proved over the
following ten years.
   Psalm 12 has a similar dynamic in that a message from
Yahweh is the turning point, though it arises out of a different
kind of situation—for me there weren't any people of double
mind involved, and the message from God is quite different.
The psalm begins with a prayer, relates a word from God, and

then closes with a response to that word. A number of stories in the Old Testament manifest the same dynamic (a problem, a prayer, a word from God, and a response), though it's almost the only example within the Psalms. Some psalms do manifest a transition from urgent prayer to confidence about God's deliverance (Psalm 6 is an example), but they leave a bit mysterious what brought about the transition. Maybe the psalm simply constitutes the words of the person praying; the word from God would have to come from God. You can write the script for prayers, but you can't write a script for God. Or maybe the reason is that people didn't receive a word from God that often. While there have been other occasions when God has given someone a message for me or has given me a message for someone else, the occasion of my installation as principal was the only time I have received a message in response to a specific need about which I and other people had been praying. Maybe it was rare for Israelites, too. Whatever the reason for the distinctiveness of Psalm 12, it's worth noting.

The psalm begins from a similar situation to others that appear in the Psalter, though it may be a prayer for people who are not so personally affected by the situation as in some preceding psalms. It again presupposes a society where the social order is near collapse. There seems to be no one you could trust; no committed people, no people who are true and on whose word you can rely. People speak smoothly and plausibly, and in regular circumstances you would trust them, but you suspect there is no substance to what they say and to the undertakings they give you. They are double-minded—they give you the impression that they intend one thing, but actually they intend something different. They are swindlers, confidence tricksters. You will lose your home and your farm to them if you're not careful.

They are too clever for ordinary people to defeat and thus are confident about their ability to achieve their ends, confident about their capacity to con people. No, an ordinary person will not be able to defeat them. So the psalm prays for God to do so. Their words are the problem, so God needs to do something about their tongues and their lips. Like chop them off. That would solve the problem. (The psalm should not be taken too literally, as when Jesus tells people to chop off their hands; it's a forceful way of saying, "You have to stop them.")

It's at that point in the psalm that God responds—intervenes, we might say. A person might pray the psalm in the context of worship, and we know from elsewhere in the Old Testament that people with prophetic gifts were involved in ministry in the temple. They might be priests, assistant ministers (Levites), or ordinary people. To someone God gives the word that comes in verse 5. God makes a commitment to act to deliver the person who is under pressure from the swindlers. Whereas these are people whose words cannot be relied on, God's words are pure. They survive being tested in the furnace whereas the swindlers' words would be all dross.

The last part of the psalm is the response of the person praying. It's a declaration of trust in God's word and a declaration of confidence in the future, a different stance from the one expressed in the first part of the psalm. The crowd of dishonest confidence tricksters who seem to run the city seem set to do so forever, but now you know God will protect you. The third element in the response is a surprise. God has spoken, and that constitutes stage one in an answer to prayer; when you leave the temple, God's having spoken changes everything. Yet it also changes nothing. The **faithless** people are still walking about doing their dishonest business, their heads held high although they are the embodiment of worthlessness. So a proper response to God's word is a reminder to God to act in accordance with his promise.

PSALM 13

How Long, How Long, How Long, How Long?

The leader's. A composition. David's.

¹ How long, Yahweh, will you ignore me forever,
    how long will you hide your face from me?
² How long must I lay up [people's] plans in my spirit,
    [lay up] trouble in my heart all day—
    how long will my enemy stand high over me?

41

³ Take note, answer me, Yahweh my God;
  give light to my eyes, lest I sleep in death,
⁴ lest my enemy says, "I have finished him off,"
  [lest] my foes celebrate because I fall down.

⁵ But I myself trust in your commitment;
  my heart will celebrate your deliverance.
 I will sing to Yahweh,
  because he has done all that should be done for me.

About the same time as the story I described in connection with Psalm 12, I had a dream or a vision—I'm not sure what it was. I was pushing Ann in her wheelchair across a bare plain toward the horizon. It was hard, but I had people who cared about us who were helping me push and who would indeed sometimes shove me out of the way so that they could push and I could simply walk. Then, as a spectator to the scene, I was lifted up on a Simon Snorkel hydraulic platform to watch the scene, and from that much greater height I saw that the horizon and the distance I had to push were much farther than I could see from ground level, though I knew it would be OK because I had those helpers. With hindsight I now know that the horizon was miles farther than I could have known—I pushed the wheelchair for twenty years. And despite the support, I often wondered, "How long, how long, how long, how long?" With hindsight, I am glad I didn't know the answer, as I'm not sure I could have lived with it.

I wouldn't say God ignored me or hid his face from me through those twenty years in the sense that those expressions have in Western thinking. I knew God was with me; God was like a father or a teacher or a coach leaving his son or his pupil or his trainee to get on with a demanding task, and God was watching, not ignoring me. But in the sense that those expressions have in biblical thinking, God was ignoring me and hiding his face from me in that he was declining to take action to relieve me and heal Ann (though God was involved with us in other ways, not least in the way other people supported us). Such is the experience that the psalm has in mind.

The psalm's background is other people's hostility rather than something like a loved one's illness, but it raises overlapping issues. It implies a knowledge that other people, powerful people, are plotting trouble, maybe some way of swindling the family out of its farm. The worry associated with these realities dominates the person's thinking. Once again Naboth's story (1 Kings 21) illustrates the scenario the psalm may imply. There, swindling someone out of his land indeed meant bringing about his death, "finishing him off."

How long, how long, how long, how long? The psalm is written for someone facing a long haul. It dares him to continue trusting in **Yahweh's commitment** and expecting to celebrate Yahweh's **deliverance**. It dares him even to talk about the moment when he will be singing to Yahweh because he *has* acted in deliverance, done that thing of which there is no sign at the moment. It's one thing to say you're confident of God's commitment, another to act as if the deliverance has already happened. The psalm nicely juxtaposes two uses of the verb "rejoice" or "celebrate." The foes think they are going to celebrate. The psalm dares the person praying to believe that it is he or she who is going to celebrate.

PSALM 14

What a Rogue Says to Himself

The leader's. David's.

1   A rogue has said to himself,
      "God is not here.
    People have become corrupt, disgusting, in their actions;
      there is nobody who does good here."

2   From the heavens Yahweh has looked down at humankind
      to see if there is someone discerning,
      inquiring after God.
3   Everyone has turned, altogether they have gone bad;
      someone who does good is not here.
4   Do they not acknowledge [Yahweh], all those who
      do wickedness?—
    the people who eat my people have eaten food;
      they have not called on Yahweh.

⁵ There, they will experience frightful terror,
    because God is among the faithful company.
⁶ You people may discredit the plan of the lowly person,
    but Yahweh is his refuge.

⁷ If only Israel's deliverance might come from Zion!
    When Yahweh restores Zion's fortunes,
    Jacob will rejoice; Israel will celebrate!

In the last decades of the twentieth century there was a thing called the charismatic movement that emphasized the felt reality of God's presence and the perceptible reality of God's speaking and acting in healing people. One of my bosses contrasted its assumptions with what he called "God-in-the-gallery" theology. Christians often picture God as really existing and caring about us yet as not really involved in the world. It's as if he is sitting in the church gallery watching us with concern yet not doing anything. The charismatic movement testified to God's being involved and acting, not merely watching.

The rogue of Psalm 14 has a God-in-the-gallery theology. The Hebrew word for "rogue" is often translated "fool," which is not exactly wrong, but there are other words for "fool," and this word has more the connotation of "scoundrel." First Samuel 25 tells the story of a successful but truculent sheep farmer called Nabal, who was not sensible enough to realize that he would be wise to kowtow to David the successful outlaw; *nabal* is this word for "stupid rogue." Translations also have the rogue in the psalm declaring that "there is no God," but this gives a misleading impression. In a traditional society like Israel, atheism hasn't been invented. The rogue's observation concerns whether God is around or not, whether God is involved, not whether or not God exists.

While the comment about people having become corrupt might be the psalmist's own comment, I have taken it as a continuation of the rogue's observation. It expresses his skepticism, or perhaps his disillusion, or his rationalization for his own behavior. When he looks around at his world, he can see only corruption. There is no one who does good here, and God is not here; God does nothing about it. It is a roguish statement; its cynicism undermines commitment to proper order in society.

Yet the psalm half grants that it cannot blame the scoundrel for his disillusion with God. It pictures God looking down on earth from the heavens, which are farther away than a mere gallery. Furthermore, God's assessment of things in the human community is the same as the scoundrel's. With some irony, God notes that there is no one with any discernment—in other words, they are all fools, not just the person of whom the psalm initially speaks. There is no one inquiring after God, looking to God, asking God what he is doing, urging God to get involved—that is what the foolish rogue has given up on. People do not acknowledge God or acknowledge the real truth about their own actions. They can devour people mercilessly (take over their farms and their livelihoods) and then enjoy the proceeds without a second thought, like a contract killer following up his murder with a good meal.

The psalm also agrees with the rogue about how things are, yet it refuses to surrender faith in God's involvement in the world: "They will experience fearful terror"—literally, "they have feared [with] fear." Like a prophet, the psalmist speaks about something that has still to happen yet speaks as if it has already happened. That is how certain it is. The oppressors are consuming the company of those who belong to Yahweh, the **faithful** company, the people with God in their midst. God is not merely in the gallery. God is on the floor, in the congregation's midst. "Where two or three are gathered together in my name, I am there in the midst" (Matthew 18:20). Their oppressors are playing with fire. The psalm then addresses these oppressors directly (one need not imagine that they are literally present, though they might be). They may belittle the hopes of the lowly person, but his reliance on **Yahweh** trumps that contempt.

The psalm closes like Psalm 12; the statements of confidence lead into a closing plea—more precisely, a closing wish—that presupposes the reality of how things are now. It may imply that the rogue is not an Israelite but the leader of another people that is oppressing Israel. But it is in **Zion** that Yahweh is among the faithful company. Yahweh's being there is ground for hope that a time of rejoicing will come.

PSALM 15

How to Dwell with God

A composition. David's.

¹ Yahweh, who may stay in your tent,
  who may dwell on your holy mountain?

² The person who walks with integrity, and acts
    with faithfulness,
  and speaks the truth in his heart.
³ He has not gone about talking,
  has not done wrong to his fellow,
  has not taken up reviling against his neighbor.
⁴ In his eyes a contemptible person is abhorrent,
  but he honors people who are in awe of Yahweh;
  he has sworn to bring trouble and not changed it.
⁵ He has not given his money on interest
  and not accepted a bribe against the innocent—
  one who does these things, who does not falter forever.

I have been in e-mail correspondence with an online student of mine in Kabul concerning the meaning of "holiness." The context in which she lives raises an odd problem. The Western Christians with whom she works are people of truthfulness, faithfulness, mercy, and peaceableness. Yet when they articulate their faith to Afghanis, they stress God's declaring us to be righteous even though we are sinners so much that they don't set up an expectation that God's forgiving grace will transform us. They make it sound as if living a moral life is optional, which is very confusing to a Muslim. "Our lives and our words are out of sync," she says. In other parts of the world, too, our Christian instinct is to keep religion and morality in separate compartments; there can be strife and backbiting between the members of a congregation, but they feel no unease about continuing in worship (possibly separately). The people involved in high-profile corruption and fraud cases and acts of slaughter often turn out to be respected members of Christian churches.

The book of Psalms began with a reminder that people couldn't separate their praise and prayer from the question of whether their lives were lived in accordance with the **Torah**. Its stress didn't rest on our feelings about our relationship with God. Repeating the teaching of the Torah and living by it had to accompany worship. Now that we have read a few psalms since that expectation expressed in Psalm 1, the Psalter reminds us of the point again in case we have come to think that honoring God in praise or prayer is possible without honoring God in one's relationships with other people and one's life in society.

While the talk of **Yahweh's** tent and Yahweh's mountain might make us think of a concrete place such as Mount Sinai or Mount **Zion**, the talk of staying and dwelling suggests that the psalm has something broader in mind. "Staying" is the word for spending the night somewhere (in modern Hebrew, it generates the word for a hotel). Dwelling likewise suggests staying somewhere for a while. While people might sometimes have camped on Zion overnight, we have no indication that it was regular practice. But the Psalms also speak of God's dwelling in a broader sense, a less focused reality, a presence of God that was a reality throughout the land of Israel.

Being in someone's tent or staying with someone implies abiding in a place of security and provision. So what kind of person must you be to enjoy that security of living in God's tent? The answer comes in a sequence of unusual three-part lines. **Parallelism** won't work with three-part lines. They keep surprising us with their third part, and thus making us think some more.

First, enjoying security with God means being characterized by integrity. Literally, you are someone who "walks whole." There is a moral consistency, constancy, and stability about you. It expresses itself in **faithfulness** in your actions; it also implies a uniformity between what you are outside and what you are inside. You speak the truth in your heart; your actions and your thinking match. You don't do one thing and think another.

Second, you don't go around talking about other people (literally, you don't go around on your tongue). The point is spelled out by the rest of the line. You don't use your tongue to wrong a fellow member of your village—for instance, by lying about someone in order to rob the family of its land or cattle. You don't use your tongue to accuse your neighbor of things.

Third, it means being discerning in the way you relate to other people in light of their own moral stances. If someone else has earned the community's contempt for such action, you don't turn a blind eye and you certainly don't honor such people. The people you honor are those who revere Yahweh in word and deed. And when you commit yourself to ensuring that wrongdoers pay for their wrongdoing, you don't go soft and let them off and thereby encourage people to assume they can get away with such wrongdoing.

Fourth, you watch what you do with your own possessions. On one hand, you are generous in lending without interest to people who (for instance) have had a bad harvest and have no seed to sew or no food to eat for the coming year. On the other hand, when you're involved in some community dispute, you don't use your wealth to get a favorable decision from the elders by bribing a witness. And you don't just maintain that stance for the short haul. This last bit of definition belongs to the last of the four three-part lines, but it wouldn't be surprising if the psalm assumes that it applies to all the psalm's constraints.

PSALM 16

The Secret of Life

An inscription. David's.

¹ Watch over me, God,
      because I rely on you.
² I have said with regard to Yahweh,
      "My Lord you are my good, none above you,"
³ to the holy ones who are in the country,
      and the leaders in whom is all my delight.

⁴ Their pains will be many,
      the people who serve another [god].
   I will not pour their blood libations;
      I will not take up their names on my lips.

⁵ Yahweh—my allotted share, my cup,
      you are the one who holds onto my allocation.

⁶ Apportionments have fallen to me in loveliness;
  yes, the estate is perfect for me.
⁷ I will worship Yahweh who has guided me;
  yes, by night my heart corrects me.
⁸ I have set Yahweh before me continually;
  because [he is] at my right hand, I shall not falter.
⁹ Therefore my heart rejoices, my spirit celebrates,
  yes, my flesh will dwell in security,
¹⁰ because you will not abandon my life to Sheol,
  you will not give over one committed to you to see
    the Abyss.
¹¹ You will make known to me the path to life;
  joyful fulfillment will be with your face,
  lovely things at your right hand forever.

As a result of a routine physical exam I was recently diagnosed with prostate cancer. Quite likely it would not develop into something actually life-threatening before I died of something else, and I might have decided to do nothing about it, but the discovery happened just after I had met, fallen in love with, and proposed to someone. Before this happened, I might have felt that I had had a good life of a reasonable length and could appropriately make way for someone else (though ideally I would like to complete the Old Testament for Everyone series). I now had reason for revising that view. In effect, we started praying that God would not abandon my life to **Sheol**, and we agreed that I would have the relevant medical procedure so that whatever I eventually die of, it will not be this condition.

When the New Testament speaks of God's not abandoning Jesus' life to Sheol, it means that God did not let Jesus stay dead. When the psalm uses that language, it means God will not let the person die. The Old Testament doesn't mind that we all eventually end up in Sheol. It's just the place where you go when you die. It's not a place of suffering; if anything, it's a place of relief from suffering. It may be a bit boring, but it's OK. At least this is the Old Testament view in connection with someone who has been able to live a full life. The Psalms do object to your ending up in Sheol before you have had the chance to live a full life; this possibility is the focus in Psalm 16.

Each morning when my wife and I wake up and have had our cup of tea, we pray the Episcopal form of family morning prayers. Where it gives you opportunity to pray your own prayers, my wife regularly thanks God for the wonderful new day God has given us together. Every day is an opportunity to start afresh with God. She takes the same attitude to life as seen in the close of Psalm 16, when it speaks of the path to life and joyful fulfillment through living before God's face and enjoying lovely things at God's right hand all through our lives. It's not referring to an afterlife (the only afterlife it expects is Sheol, which is OK, but not wonderful). It's referring to the wonder of this life that God has given us to enjoy.

The German theologian and martyr Dietrich Bonhoeffer said in his *Letters and Papers from Prison* (New York: Simon & Schuster, 1997) that the reason God didn't tell Israel that there was going to be resurrection life was that once people know that fact, they will stop taking this life seriously. The church's history shows he was right. Of course, our failing to take this life seriously was illogical; the New Testament declares that our eternal life will involve the resurrection of the body. It will be a new form of this life, not an eternal bodiless life for a bodiless soul. It's also illogical because God created our this-worldly, bodily life, so presumably God likes it.

The psalm knows that if you want to enjoy a full life in this world, you are wise to look to the God who devised this bodily life for us. It's tempting, however, to look in other directions. In Israel it was tempting to look to other gods, to offer blood libations to them (that is, offer sacrifices that involve pouring out the animal's blood), to call on them, to rely on them, to see them as the ones who give good things. The psalm knows this way leads to trouble, not fulfillment. The person who prays needs to make a public commitment to **Yahweh** alone before the holy ones in the country (that is, the rest of those who belong to God's holy people) and to their leaders (who have responsibility to keep an eye open for people who turn to other gods). Sometimes the background might be an accusation that an Israelite has turned to other gods, and such a declaration constitutes a solemn denial of apostasy. The declaration affirms the confession in Deuteronomy 5 that Yahweh is our God,

Yahweh alone, but it provides further ways of publicly making that declaration. It thus helps strengthen the commitment, as does the reminder of how beautiful this commitment is. The psalm's distinctive way of making the point is to say that I always have my eye on Yahweh, or (to mix metaphors) I always have Yahweh at my right hand. I am confident that I will be OK, not because I secretly turn to other deities but because I do rely on Yahweh, the one who guides me, the one whose voice I heed in the darkness of night when some people might secretly look in other directions. Uttering the public commitment perhaps makes it harder to slip into secret apostasy.

Apostasy could mean forfeiting your share in the land. The psalm takes up the image of each Israelite family having an allocation within the promised land as a whole. That's my allotted share, my cup, my allocation, my apportionment, my estate. It's lovely and precious to me. Every Israelite would be able to make that statement—it doesn't imply that my land is better than other people's. But it's mine, so it's precious, lovely, perfect to me. The psalm reminds us that we have a lovely place in a promised land in this life, not just in the resurrection life.

PSALM 17

Go On, Look into My Heart

A plea. David's.

1. Listen in faithfulness, Yahweh, attend to my resounding cry;
   give ear to my plea on lips that are not deceitful.
2. May a decision for me come forth from your presence;
   may your eyes behold what is upright.
3. Were you to test my heart, visit me by night,
   try me, you would not have found [anything]—
   I had decided that my mouth would not transgress.
4. As for human actions, in accord with the word of your lips,
   I indeed have watched for the ways of the robber.
5. My steps have held onto your tracks,
   my feet have not faltered.
6. I myself call you, because you will answer me, God;
   bend your ear to me, listen to my word.

⁷ Act wondrously with deeds of commitment,
  you who deliver those who rely on you
  from the people who rise up against them, by your
    right hand.

⁸ Watch over me like the apple of your eye,
  in the shadow of your wings hide me
⁹ from the faithless who have assaulted me,
  the enemies of my life who surround me.
¹⁰ They have closed their hearts,
  with their mouth they have spoken grandiosely.
¹¹ Our steps—they have now surrounded us;
  their eyes—they set them to extend through the country.
¹² His appearance is like a lion that is eager to tear,
  like a great lion that sits in ambush.
¹³ Rise up, Yahweh, meet him face to face,
  bring him down!
  Rescue my life from the faithless person with your sword,
¹⁴   from human beings by your hand, Yahweh.
  From human beings in their lifetime, with their share in life
    and with what you have stored up, will you fill their belly.
  Their children will be full
    and they will leave what they have over to their children.
¹⁵ But when I behold your face in faithfulness,
  I will be full with your form when I awake.

From time to time my wife asks me what I'm thinking. She has to do so because whereas she instinctively tells me what she's thinking, I'm not good at doing so. But it's a potentially scary question. Occasionally I might be thinking something that could be hurtful or could otherwise get me into trouble. I then have to decide whether to tell the truth or lie. Then sometimes she sees though me anyway. Just now I claimed to have blanked out everything from before we got married six months ago, and she responded, "That's the biggest lie of all time." The Bible makes clear that God can see through us, but it also implies that God doesn't always choose to do so, because it indicates that God has surprises, and especially disappointments—though not ones that he can't handle.

What kind of person do you have to be in order to be at ease with the idea of God's testing your heart—that is, looking inside you and examining your thinking, or visiting you by night when other people can't see what you're doing so that you can get away with things you couldn't get away with by daylight? Or with the idea that God might test you? The psalm uses the word for refining silver, heating it to huge temperatures to reveal and remove dross. If you are to invite such testing, examining, and proving with a confidence that it will not uncover anything shameful, you have to be a person who has looked unflinchingly at your own life and not hidden from the truth about yourself. One challenge of the Psalms is that they expect us to be people who do so and who can then claim to be committed people—which doesn't mean sinless, but it does mean that we have a proper orientation to our lives.

Being such people is often the background to the prayers that the Psalms offer us to pray. So this psalm appeals to God's **faithfulness** and God's **commitment**, an appeal you can only make if you can claim that faithfulness and commitment to God characterize your own life (the idea of the apple of the eye is that in someone else's eye you can see a tiny image of yourself). There is no point appealing for **deliverance** as one who relies on **Yahweh** unless you actually are a person who relies on Yahweh rather than looking to other gods—in Western culture, we ourselves might be the god on which we rely. To put it more concretely, the psalm speaks of being like a baby bird hiding under its mother's wings. In connection with one's relationships with other people, there is no point in asking God to honor uprightness unless you are upright, and no point in asking for protection from robbers if you are a robber.

The background in the pleas of the Psalms often seems to be a false accusation. Someone fancies your farm and "rises up against you," making up a story about your stealing his sheep or turning to other gods, and thereby imperiling your life. The switch between "I" and "we" in the psalm allows for the possibility that the person who is accused is the head of the family, but it is the whole family's life that is imperiled by the accusations. On the other hand, the switch between "they" and "he" allows for there being a conspiracy of accusers but also a front man. The family feels surrounded by assailants operating like people with grandiose ambitions, with their eyes on a takeover of all the farms in the country. The way prophets such as Isaiah talk implies that such fears are only slightly exaggerated.

The psalm presents God with a closing challenge. He should put the assailants and their families down. Their plan is to take over an innocent family's share in life, its share in the land. The psalm takes up the image of a "share" and uses it in more sinister fashion. God surely has a "share" in store for faithless people: well, God should fill them and their family with it. It's not a nice prayer, but like other psalms it leaves the judgment to God and provides people who are helpless and scared stiff with somewhere to go with their fear and their helplessness. It enables them to envision a scenario that is more encouraging than the one that confronts them. They can imagine seeing God's face shining out in love and faithfulness and rescuing them. They can imagine waking in the morning as if they are beginning a whole new life, waking up as from a nightmare, and realizing that they have indeed seen God in person acting to deliver, so they will be full to satisfaction in a quite different way from the experience that comes to their assailants.

PSALM 18:1–24

We've Probably All Been Rescued from Death a Few Times

The leader's. Yahweh's servant's. David's, when he spoke to Yahweh the words of this song on the day Yahweh saved him from the hand of all his enemies and from the hand of Saul. He said:

¹ I give myself to you, Yahweh, my strength,
²   Yahweh my cliff, my fortress, my rescuer,
   my god, my crag on whom I rely,
      my shield, the horn that delivers me, my haven.
³ As one to be worshiped, I called Yahweh,
    and from my enemies I found deliverance.
⁴ Death's ropes have encompassed me,
    Belial's torrents overwhelmed me,
⁵ Sheol's ropes have encircled me,
    death's snares have confronted me.
⁶ In my trouble I called Yahweh,
    I cried for help to my God.

⁷ And the earth has rocked and vibrated,
    the mountains' foundations shook.
  They have rocked because he has raged;
⁸   smoke has gone up in his anger.
  Fire from his mouth consumed,
    coals have blazed from him.
⁹ He has spread the heavens and come down,
    thundercloud beneath his feet.
¹⁰ He has ridden on a cherub and flown,
    swooped on the wings of the wind.
¹¹ He has made darkness his screen,
    his shelter around him rain cloud, masses of mist.
¹² Out of the brightness before him,
    through his masses there have passed hail and
      burning coals.
¹³ Yahweh has thundered in the heavens,
    the One on High gave forth his voice.
  Hail and burning coals:
¹⁴   he has sent off his arrows and scattered them,
    shot lightning and routed them.
¹⁵ Streams of water have appeared,
    the foundations of the world have come into sight
  at your roar, Yahweh,
    at the blast of your angry breath.

¹⁶ He sent from on high so that he might take me,
    drew me out of great waters.
¹⁷ He saved me from my strong enemy,
    from people who were against me,
    because they were stronger than me.
¹⁸ They confronted me on the day of my calamity,
    but Yahweh has become a support for me.
¹⁹ He has brought me out into roominess;
    he has rescued me because he delights in me.
²⁰ Yahweh has dealt with me in accordance with
      my faithfulness;
    in accordance with the cleanness of my hands he has
      recompensed me,
²¹ because I have kept Yahweh's ways
    and not been faithless to my God,
²² because all his decisions have been before me;
    his laws I have not put away from me.

²³ I have been a person of integrity with him;
    I have guarded myself from my waywardness.
²⁴ So Yahweh has recompensed me in accordance with
        my faithfulness,
    in accordance with the cleanness of my hands before
        his eyes.

Between us my wife and I have had four or five illnesses that would have left us dead had we lived in most contexts in human history. We have both had appendicitis that might have killed us without medical intervention. My wife's appendicitis then turned into something more unpleasant, which might also have killed her. When she was giving birth to her daughter, she almost died. This year I have had an illness that would have been life-threatening in the past. One of my sons had appendicitis and peritonitis when he was a teenager; the other recently developed diabetes. In the West, we take for granted that medicine can cope with all these illnesses or events, which in most contexts would most likely have led to death, but we don't think much about it.

It would be appropriate for us to talk in the terms that this psalm uses. From time to time, death's ropes have encompassed us, Belial's torrents have overwhelmed us, **Sheol's** ropes have encircled us, and death's snares have confronted us; the psalm is talking about **deliverance** from enemy attack, but the threat of death is the same. Death's ropes have encompassed us, all right, but we who live on can say, "God drew me out of great waters; God saved me from my strong enemy."

It's hardly surprising that the psalmist invites us to respond, "I give myself to you, **Yahweh**." Translations often have "I love you," but the verb is not the regular word for love—in fact this is the only time it comes with this sense in the Bible (and actually it's hard to find passages in the Bible where people tell God they love him). It suggests an act of commitment more than an emotion—though the psalm indicates that it implies lots of emotion. The psalm goes on to put end to end all the words you could think of to describe God as protector, preserver, and rescuer. When threatened by death, you need to reach out for something to hold on to, and God is that reality. In this psalm, it is not merely a hope or a conviction of faith but a proven reality.

So the psalm can go on to give a testimony to God's rescue. It gives a dramatic picture of God's acting. It was so extraordinary that it was as if God had swooped down dramatically from the heavens. The stupendous power of a Middle Eastern thunderstorm provides an image for understanding such an event. The clouds suggest the reality of God's presence yet also protect us from seeing that presence and being blinded by its brightness; it's easy to have a too-exclusively warm and fuzzy view of God as our buddy. Thunder that seems to shake the earth suggests the overwhelming effect of God's action in the world. Lightning suggests the fiery and devastating nature of God's intervention to put down wickedness. Storming rain suggests disturbing the separation of land and water established at creation.

The point about a testimony is to glorify God. Testimony psalms are also expressions of thanksgiving to God, but if we simply wanted to give our thanks to God, we could do so silently. We wouldn't need other people to hear. Giving thanks aloud makes our thanksgiving something other people join. It becomes a corporate act of praise. The community rejoices in God together because everyone is glad about what God has done for some members of the family. Further, describing a psalm as a testimony reflects how God's acting on behalf of someone else is also an encouragement to me. It suggests what God might do for me. The psalm functions to encourage the whole community to turn to Yahweh as one who can be our refuge and fortress when death threatens us before our time.

PSALM 18:25–50

Self-Knowledge or Self-Deception

25 With the committed you show commitment;
   with the man of integrity you show integrity.
26 With the pure you show yourself pure;
   with the crooked you show yourself antagonistic.

27 Because you are one who delivers a lowly people
   but puts down those whose eyes are superior.
28 Because you are the one who keeps my lamp alight;
   Yahweh my God lights up my darkness.
29 Because with you I can rush a barricade;
   with my God I can jump a wall.
30 God: his way has integrity;
   Yahweh's word is proven.
   He is a shield to all who rely on him.

31 Because who is God apart from Yahweh,
   who is a crag except our God?
32 God is one who girds me with strength
   and makes my way upright,
33 who makes my feet like deer
   and enables me to stand on the heights,
34 who trains my hands for battle
   so that my arms could bend a bow of bronze.
35 You gave me a shield that would be my deliverance;
   your right hand sustains me, your response made
      me great.
36 You give my steps room beneath me
   and my ankles have not given way.

37 I pursue my enemies so as to overtake them;
   I do not turn back until I have finished them off.
38 I strike them down so that they are not able to stand;
   they fall beneath my feet.
39 So you girded me with strength for battle;
   you bring low beneath me the people who arise against me.
40 You made my enemies turn tail for me;
   the people against me—I destroy them.
41 They cried for deliverance, but there was no deliverer—
   [they cried] to Yahweh, but he did not answer them.
42 I ground them fine like dirt on the wind,
   flattened them like mud in the streets.
43 You rescue me from the contentiousness of the people,
   you set me at the head of nations.
   A people that I did not acknowledge serve me;
44   on hearing with the ear, they obey me.
   Foreigners wither before me,

⁴⁵   foreigners wilt and come trembling out of their strongholds.
⁴⁶ Yahweh lives, my crag is to be worshiped,
        may God my deliverer be on high,
⁴⁷ the God who gives me total redress
        and subjects peoples under me,
⁴⁸ the one who saves me from my enemies,
        yes, exalts me above the people who rise up against me,
        enables me to escape from violent people!

⁴⁹ Therefore I will confess Yahweh among the nations
        and proclaim his name,
⁵⁰ the one who gives great acts of deliverance to his king,
        keeps commitment with his anointed,
        with David and with his offspring forever!

I know some Christians who have had affairs, and I have
come closer to doing so than I should have done. When
Christians talk about their affairs, the story regularly involves
an element of denial and/or self-deception. Maybe the people
now have some insight about what they did, but they acknowledge that at the time they were deceiving themselves; they
were denying the nature of their actions. Their marriage had
gone stale; their spouses were no longer interested in them;
this new love was so creative and life-giving, it surely must be
a gift from God.

The introduction to Psalm 18 invites us to read it in light of
David's experience; he had many brushes with death before he
became king (hence the reference to Saul) and after he became
king and commander-in-chief. So reading his story helps us
appreciate why someone might pray the way Psalm 18 does.
At the same time, it raises questions for us. When the Old
Testament tells the story of how David became king, he could
indeed say that he had behaved with integrity and **faithfulness**
in relation to Saul. But he could hardly make that claim about
the second half of his life (see **David's story**). The turning point
in his story is when he has an affair. So if we are to imagine
David praying this psalm, we also need to imagine God raising an eyebrow and sighing about his lack of self-knowledge.
David did come to acknowledge that he had done wrong in

having an affair (see 2 Samuel 12), though it's not clear how deep the acknowledgment went, and while God "puts away his sin," it doesn't stop God from taking away his son, nor does it prevent David's life unraveling from then on. Such considerations heighten the question about David's self-knowledge if we imagine David saying this psalm, and they heighten the importance of our asking questions about our own self-knowledge and our part in cleaning up the messes we make and facing how repentance and forgiveness may not sort out the messes or our actions' impact on other people.

So reading the psalm in light of David's story makes it possible for God to speak to us. Reading the psalm in its own right makes it possible for God to speak to us in other ways. This second half of the psalm spells out the implications of Psalm 1. Between us and God there's a two-way relationship of **commitment**, integrity, and purity. If those are features of your life and you are under attack or sick, you can expect them to be features of the way God relates to you. The psalm indicates that this is not mere theological theory, because it is a testimony to God's making things work out in this way in someone's life—as God did in the first half of David's life when he could claim to have been upright and pure.

Western readers of the psalm may be uneasy about its conviction that God made it possible for someone to win victories in war. The psalm assumes that God is involved with Israel as a nation and with the Davidic king as its ruler, and that God then doesn't go in for half measures in pursuing his purpose in the world. That involvement with the king is for the sake of the people, and the involvement with the people is ultimately for the sake of the world. The psalm is concerned for **Yahweh**'s **name** to be proclaimed among the nations. The psalm doesn't imply that any ruler or any people can claim that God is on their side, though maybe sometimes a ruler or a people may be able to make this claim when they are the underdogs but have right on their side. Once again the psalm's readers have to exercise some self-knowledge and think about their actions' impact on other people if they claim they can apply the psalm to themselves.

PSALM 19

The Mystery of Sin

The leader's. A composition. David's.

¹ The heavens are declaring God's splendor,
   the sky is announcing the work of his hands.
² Day by day it pours out speech,
   night by night it proclaims knowledge.
³ There is no speech, there are no words,
   whose voice does not make itself heard.
⁴ In all the earth their noise has gone out,
   at the end of the world their words.
   For the sun he put a tent in [the heavens];
⁵   it is like a groom departing from his chamber.
   It rejoices to run the path, like a warrior
⁶   when its departure is from the end of the heavens.
   Its completed circuit is at their [other] end,
   and there is nothing hidden from its fierceness.

⁷ Yahweh's teaching has integrity, restoring life.
   Yahweh's declaration is trustworthy, giving insight
      to the naive.
⁸ Yahweh's precepts are upright, rejoicing the mind.
   Yahweh's command is clean, enlightening the eyes.
⁹ Awe of Yahweh is pure, standing forever.
   Yahweh's decisions are true; they are faithful altogether.
¹⁰ They are more desirable than gold, than much pure gold,
   sweeter than honey, than the juice of honeycombs.
¹¹ Yes, your servant takes warning from them,
   and in keeping them there are great results.

¹² Who can understand mistakes?—
   free me of things that are hidden;
¹³   yes, hold your servant back from willful deeds.
   May they not rule over me,
   then I will be whole, and free of great rebellion.
¹⁴ May the words of my mouth be favorable to you,
   and may the talk of my mind come before you,
   Yahweh, my crag and my restorer.

One of the Christians I know who have had affairs had three such relationships and got away with two without anyone knowing. Then some people discovered about the third (I don't know what his wife might have suspected), which was how he came to be talking to me. I didn't know whether he was repentant or just remorseful about getting found out, but I was struck by what he said about not recognizing temptation as temptation because he was able to rationalize his way into believing that it was OK for him to act in a way that the Christian community would regard as wrong (and that you would think Scripture was pretty clear about). Yet I know he was only an extreme example of something most of us experience. It's what Romans 7 refers to as failing to do the things we theoretically want to do and doing the things that we theoretically don't want to do.

Psalm 19 is concerned about something along these lines. When it talks about mistakes, it's likely not referring to (say) forgetting to pay your fare on the bus, but instead to moral or religious mistakes, to wandering off the right moral or religious path. Why do we wander in this way? It's hard to understand. The psalm spells out the idea in asking to be freed of things that are hidden, things we do in secret because we know they're wrong. They might be an affair (funny how we keep such things secret even when we've convinced ourselves they're not wrong), or they might be something in our relationship with God—for an Israelite it might be seeking blessing from gods other than **Yahweh** in the privacy of one's home. The expression "great rebellion" is one used in Israel and elsewhere of having an affair. It's as if marital unfaithfulness is one of the really terrible "mistakes"—hence its appearing in the Ten Commandments. There's a link with Israel's use of the marriage relationship as an image for its relationship with God. The two most terrible "mistakes" are unfaithfulness to one's spouse and unfaithfulness to God.

If we start facing facts, we will recognize that these are willful deeds. There is a mystery about our willingness to do them; it is as if they control us rather than that we control ourselves. Yet the "great rebellion" commonly starts as an act that seems small and innocent but perhaps conceals an openness to something big and not so innocent. In due course it means that we have to throw ourselves on God's mercy and implore God to hold us back from such temptations. We need God to enable us to say the right words to other people (e.g., I can't say, "I love you" to someone other than my spouse) and to God (e.g., I can't say, "I trust you" to a god other than Yahweh). And we need God to help us with the words we say inwardly as well as the words we say outwardly.

How do the first two parts of the psalm lead into that closing reflection and prayer? The first part talks about the cosmos declaring God's splendor. In a sense the cosmos gives out a clear message, but it doesn't get you very far. In traditional societies and in the Western world people end up admiring and trusting in the creation rather than the creator (as Romans 1 puts it). In connection with the question of what makes people live their lives God's way, the middle part of the psalm thus attaches importance to the concrete teaching you find in the **Torah**—so it is another psalm that spells out the implications of Psalm 1. Its insight is the typical Israelite and Jewish one that the Torah isn't a burden but a blessing. It's a terrific thing that God has told us in detail how to live our lives. That heightens the mystery of our ignoring what God says and the importance of the reflection and prayer that close the psalm.

How fortunate that God is the crag that protects us from ourselves as well as from other people and that God is our restorer.

PSALM 20

How to Be Codependent

The leader's. A composition. David's.

¹ May Yahweh answer you on the day of trouble,
  the name of Jacob's God shelter you.
² May he send you help from the sanctuary,
  support you from Zion.
³ May he be mindful of all your offerings,
  accept all your burnt sacrifices.   (*Rise*)
⁴ May he give to you in accordance with your thinking,
  fulfill every plan of yours.

63

5 May we resound at your deliverance,
    in the name of our God we will lift our banners:
    may Yahweh fulfill all your requests.

6 Now I acknowledge
    that God has delivered his anointed.
  He answers him from his holy heavens
    with the mighty acts of deliverance of his right hand.
7 Those people [eulogize] about chariotry and those people
    about horses,
    but as for us—we eulogize about the name of Yahweh
    our God.
8 Those people have knelt and fallen,
    but as for us—we have risen up and taken our stand.
9 "Yahweh, deliver the king!"
    May he answer us on the day that we call.

In our church we are in the midst of accepting that we can no longer afford a full-time rector. As a result I am becoming the only priest involved with the church on a regular basis, presiding at services and preaching except on occasions when I ask someone else to do so. I'm sad about the circumstances, but I'm looking forward to presiding and preaching. I'm also aware of the responsibility. There is a two-way relationship between people involved in leadership and the people who are being led, and it applies to the lay leaders of the congregation as well as to me in our relationship with the congregation as a whole. You could call it a codependent relationship if you use that expression in a positive way. It's a mutual, reciprocal relationship. There is responsibility that the leaders accept and responsibility exercised by the congregation as a whole. Each depends on the other to make things work. Codependency doesn't mean being passive, expecting that the person you depend on will "just do something." Codependency means co-responsibility.

In the way Psalm 20 pictures this codependency, the responsibility it attributes to the people as a whole is to pray for God's blessing on their leader. As the last line makes explicit, the leader was their king, and a key aspect of the king's responsibility was leading the army in battle. You couldn't be commander-in-chief sitting in Washington. The king directly faces the enemy when trouble comes to the people. So they pray that God may answer his prayers when that day comes. The **parallelism** in the first line suggests that such answering involves action as well as reassurance—it involves God's protection. The second line spells out the point. While God dwells among the people on Mount **Zion**, the king may have to fight all over the place—so may God send help and support from there to wherever it is needed. The third line returns to the idea of the king's praying for help. Prayer is not just a matter of words but of actions; the king will appeal to God by making offerings as well as by using words. So his people pray for God to accept those offerings. The fourth line recognizes that the king will have to make the battle plans, but Proverbs likes to emphasize that it is fine to make plans, but whether they get implemented depends on God. So there's further reason to pray for God to be involved in events. After all (the psalm later notes), it's customary to believe that your military hardware decides the result of battles, but in reality things often work out otherwise.

The second half of the psalm begins, at least, with the king's response to the people's prayer of blessing. It would evidently be encouraging to hear it. To know people are praying for you is a blessing, not just because it indicates their concern but because you know that God's cabinet in the heavens takes note of submissions that come to it. God answers not merely from his abode on Mount Zion but from his abode in the heavens where the cabinet meets and where decisions are made.

The mixture of tenses in verses 6–8 means people could use this psalm on more than one kind of occasion. They could use it when trouble threatened, when the king had just experienced a great **deliverance**, and when there was no crisis but they were giving praise for the ongoing nature of God's commitment to them and their king.

PSALM 21

Being Blessed and Being a Blessing

The leader's. A composition. David's.

1 Yahweh, the king rejoices in your strength;
    how greatly he exults in your deliverance!

² You gave him the longing of his heart;
    the request of his lips you did not deny.
³ Because you meet him with blessings of good,
    set on his head a crown of pure gold.
⁴ When he asked for life from you,
    you gave him length of days for ever and ever.
⁵ Great is his honor through your deliverance,
    splendor and majesty you bestow on him.
⁶ Because you make him an [embodiment of] great
      blessing forever,
    you gladden him with joy through your presence.
⁷ Because the king trusts in Yahweh,
    and by the commitment of Elyon he does not falter.

⁸ Your hand finds all your enemies,
    your right hand finds your opponents.
⁹ You make them like a blazing furnace
    at the time of your appearing.
Yahweh in anger swallows them;
    fire consumes them.
¹⁰ Their offspring you destroy from the earth,
    their posterity from among humanity.
¹¹ When they have directed evil against you,
    thought up a scheme, they do not succeed.
¹² Because you set them back
    when you aim at their faces with your bows.
¹³ Be on high, Yahweh, in your strength—
    we will sing and make music about your might.

Yesterday a young Christian man set off an explosion in Oslo, Norway, to preoccupy security forces, then took a ferry to a nearby small island. Hundreds of young people with political connections or political involvement were at camp there, with no escape from him, and he shot and killed nearly a hundred. He took the action in God's name because he believed that God's purpose in the Christian West was imperiled by the spread of multiculturalism, and specifically by the growing numbers of Muslims living in Europe, which he feared might turn Europe into a Muslim rather than a Christian culture. One of the host of questions that the man's action raises is whether the Old Testament provides justification for the kind of stance he took.

Psalm 21 says nothing about human beings taking initiatives to safeguard God's purpose in the world. There are other psalms that may presuppose such human action, but here, at least, all the emphasis lies on God's action. Maybe the king went out to initiate a battle, but if so, that fact is not seen as the key factor in the situation. The word that recurs in the psalm is *deliverance*. This word and related ones such as the verb *deliver* came a number of times in the previous psalm, and they will come again in the next (they also recurred in Psalm 18). It's sometimes possible to see links of this kind between successive psalms so that here (for instance) the sequence invites us to see Psalm 20 as the way you pray for your leader before a crisis and to see Psalm 21 as the way you pray when God has answered that prayer. The point about the word *deliverance* is that it denotes something that happens such as you could not have made happen. It involves God's delivering you, saving you, rescuing you. The Old Testament tells many stories about Israel's winning a battle against crazy odds, or sometimes winning without fighting at all (as at the exodus and at Jericho). The other side had the submachine gun, but somehow it jammed.

While it would be possible to read the second half of the psalm as addressed to the king, it speaks in a way more reminiscent of talk concerning **Yahweh's** activity in battle, which fits with the stress on deliverance and with the psalm's closing declaration to Yahweh. The whole psalm addresses Yahweh as someone with the resources to implement his purpose in the world and protect his people. It functions to challenge king and people to trust in those resources rather than in their tanks.

Its talk about blessing points to the common Old Testament assumption that God's actions toward Israel are not only undertaken for Israel's benefit. On one hand, God meets the king with "blessings of good." Literally understood, the phrase sounds like a tautology—there is no such thing as blessings of evil. The two words build on each other; these are rich blessings with which God goes out to meet the king (as he returns from battle?). They include wondrously long life; living "forever" may imply living to the very end of a regular human life span instead of dying before one's time, or it may be purely conventional (in 1 Kings 1 Bathsheba expresses this wish when David is on his deathbed).

On the other hand, as well as blessing the king God has "made him blessings"—as verse 6 literally puts it. The expression means more than "You gave him blessings." It implies, "You made him into blessings," or into "great blessing." It is a similar phrase to the one in God's promise to Abraham that he would be a blessing (Genesis 12). The idea is that Abraham (and now Israel's king) would be so blessed that other people would take him as their standard of blessing and would ask God to be blessed in the same fashion as he had been. It doesn't imply that Abraham or the king has to do something in order to be a blessing. They just have to let people see how they are blessed. So Israel's gaining deliverance from particular enemies whom Yahweh annihilates doesn't imply that Yahweh is unconcerned about other peoples. Indeed, it implies the opposite. Peoples who submit to Yahweh rather than acting as his enemies find the same blessing as Israel.

PSALM 22:1–18

My God, My God, Why?

The leader's. On Dawn Help [perhaps a tune]. A composition. David's.

¹ My God, my God, why have you abandoned me,
    far away from delivering me, from the word I yell?
² My God, I call by day but you do not answer,
    and by night—there is no quietness for me.

³ But you are enthroned as the holy one,
    the great praise of Israel.
⁴ In you our ancestors trusted—
    they trusted and you rescued them.
⁵ To you they cried out and they escaped;
    in you they trusted and they were not shamed.

⁶ But I am a worm, not a person,
    an object of reviling for humanity,
    an object of contempt for the people.

⁷ All who see me mock me,
    open their mouth, shake their head.
⁸ "He should commit it to Yahweh, he must rescue him,
    he must save him, because he delights in him."

⁹ Because you are the one who enabled me to break out
        of the womb,
    enabled me to trust at my mother's breast.
¹⁰ On you I was thrown from birth;
    from my mother's womb you were my God.

¹¹ Do not be far from me,
    because trouble is near,
    and there is no one to help.
¹² Many bulls have surrounded me,
    mighty Bashan steers have encircled me.
¹³ Tearing and roaring lions
    have opened their mouth at me.

¹⁴ I have spilled out like water,
    all my bones have become loose.
My mind has become like wax;
    it has melted inside me.
¹⁵ My strength has withered like a piece of pot,
    my tongue sticks to my palate.
You have put me into death's dirt,
¹⁶   because dogs have surrounded me.
An assembly of evil people has surrounded me;
    my hands and feet have shriveled.
¹⁷ I can count all my bones,
    while those people take note and see me.
¹⁸ They divide my clothes for themselves;
    for my garments they cast lots.

Each Palm Sunday as part of our church's worship we read the
story of Jesus' trial and execution, with members of the congregation taking different parts. There are a number of frightening
moments in the story. Particularly sickening is the point when
we all join in the cry "Crucify him," and when Pilate resists,
we cry again, "Crucify him." Equally horrifying is the moment
when Jesus cries out in the opening words of this psalm, "My

God, my God, why have you abandoned me?" It's not the only point where the Gospels take up the language of Psalm 22. When the executioners divide Jesus' clothes among themselves, John 19 sees a fulfillment of verse 18. Some translations of verse 16 speak of piercing the victim's hands and feet, which reminds one of what happened in the course of the crucifixion.

The psalm isn't a prophecy in the sense of a passage that says, "One day there will be a messiah to whom this happens." It's a prayer for Israelites to pray when they need to, so it is hugely encouraging because it gives them permission to acknowledge their sense of abandonment and their fears without shame. But it is also one of the most horrifying of the prayers that the Psalter gives Israelites to pray, so it's not so surprising that when Israel's Messiah goes through his martyrdom, the prayer fits uniquely on his lips. In a paradoxical way, his praying this psalm helps us see what we would mean by praying it. Jesus was not abandoned by God in the sense that God was not present at his execution. God was there all right, as is implied by the fact that Jesus prays; you can't address someone who has gone off. God is watching steadfastly as Jesus is executed, suffering as profoundly in his spirit as Jesus is suffering in body and spirit. Indeed, it is hard to imagine the depth of the agony involved in watching your son be executed when you could stop it. As some of the witnesses at the execution declare, it would be appropriate for God to rescue Jesus if Jesus is really God's son. But God doesn't do so. God listens to Jesus asking, "Why have you abandoned me?" and does nothing. God's abandonment lies not in going away but in being present and yet doing nothing.

Such is also the nature of God's abandonment of other people. When women get raped or children get abducted and abused and killed, God abandons them. God sits in heaven aware of what is going on but does nothing. How could that be?

In one sense, when Jesus asks the question "Why?" he knows the answer. He has been seeking to get his disciples to see the inevitability and the logic of the martyrdom he knows is his destiny. There is a specific answer to the question as applied to Jesus. Thus when he asks, "Why?" it likely has the same meaning as attaches to it when anyone else asks it. We noted in connection with Psalm 10 that the question is more a cry

70

of pain and protest than a request for information, but there is a general answer to the question why God does not intervene. God did not make the world a place where he would be continually stopping people from doing wrong to one another. Maybe you think God should have made the world that kind of place, but God did not do so. Sometimes God intervenes; often God doesn't. The presence of Psalm 22 in the Psalter as a prayer for people to pray makes it possible for us to ask, "Why?" and to utter our protest; the fact that Jesus takes up the question encourages us to assume that we can ask it too. It presupposes that God is there and is listening. As was the case at the cross, God is not miles away in an aseptic environment in heaven. God is listening and watching and suffering with us.

PSALM 22:19-31

On Facing Two Sets of Facts

19 But you, Yahweh, do not be far away—
   my strength, come quickly as my help.
20 Save my life from the sword,
   my very self from the dog's power.
21 Deliver me from the lion's mouth;
   may you have answered me from the buffalos' horns.

22 I will tell of your name to my kindred;
   in the midst of the congregation I will praise you.
23 You who are in awe of Yahweh, praise him,
   all Jacob's offspring honor him,
   be in awe of him, all Israel's offspring!
24 Because he has not despised,
   he has not scorned the lament of the lowly.
   He has not turned his face from him
   but listened to his cry for help to him.
25 From you will be my praise in the great congregation;
   my promises I will fulfill before the people who are in
      awe of him.
26 Lowly people will eat and be full;
   people who inquire of Yahweh will praise him—
   may your heart live forever.

²⁷ All the ends of the earth will be mindful and turn to
    Yahweh;
  all the families of the nations will bow low before you.
²⁸ Because sovereignty belongs to Yahweh;
  he rules over the nations.
²⁹ All the well-to-do of the earth have eaten, and bowed low;
  before him all the people who go down into the dirt
    will kneel,
  and the person who has not been able to keep
    himself alive.
³⁰ Offspring will serve him;
  a generation to come will be told of my Lord.
³¹ They will proclaim his faithfulness to a people to be born,
  because he has acted.

Two friends of ours were giving us an amusing account of a
difference they had discerned between the way they approach
problems in their relationship and in other aspects of life. It
was amusing yet also serious and profound. When there is a
problem, the guy is inclined to look the other way, to pretend it
isn't there, because his confidence in life or in the relationship
is imperiled by the possibility of a problem. In contrast, the girl
is inclined to feel that the problem occupies the entire horizon,
so that for her, too, the problem imperils her confidence in life
and in the relationship, though she sees it as he doesn't. It is
somewhat analogous to the way we react to God when some
tragedy happens. Some people avoid facing what has happened
because it imperils their fundamental understanding of God
as one who is faithful and loving and involved. Other people
face the nature of what has happened and indeed find that their
fundamental understanding of God is imperiled.

The genius of Psalm 22 is that it refuses to take either of
those alternatives. It resolutely insists on facing two sets of
facts. It invites people to look directly in the face the adver-
sity that has happened to them but also to stay attentive to the
facts about God that they already knew. It thus moves between
"Why have you abandoned me?" and "You are enthroned as
the holy one"; between "I am a worm, not a person" and "You
are the one who enabled me to break out of the womb"; and
between "You have put me into death's dirt" and "My strength,

come quickly as my help." (As is often the case, the description of the sufferer's predicament in verses 19–21 is expressed in metaphors rather than in literal terms; the effect is to make it easier for other people to pray the psalm because it is not too specific about the kind of trouble to which it refers. Whatever are the "wild animals" that threaten us, we can use the psalm's words.) Then the last third of the psalm stands in contrast to the first two-thirds, in that the first two-thirds includes much material that suggests hopelessness, but the last third is so confident of **Yahweh**'s **deliverance** that it can speak of that deliverance as if it has already happened.

The psalm thus invites us neither to deny the reality of what we already know about God nor to deny the reality of what has happened. It also invites us not to deny the reality of the present but neither to think that the present is all there is. Like other psalms, but at greater length and arguably therefore with greater depth, Psalm 22 makes an extraordinary final transition from speaking of the grim facts about the present to speaking of the glorious facts about the future in the conviction that God has heard this prayer, even though God has not yet acted. It gives no indication that anything has changed after verse 21. The grimness of the present has the first word; the praise of the future has the last word. The psalm thus again models something.

As is often the case, Psalm 22 also makes clear that it is not only looking forward to thanking God for the act of deliverance that will surely come. It is looking forward to giving a testimony to other people to that act of deliverance, because that testimony will build up their faith and make it more possible for them to face both sets of facts when they need to do so. It speaks in outrageously ambitious terms about people from all over the world hearing of what God has done, in future generations as well as in the present. Its ambitiousness, however, has been more than justified, for the psalm has been used by people all over the world for two or three millennia.

As we hear in Mark and Matthew the first words of Psalm 22 on Jesus' lips when he is being executed, so we hear in Hebrews 2 the opening words of the last third of the psalm on the lips of the risen Jesus as he says, "I will tell of your **name** to my kindred; in the midst of the congregation I will praise you." Jesus had worked hard to prepare his disciples for his martyrdom, partly by assuring them that it would not be the end, though he had not succeeded in enabling them to be ready when it came. Before his death he had known that his death would not be the end—he knew it because of what he knew about God and because of what he had read in the Scriptures. He could thus face both sets of facts.

PSALM 23

In the Dark of the Canyon

A composition. David's.

¹ My shepherd being Yahweh, I do not lack;
²   he enables me to lie down in grassy pastures.
  He leads me to waters that are totally still;
³   he restores my life.
  He guides me in faithful tracks
    for the sake of his name.
⁴ Even when I walk in a deathly dark canyon,
    I am not afraid of disaster,
  because you are with me;
    your club and your cane—they comfort me.

⁵ You spread a table in front of me
    in full view of the people watching for me.
  You have bathed my head in oil;
    my cup fills me up.
⁶ Yes, goodness and commitment pursue me
    all the days of my life.
  I will return to Yahweh's house
    for long days.

In the foothills of the mountains near where we live is a retreat center where we have a faculty gathering each fall. Two years ago a new director at the center gave us some advice we had not been given before. If we met a bear on the grounds, we were advised not to try running away; bears can run faster than we can. I've forgotten what we were supposed to do instead, but in any case I decided I wasn't going for a walk, especially as the director also told us that we would probably not get attacked by a rattlesnake if we stuck to the path and that there had been no cougar sightings lately. From a location like that of the retreat center many canyons lead up into the mountains, and I can imagine shepherds once leading sheep up the canyons. Shepherds would know about bears, cougars, and rattlesnakes and would know the best way to deal with them. In relation to some creatures, a club would be an important part of their security.

The canyons are deep and often have streams running through them, at least in winter and spring, and they are thus densely wooded—they have the water supply lacking in the countryside outside the canyons. They are thus dark and a bit sinister, and their deep darkness contrasts sharply with the bright sunshine above them. Maybe the swiftly running water would be a bit scary for the sheep, but the shepherd would know where it flows into quieter pools. He would also know where the presence of moisture makes some grass grow and where the presence of shade stops it withering in the blistering heat. He would know where there are some trees or other bushes whose fruit he can knock down with his cane. So the flock is secure and also provided for. Their shepherd is **faithful** in his care for it. So it is for a human being who has **Yahweh** as shepherd. To be Yahweh means to be the God who is faithful, active in seeing that his people are provided for and protected. So Yahweh acts in this way "for the sake of his **name**" in order to be the person his name proclaims him to be.

In the second half of the psalm, literal reality pokes through. The psalm is encouraging us to declare our trust that we can face being threatened by the human equivalent of bears, rattlesnakes, and cougars (compare the bulls, steers, lions, and dogs of Psalm 22), because God protects us with his club like a shepherd protecting his sheep. Like a shepherd providing his sheep with pasture, Yahweh provides us with what we need—indeed, provides us abundantly. The psalm imagines the enemies outside our camp able to see us within it, clean-shaven and smart and enjoying our meal, but they are unable to get access to us, like animals on the edge of a clearing unable to get to the sheepfold. Whereas sheep can be chased by wild animals, and human beings by their enemies, on the battlefield we are chased only by two of God's agents, goodness and **commitment**. On the battle-field we are cut off from the place of worship where we meet with God and from the place of fellowship where we meet with God's people, but we know this will not be the end of the story.

PSALM 24

Will God Let You In? Will You Let God In?

David's. A composition.

1 The earth and what fills it are Yahweh's,
    the world and the people who live in it.
2 Because he founded it upon the seas,
    sets it on the rivers.

3 Who goes up on Yahweh's mountain,
    who stands up in his holy place?
4 The person who has been clean of hands and pure of mind,
    who has not lifted up himself to emptiness
    and not sworn in such a way as to deceive.
5 He will receive a blessing from Yahweh
    and faithfulness from God his deliverer.
6 This is the company of people who inquire of him,
    [This is] Jacob who look to your face.   (*Rise*)

7 Lift your heads, you gates;
    lift up, age-old doors,
    so that the glorious King may come in.
8 "Who is he, the glorious King?"—
    Yahweh the strong one and warrior,
    Yahweh the battle warrior.
9 Lift up your heads, you gates;
    lift up, age-old doors,
    so that the glorious King may come in.
10 "Who is he, then, the glorious King?"—
    the glorious King is Yahweh Armies.   (*Rise*)

Five days before the Egyptian army crossed the Suez Canal in September 1973, aiming to recapture Sinai from Israel, I was in Sinai climbing what in Arabic is called "Mount Moses," the mountain traditionally regarded as Mount Sinai in the Old Testament. From our campsite at the foot of the mountain we began the climb at dawn. Most of the group were Israelis, but as far as I could tell, there were few other people for whom climbing Mount Sinai had a religious significance; the weekend was part of the program of the Society for the Protection of Nature in Israel. For me, it was a climb that inspired awe. All the way up the four thousand feet from our base camp, I found myself repeating words from Psalm 24. Who can ascend the hill of the Lord? The psalm refers to Mount **Zion**, but instinctively I felt that the same issues were raised by my setting foot on Mount Sinai.

Like Psalm 15, the middle part of Psalm 24 reminds us again of the Psalter's opening assertion that you can't expect to be involved in praise and prayer unless you are also living in a morally and religiously authentic way with other people and with **Yahweh**. Do you want to be on the receiving end of the kind of blessing and faithfulness of which Psalm 23 speaks and to return for long days to Yahweh's house? OK, pay attention to verse 4, which makes four brisk, interwoven points about relationships with other people and with God. First, our hands need to be clean—that is, they mustn't have blood on them (compare Isaiah 1:15–16). That's a challenging demand for people in Western countries when we have so much blood on our hands through our involvement in war and neglect in relation to other parts of the world. Second, our cleanness needs to be not just a matter of outward act but of inner attitude. Third, we mustn't lift ourselves up to emptiness—that is, lift our faces and our prayers to gods that have no real existence, looking elsewhere than to God as our reliance. Fourth, we mustn't take oaths in God's **name** that actually contain untruths. When the people of God come before God, they have to be able to say, "That's the kind of people we are."

The tricky question in Psalm 24 is the relationship between that middle section and the opening and closing verses. Maybe the psalm is a liturgy, with the opening verses being a song of praise uttered by the congregation. They affirm that Yahweh is the creator of the world and thus its owner. They work with the common picture of the world as a kind of island floating over the seas or rivers that flow beneath, secure because Yahweh anchored it safely there. Paradoxically, the fact that Yahweh is the creator of the world is accompanied by the fact that Yahweh has a particular mountain, a particular holy place, where you can meet him. As they draw near the presence of the creator of the world there, the question arises of what sort of people you need to be in order to do so.

With further paradox the psalm's last paragraph has Yahweh outside the city and has people urging the city's inhabitants to welcome him into the city. While there is a sense in which God is everywhere, there is also a sense in which God can be specially known in certain places and contexts; we noted in connection with Psalm 14 Jesus' promise: "Where two or three are gathered in my name, I am among them" (Matthew 18). And while there is a sense in which God can be specially known in certain places and contexts, this fact does not stop God from appearing elsewhere. Maybe the psalm thus presupposes the way **Yahweh Armies** goes out with Israel's army in battle; he and they now return. It also presupposes that one way or another it's quite possible for the people of God to keep God out of its midst, as Revelation 3 indicates with its picture of Jesus standing outside the door of a church and knocking to see if he will be admitted.

PSALM 25

I Can't Wait

David's.

¹ To you, Yahweh, I lift my heart.
²   My God, I have trusted in you.
I must not be shamed;
  my enemies must not exult over me.
³ Yes, all the people who wait for you will not shamed;
  the people who are false without reason will be shamed.

⁴ Enable me to acknowledge your ways, Yahweh,
  teach me your paths.

⁵ Direct me in your truthfulness and teach me,
    because you are my God who delivers;
    for you I have waited all day.
⁶ Be mindful of your compassion, Yahweh,
    and your commitment, because they are age-old.
⁷ Do not be mindful of the wrongs of my youth
    and my acts of rebellion.
  In accordance with your commitment be mindful
      of me yourself,
    for the sake of your goodness, Yahweh.

⁸ Yahweh is good and upright;
    therefore he instructs wrongdoers in the way.
⁹ He directs the lowly with authority,
    teaches the lowly his way.
¹⁰ All Yahweh's paths are commitment and truthfulness
    to people who keep his covenant, his declarations.

¹¹ For the sake of your name, Yahweh,
    pardon my waywardness, because it is great.
¹² Who, then, is the person who is in awe of Yahweh?—
    he instructs him in the way he should choose.
¹³ His life abides in goodness,
    and his offspring possess the country.
¹⁴ Yahweh's counsel comes to people who are in awe of him,
    and his covenant, in enabling them to acknowledge him.
¹⁵ My eyes are continually toward Yahweh,
    because he is the one who brings my feet out of the net.

¹⁶ Turn your face to me and be gracious to me,
    because I am alone and lowly.
¹⁷ The troubles in my mind have spread;
    bring me out from my straits.
¹⁸ Look at my lowliness and pressure;
    carry all my offenses.
¹⁹ Look at my enemies, how they are many;
    with violent opposition they are against me.
²⁰ Guard my life, rescue me;
    I must not be shamed, because I have relied on you.
²¹ Integrity and uprightness must watch over me,
    because I have waited for you.

 [22] God, redeem Israel
        from all its troubles.

"We can't wait till you come to see us next year," a friend in the Philippines said. "I can't wait till the concert on Saturday," a singer-songwriter said. "We can't wait to meet your new wife," a friend said. "I can't wait for Christmas," another friend said. "We can't wait to move into our own house," my son said. "I can't wait for the party," a friend said. "I can't wait for our wedding," my then-fiancée said. "I can't wait for the end of the quarter," a student said. I am amused each time someone uses this common U.S. expression; it makes me want to respond, "You will just have to," which would be to miss the point. If I say, "I can't wait for the end of the quarter" (for instance), I mean I am not going to wait; I am going to the beach *now*. But the expression simply means "I'm really looking forward to it and wish I didn't have to wait."

In the Psalms, thinking about the future is important, and so is waiting. This psalm alone refers three times to waiting. Waiting is related to hope, but in English the word *hope* suggests an attitude that may or may not be justified by events. You try to be hopeful as a way of keeping going (unless you are like me and just avoid thinking about the future). Waiting is more like expectancy. It relates to something you know or believe is going to happen. All those "can't wait" comments are related to events that people knew would come. The "problem" wasn't whether they would come; it was that they weren't going to come immediately. But because the people knew the events would come, their waiting could be reassuring and agreeable in its own way.

The waiting in the psalm is expectant in that concrete way and not hard to live with, but its particular expectancy and its grounds for confidence are quite different. Like so many psalms, it presupposes trouble, conflict, and pressure, and when these are your experience, you may not have a concrete, tangible reason for confidence that you will come out the other side. You may try to be hopeful, but you may not be able to justify expectancy. The psalm's basis for confidence lies in who God is: the God who **delivers**, the one characterized by compassion, **commitment**, and truthfulness.

It is on that basis that the psalm invites us to wait for God to act. This attitude is expressed in a variety of other ways. It means lifting our hearts to God—more literally, lifting ourselves to God; we are putting ourselves before God's eyes so that God looks at us and is bound to take action. It means trusting in God. It means lifting our eyes to God so that we look at God imploringly; we do not look just at the troubles, and we do not look at all at other resources. It thus means relying on **Yahweh**.

The psalm expresses two other attitudes to God that themselves might have seemed in tension with each other. It is more forthcoming than most psalms with an awareness of shortcomings, waywardness, and rebelliousness in the past and in adulthood. It knows that when we are aware of those realties, we have to cast ourselves on God's mercy and ask God not to be mindful of them, like a friend or spouse who is willing to forget things we do wrong, to pardon them like a king or president, to carry them like parents accepting responsibility for the actions of their child even though it was not they who did what was wrong. On the other hand, in tension with those appeals, the psalm emphasizes the importance of being committed to God's ways if we are to have a basis for appealing to God to answer our prayers; we have to accept responsibility for our actions. Yet with further tension, it also recognizes that we need God to teach us if we are to live the life God looks for. God has to work on us if we are to acknowledge God's ways by walking in them.

Psalm 25 is another alphabetical psalm; allowing for a little untidiness at the edges of its making the alphabetical structure work, it covers the nature of prayer from *A* to *Z*. Its leaving unresolved those tensions is part of its strength.

PSALM 26

I Wash My Hands in Innocence

David's.

¹ Decide for me, Yahweh,
    because I—I have walked in integrity.
  In Yahweh I have trusted;
    I do not falter.

² Probe me, Yahweh, try me,
    test my heart and mind.
³ Because your commitment is in front of my eyes;
    I walk about by your truthfulness.

⁴ I have not sat with empty men;
    I do not go with deceitful people.
⁵ I oppose the congregation of evil people;
    I do not sit with the faithless.
⁶ I wash my hands in innocence
    so that I may go about your altar, Yahweh,
⁷ to let people hear the sound of testimony,
    to declare all your wonders.

⁸ Yahweh, I love the abode that is your house,
    the dwelling place of your splendor.
⁹ Do not gather me up with wrongdoers,
    my life with men of blood,
¹⁰ who have scheming in their hands,
    whose right hand is full of bribery.
¹¹ But I walk in accordance with my integrity;
    redeem me, be gracious to me!
¹² My foot has stood on level ground;
    in the great congregation I will worship Yahweh.

In the Episcopal church, when we move from the first part of a service, which focuses on the reading of Scripture, to the celebration of communion, someone pours a little water over my hands as the priest and I say some words from Psalm 26: "I wash my hands in innocence so that I may go about your **altar** and tell of all your wondrous deeds." The practice, going back to the time of Cyril, Bishop of Jerusalem in the fourth century, means a lot to me, because telling of God's wondrous deeds (in this context, telling of Jesus' Passover celebration with his disciples, his dying for us, and his rising from death) is a responsible activity, designed to glorify God and be a blessing to his people. In the same century, John Chrysostom, Archbishop of Constantinople, mentions a practice whereby everyone washed their hands before going into church for worship. We all need to be prepared for listening to this story. Our church has a bowl of holy water just inside the door for people to dip a finger into and cross themselves, which can fulfill a similar function.

It is an even more solemn prayer when we think about the meaning of "washing our hands in innocence." In between Jesus' last supper and his execution, Pilate seeks to excuse himself from blame for Jesus' death by washing his hands and declaring his innocence with regard to it. The alternative to having clean hands is having blood on them. The psalmist thus asks not to be gathered up (to be buried with one's ancestors) with men of blood, people who do have blood on their hands. We have noted that it is hard for the citizens of powerful countries such as Britain and the United States to evade responsibility for much bloodshed in the world. When we come to worship, we indeed need to wash our hands in innocence, to repent of the blood on our hands and commit ourselves to working for policies that do not keep staining our hands with blood. We can't come to worship or pray the prayer if we intend to continue to stain our hands.

The psalm itself is intended for people who are in danger of having their blood shed, possibly because they are falsely accused of some capital offense. They need God to exercise his **authority** and decide for them. They also need to be able to let God check that their integrity holds in their hearts as well as in their outward behavior (the capital offense might involve looking to other gods, which they might not be doing publicly but might be doing secretly).

When priests talk about God's wondrous deeds while praying that prayer, they are referring to Jesus' dying and rising for us; however, the psalm has something different in mind. The proclamation of God's wondrous deeds will be "the sound of testimony." In other words, the psalm invites us to look forward to the time when God has made the kind of **decision** that it urges and has vindicated us so that we have been delivered from the pressure of false accusation. We then have a testimony to give concerning God's wondrous deeds for us. God's deeds are not just ones done long ago for the whole people but ones done right now for us. Such is the expectation the psalm invites.

PSALM 27

One Thing

David's.

¹ Yahweh is my light, my deliverance—
    whom should I fear?
Yahweh is the stronghold of my life—
    of whom should I be afraid?
² When evil people drew near me
    to devour my flesh—
my adversaries and my enemies—
    they collapsed, fell.
³ If an army camps against me,
    my heart will not fear.
If battle arises against me,
    in this I trust.

⁴ One thing I have asked from Yahweh,
    this I look for,
that I may live in Yahweh's house
    all the days of my life,
to gaze at Yahweh's loveliness,
    and come each morning into his palace.
⁵ Because he keeps me safe in his shelter
    on the day of trouble.
He hides me in his tent as a hiding place;
    he lifts me high on a rock.
⁶ So now my head is high
    above my enemies around me.
In his tent I will offer noisy sacrifices;
    I will sing and make music for Yahweh.

⁷ Listen, Yahweh, to my voice when I call;
    be gracious to me, answer me.
⁸ In respect of you my mind said,
    "Inquire of his face!"
Of your face I inquire, Yahweh:
⁹   do not hide your face from me.
Do not turn aside your servant in anger;
    you have been my help.

Do not forsake me, do not abandon me,
   God my deliverer.
¹⁰ If my father and my mother have abandoned me,
   then Yahweh will take me in.
¹¹ Teach me your way, Yahweh,
   lead me on a level path.
   In view of the people watching for me,
¹²   do not give me over to the will of those who trouble me.
   Because there have arisen against me false witnesses,
   a person who testifies violence.

¹³ Unless I believed I would see good things from Yahweh
   in the country of the living. . .
¹⁴ Wait for Yahweh,
   be strong, may your mind take courage,
   wait for Yahweh!

Soon after I came to the United States, I attended an inaugural lecture by a man who (we were told) was a full-time pastor and a half-time professor. I laughed because I assumed it was a joke—how could you be a full-time this and a half-time that? (He also told us that he was writing a book on "rest," which he subsequently published.) How naive I was about the United States! How many things people here are capable of doing at the same time! How inferior it makes me feel! A young man I know works at two jobs, is our church organist, is engaged in graduate study in engineering, and has a wife and baby to try to give time and attention to. It's not surprising that it's hard for us to arrange a time to discuss what hymns we should sing in church over the next month. Another young man I know is a graduate student in theology, works as a waiter in a restaurant (or maybe it's two restaurants), belongs to an Ignatian study group, has been candidating for Baptist ministry, and is in a dating relationship. It's not surprising that he sometimes can't show up for our Bible study group.

   "One thing," says the psalm. "One thing I do," says Paul (Philippians 3). "You lack one thing," says Jesus to a rich man (Mark 10). "Only one thing is needed," says Jesus to Martha (Luke 10). "I know one thing," says the blind man whom Jesus had healed (John 9). These declarations about "one thing" vary, but all recognize that there are moments when you have to focus. In Western culture we have gotten used to "multitasking," partly out of apparent necessity, partly out of choice. We think we can keep adding one more thing to our schedules without asking what we are going to abandon to create the room, and we aren't very good at standing back and asking what has priority. It's hard to perceive the moment when you have to focus, and it's hard to do the focusing. Perhaps the recurrence in Scripture of the expression "one thing" indicates that it's not just a Western problem.

The fuller expression in the psalm is "one thing I have asked for." What you ask for tells you who you are. "What do you want?" is thus a telling question when God asks it of Solomon (1 Kings 3) and when Jesus asks it of another blind man (also in Mark 10). Both stories indicate that the person could have given other answers to the question. The psalm is yet another psalm that presupposes a situation of being under attack; people are watching me, and I want them to be given their comeuppance and to be protected. But the psalm's "one thing" lies somewhere else, somewhere beyond those practicalities, or somewhere behind them. The "one thing" is to dwell in **Yahweh's** house. This hardly means living in the temple; as far as we know, no one lived there apart from Yahweh. The expression is an image for living in Yahweh's presence, living in Yahweh's household, and therefore being under Yahweh's protection. It makes everything else but the "one thing" fall away.

To judge from Psalm 90, Yahweh's "loveliness" denotes the beautiful things Yahweh has in store and intends to do, the "good things" to which verse 13 refers. These expressions suggest another angle on the psalm's understanding of how life with God works. It presupposes that we have past experience of God's **delivering** us; coming into God's presence reminds us of that reality. It also brings home the reality of what God intends to do for us and thus builds up our confidence and our capacity to live in hope, to look forward. But living in hope relates to living with a focus on "one thing"—not living in hope that we will be able to achieve and get everything but living in hope of gaining the "one thing."

PSALM 28
Our Handiwork and God's

David's.

1 Yahweh, I call to you;
    my crag, do not be deaf toward me,
  lest you be silent in relation to me
    and I am like the people who go down to the Pit.
2 Listen to the sound of my prayers for grace
    when I cry for help to you,
    when I lift up my hands to your holy room.
3 Do not drag me off with faithless people,
    with people who do wickedness,
  people who speak of well-being with their neighbors
    when there is evil in their minds.
4 Give to them in accordance with their action,
    in accordance with the evil of their deeds.
  In accordance with the work of their hands,
    render their wages to them.
5 Because they do not consider Yahweh's acts,
    the work of his hands;
    may he tear them down and not build them up.

6 Yahweh be worshiped,
    because he has heard the sound of my prayers for grace.
7 Yahweh is my strength and my shield;
    in him my soul has trusted, and I will find help.
  My soul has exulted
    and I will glorify him with my song.
8 Yahweh is his [people's] strength and stronghold;
    he is the great deliverance of his anointed.
9 Deliver your people, bless your very own,
    shepherd them and carry them forever.

In the news last weekend was a story about an unemployed and
deep-in-debt hairdresser in his forties who went to a "Money
Cometh to You" conference at a church in Vermont to listen to
a visiting preacher who promised that the Lord could not only
save him and take him to heaven but also give him good health

and solve even the worst financial problems—indeed, make him wealthy. The preacher spoke about his own 20,000-square-foot house and his Falcon 900B airplane for delivering his message. After all, he said, Matthew speaks of seeking the kingdom of God and his righteousness and of how all these things will be added to you. The hairdresser pulled out the sixty dollars with which he came to the service and left with none of it, yet he also left with his guilt and shame gone.

The trouble with heresy is that it is half right; things would be easier if it were simply wrong. Jesus does speak of having "all these things." They don't actually include a big house, but they do include food, drink, and clothing, which would suit the hairdresser. Psalm 28 makes the same assumption about the way God relates to his people. Reference to "the anointed" in a psalm sometimes implies that it is a prayer for the king to pray, but in Psalm 28 nothing else suggests this particular usage. The psalm is a prayer for ordinary individuals. It makes no reference to specific problems that they would be bringing to God, which means it can easily be used by people in many different circumstances. It does imply that the people who pray this psalm have some problems. They need help, and they need **deliverance**; they need a crag to climb onto; they are in danger of death, of ending up in the pit before their time. It's in this connection that they need God's grace. Some people deserve that fate; the psalm is for people who can claim that they do not.

The psalm assumes that you belong to one of two communities and that God relates to these two communities in two different ways. On one hand, there are the **faithless**, the people who do wickedness, the people who talk nice but are actually planning wrongdoing. If such people die before their time, it's quite appropriate. On the other hand, there is the community that is **Yahweh's** possession, the people headed up by the one Yahweh anointed. They are the people who find Yahweh to be their strength and stronghold, to be the one who shepherds them and carries them. They are the people whom Jesus will describe as those who prove that seeking God's reign does mean you also receive food and drink and clothing. Neither the psalm nor Jesus assume that such people are perfect; both the

Old and New Testaments show that people who are basically faithful sometimes act faithlessly.

The psalm has a distinctive way of differentiating between the two groups in the way it speaks of actions and handiwork. The first group comprises people who deserve to see the results of their own actions, of the ways that they say one thing but do another; such is "the work of their hands." It's as if they do a solid week's work, and the psalm thinks they ought to get the proper wages; but while it's a solid week's work, it's not a good week's work.

The second group comprises people who recognize the nature of God's acts, the work of God's hands. There might be two ways in which the psalm expects people to do so. One is that our lives should be lived in light of what God has done. They are expressions of gratitude for what God has done for us; they are lived in imitation of the priorities that God has, such as faithfulness rather than faithlessness. The other is that we live our lives in light of what God is going to do. If we live faithless lives, we will find God tearing us down, not building us up. This phrase recurs in Jeremiah in connection with the choice that stands before Israel, and Israel's story shows how the people of God may experience either destiny. The psalm presupposes that you have to decide which group to belong to, but you can expect to pray for deliverance only if you belong to the second group. The prayer for deliverance that closes the psalm places it between stage one and stage two of an answer to prayer. It knows that God has listened and responded to the raised hands; it still prays for stage two. It knows that Jesus has promised "all these things," and it asks God to fulfill that promise. When we know of Christians for whom life does not work out that way, the prayer drives us to pray in the way it prays.

PSALM 29

Who Is Really God (and Do You Treat Him as Such)?

A composition. David's.

¹ Give Yahweh, you divine beings,
   give Yahweh honor and strength.

2 Give Yahweh the glory of his name,
      bow low to Yahweh in holy array.

3 Yahweh's voice was over the waters,
      the glorious God thundered,
      Yahweh was over mighty waters.
4 Yahweh's voice was with power;
      Yahweh's voice was with majesty.
5 Yahweh's voice breaks cedars;
      Yahweh breaks off cedars of Lebanon.
6 He makes them jump like a calf,
      Lebanon and Sirion—like a young buffalo.
7 Yahweh's voice splits flames of fire,
8   Yahweh's voice convulses the wilderness,
      Yahweh convulses the Kadesh Wilderness.
9 Yahweh's voice convulses oaks, strips forests;
      in his palace everyone in it says,
10 "In glory Yahweh sat on high;
      Yahweh sat as king forever."

11 Yahweh gives strength to his people;
      Yahweh blesses his people with well-being.

Without being fully aware of what she was doing, on the eve of her daughter's wedding my innocent, soon-to-be wife agreed with her prospective son-in-law's mother (who was the matriarch of a large, Mexican, Roman Catholic family) that the two of them would say a novena for the next generation—for their children and grandchildren. Strictly speaking, a novena is a prayer you say for nine days, but my soon-to-be stepson's mother maneuvered my fiancée into making this commitment for two years, so when we married I inherited it. However, it has turned out to be a fine discipline. Part of this particular novena involves saying the Lord's Prayer twice, which has focused my prayer, especially the petition "Your kingdom come; your will be done, on earth as in heaven." Yet I find this petition puzzling, because both the Old and New Testaments make clear that there are forces in heaven (at least, in the supernatural world) opposing God's will just as there are on earth. Perhaps the implication is that we need to urge God to implement his will both in heaven and on earth.

Psalm 29 begins from the awareness that there are many divine beings and that they don't necessarily honor the one real God. Whereas English has a conventional way of distinguishing between *God* and *gods* by using a capital *G*, Hebrew and Greek don't have that convention, so Paul can speak in 1 Corinthians 8 about there being many gods and lords, and the psalm can do the same. As the psalm makes clear, this doesn't mean all these divine beings have the same status as **Yahweh**; Yahweh is so different from them that it is very useful to have a way of differentiating between gods and God. But the divine beings are like Yahweh in being supernatural and otherworldly. They have some power in the heavens and on the earth, and they are capable of misusing it. Hence the Lord's Prayer presupposes that they have some power but that it is ultimately subordinate to God's power (it's an enhanced version of human power, in fact).

In worship, then, Israelites challenge them to recognize who they are and who God is—in other words, who is really God. Maybe one implication is that there is some sense in which worshipers have power in relation to them. Perhaps they are like the rulers of countries where rulers are not elected and have power only as long as their people acquiesce in their power such that when people realize they do not have to acquiesce in this way, the rulers lose their authority. If the parallel holds, then when worshipers tell the supernatural beings that they must acknowledge the real God, they too have lost their power. These world rulers have power only as long as we agree to their having power.

The Bible isn't interested in monotheism, the question of how many gods there are. It's interested in the question "Who is God?" Its concern is to affirm not that there is only one God but that Yahweh is the only God. Although that implies monotheism, monotheism isn't the issue that interests the Bible. So Psalm 29 is interested in affirming that Yahweh alone is God and in pressing other divine beings to recognize the fact and honor Yahweh in the way Yahweh deserves. They should do so because their power is nothing compared with Yahweh's power. Just look at the way the created world is, the psalm says. Look at the way it convulses in a thunderstorm when lightning flashes, the ground shakes, and the wind blows so hard it makes huge trees crash to the ground. Think about how that assertion of divine power links with the way Yahweh acted back at creation, when Yahweh exercised authority over the other dynamic forces that might have tried to assert themselves, and took his seat on his throne where he would sit as king forever.

Formally, the psalm thus addresses supernatural beings in the heavens. But the presence of the psalm in the Psalter suggests that it belongs in the context of Israel's worship, and whether or not the divine beings are paying attention, the earthly beings who worship in the temple are overhearing. Maybe that is the real point of the psalm; we sometimes listen more intently when we are overhearing something not directly addressed to us. Through most of Israel's history, Israelites were tempted to hedge their bets by praying to other gods as well as to Yahweh. But if the divine beings ought to acknowledge that Yahweh is the only God with real power, then worshipers in the temple who slid off home after the service and made a surreptitious offering to some other deity are really stupid. There are many gods, but there is only one God. The last line points to a corollary. Yahweh is the only real God, and Yahweh is committed to Israel. He is its source of strength, blessing, and **wellbeing**. The message to the worshipers in the temple then is, "Look to Yahweh for those gifts. Your God is such a great God!"

PSALM 30

Answer to Prayer Phase Two

A composition. A song at the dedication of the house. David's.

1 I will extol you, Yahweh, because you put me down,
     but did not let my enemies rejoice over me.
2 Yahweh my God, I cried for help to you,
     and you healed me.
3 Yahweh, you brought my life up from Sheol,
     you kept me alive from going down to the Pit.
4 Make music for Yahweh, you who are committed to him,
     confess his holy remembrance,
5 Because there is a moment in his anger,
     a life in his favor.

In the evening weeping lodges,
   but at morning there is resounding.

6 I—I had said when I was at ease,
   "I shall not collapse ever."
7 Yahweh, in your favor
   you had established strength for my mountain.
   You hid your face;
   I became distraught.
8 To you, Yahweh, I would call,
   to my Lord I would plead for grace.
9 What would be the gain from my being killed,
   from my going down to Sheol?
   Can dirt confess you,
   can it declare your truthfulness?
10 Listen, Yahweh, be gracious to me;
   Yahweh, be my help.
11 You turned my lament into dancing for me,
   you undid my sackcloth and girded me with joy,
12 so that my heart might make music and not stop;
   Yahweh my God, I will confess you forever.

In connection with Psalm 16, I have mentioned how a few months ago I met, fell in love with, and proposed to someone, then discovered I had prostate cancer and arranged to have surgery. We had a very moving prayer time in church, and I knew God had heard people's prayers. It was phase one in having a prayer answered in the way the Psalms portray it. It means you start praising God for answering your prayer, but you recognize that phase one is only phase one, and you don't stop praying. Only after phase two, when you have seen God's answer and not merely heard it, do you stop praying and start simply praising. For me, even that process felt a bit more complicated, in that the doctors were very pleased with themselves after the surgery. In this sense you could say phase two had come, but for me, getting back to feeling normal took a few more weeks, and having the test last week that established that the level of the relevant antigen in my blood was now correct felt like the real phase two. Now I *really* know God answered those prayers. (Well, unless you hear in a year or two that I have died because the cancer has spread. . . .)

Psalm 30 illustrates the way you pray after phase two—or rather, it illustrates the way you thank God for answering your prayers and other people's prayers after phase two, and the way you give your testimony to what God has done. One reason for using the word "testimony" is that thanksgiving involves telling a story. The story comes in three parts: you relate how things went wrong for you, how you prayed, and how God answered. The psalm illustrates another feature that recurs in the psalms: it says what it needs to say but then says it again. It could have stopped after verse 5, and we would not have thought that the psalm was truncated, but it starts again in verse 6. Maybe the psalmist felt that what verses 1–5 say just isn't enough to do justice to what God has done.

When the second half of the psalm tells the story again, it goes behind the first account by recalling how fine things were before trouble struck. Maybe the words imply that the psalmist was overly confident, though I don't think I was wrongly excited with the way my life was unfolding before I discovered I had cancer. But the opening line in version two of the testimony raises a question we should think about. Version two also gives us more information on the way the psalmist prayed, which resembles Psalm 6 (you could imagine someone praying Psalm 6 after phase one of an answer to prayer and praying Psalm 30 after phase two).

The psalm illustrates three other interrelated aspects to giving one's testimony. First, the psalm assumes that an experience of God's deliverance is not a mere one-time, odd event. It constitutes a concrete illustration of who God really is. God is one who puts down, but his anger lasts only a moment (perhaps because it doesn't take long to make the point that wrongdoing is a serious business), and his loving acceptance of his people is more characteristic of him. The second is that experiencing God's deliverance isn't something that just affects you at the time. It changes you and changes the way you pray forever. The third is that you are not the only person it affects. A thanksgiving psalm is also a testimony psalm because it is designed for other people to hear and for them to join in, because the facts about God that it illustrates are relevant to the rest of the congregation as well as to the person who is healed.

It's easy to see how someone might use the psalm to praise
God for an experience of healing or deliverance. But what
about the introduction? What's its link with the dedication of
the house? The house is presumably the house of God (a link
with a royal palace or an ordinary person's house is harder to
make sense of). So maybe the psalm was used at the dedication
of the temple in the time of Haggai and Zechariah in 515 BC,
when people have been freed to return from **exile**. Or maybe
it was used at the rededication of the temple after its desecra-
tion by Antiochus Epiphanes in 167 BC, in fulfillment of the
visions in Daniel. The Hebrew word for dedication is *hanuk-
kah*, and that is the name of the Jewish festival celebrating the
deliverance from Antiochus. Either way, a psalm devised with
an individual's testimony in mind became a means of giving
the congregation's testimony, which illustrates the flexible way
the Psalms could be used.

PSALM 31

They're Trying to Wash Us Away

The leader's. A composition. David's.

1   Since I have relied on you, Yahweh,
        may I never be shamed;
        rescue me in your faithfulness.
2   Incline your ear to me,
        hurry and save me.
    Be for me a crag, a stronghold,
        a fortress to deliver me.
3   Because you are my rock, my stronghold;
        for your name's sake lead me and guide me.
4   You could take me out of the net that they concealed for me,
        because you are my stronghold.
5   Into your hand I assign my spirit;
        you have redeemed me, Yahweh, truthful God.
6   I oppose people who hold onto empty vanities;
        I myself trust in Yahweh.
7   I will celebrate and rejoice in your commitment,
        you who have seen my lowliness;
        you have acknowledged my deep troubles.

⁸ You have not delivered me into the hand of the enemy;
   you have stood my feet in a wide place.

⁹ Be gracious to me, Yahweh,
      because I am in trouble.
   My eye wastes away because of vexation—
      my spirit and my body, too.
¹⁰ Because my life spends itself in sorrow,
      my years in groaning.
   My strength falters because of my waywardness,
      my bones waste away.
¹¹ Before all the people watching for me I have become an
         object of reviling,
      and very much so to my neighbors.
   A terror to my acquaintances,
      people who see me in the street flee away from me.
¹² I am put out of mind like someone who has died;
      I have become like a vessel, perishing.
¹³ Because I have heard the smears of many people,
      alarm all around.
   As they scheme together against me,
      they have plotted to take my life.

¹⁴ But I—I have trusted in you, Yahweh;
      I have said, "You are my God."
¹⁵ My times are in your hand;
      rescue me from the hand of my enemies, from my pursuers.
¹⁶ May your face shine upon your servant;
      deliver me, out of your commitment.
¹⁷ Yahweh, may I not be shamed, because I have called you;
      may the faithless people be shamed.
   As they go silent to Sheol
¹⁸   may lying lips be quiet,
   which speak arrogantly against the faithful,
      with pride and contempt.

¹⁹ How much good you have,
      which you have stored up for those who are in awe of you,
   which you have done for those who rely on you,
      before people.
²⁰ You protect them in a place of protection in your presence
      from human plots.

You hide them in a shelter
    from contentious tongues.
21 Yahweh be worshiped,
    because he has been wonderful in his commitment to me,
    like a city besieged.
22 I myself had said in my alarm,
    "I am cut off from before your eyes."
    On the contrary, you heard my voice pleading for grace
    when I cried out for help to you.
23 Give yourselves to Yahweh, all you who are committed
      to him;
    Yahweh guards the people who are true,
    but requites in full the person who acts with pride.
24 Be strong; your heart should take courage,
    all you who wait for Yahweh.

Last night we went to a concert by the great honky-tonk/blues singer Marcia Ball, who grew up in Louisiana. Her closing song was Randy Newman's unbearably moving "Louisiana." The song describes how the Mississippi River rose all day and all night, and it pictures the sheer volume of water with the recurring phrase "six feet of water in the streets of Evangeline." It describes the at-best indifferent response of the federal government, and it keeps repeating the lament "They're trying to wash us away." The first time I heard the song was after Hurricane Katrina, and I didn't realize that it was not written in light of that event. Newman had written it three decades previously to tell the story of the Mississippi flood of 1927, which left 700,000 people homeless.

One could imagine lines from Psalm 31 on the lips of people watching helplessly as the river rose all day and all night. They have little alternative but to say to God, "Into your hand I commit my spirit." These words from verse 5 recur on Jesus' lips, as does the line from Psalm 22: "My God, my God, why have you forsaken me?" More literally it's "Into your hand I assign/ delegate my spirit." The expression is striking. Usually someone powerful designates or appoints a subordinate to have some office or to be in charge of something. Perhaps the psalm implies that the last thing even weak people keep hold of is their spirit. You can hold onto it or be prepared to surrender it.

When there are six feet of water in the streets of Evangeline, you feel the need to find somewhere that is seven feet higher than Evangeline. In the psalm, God is the crag onto which people climb for safety as the waters swirl. For Israelites, it is always tempting to trust in someone other than **Yahweh**, and the swirling of the waters increases that temptation. The psalm declares, "We will continue to trust."

As usual, the psalm declines to be confined to thinking about the present. When it uses expressions such as "You have redeemed me," people who use the psalm could be recalling occasions in the past when God has brought about a rescue. Such recollection reminds God, "You have rescued us in the past; you could do so once again." It also keeps those events in the awareness of the people praying and thus makes it more possible for them to hold on as the waters rise. But maybe they are not people who have had that experience; the statements about what God has done are then statements made by faith. They refer to acts God has not yet undertaken but that God has decided on and thereby initiated. They are like the statements that prophets sometimes make when they speak of coming events as if they have already happened. Either way, the psalm envisages that people praying will look to the future as well as to the past and will thus allow for the prospect of a rescue. Maybe there's a possibility we can't think of, a rescue that only God could devise. We might miss or negate it if we don't believe it's possible. Thinking about the past makes it possible to think about the good things that God has in store for his people.

As Psalm 30 cannot confine itself to telling only once the story of God's rescue, Psalm 31 cannot confine itself to praying its prayer only once. If the psalm stopped after verse 8, it would be quite complete. It has pleaded with God to listen and act, declared faith in God, looked forward to what God could do, and looked forward to celebrating God's standing our feet in a broad or dry place instead of the narrow or wet one where they now stand. Verses 9–20 could equally stand alone. Maybe it's significant that this second section gives more space to pained and anxious description of the situation; we sometimes need time to feel free to say what is said here. Yet as the protest is louder, so are the statements of trust and hope. They come to a climax with lines that speak as if **deliverance** has already come but do so when the water is still rising. People praying are invited to believe and declare that God has heard their prayer even when there is yet no evidence, to urge one another to believe that this is so, and to take courage accordingly. Sometimes it takes the repeating of a prayer over and over for the people praying to believe what they are saying, especially when the situation doesn't change immediately. And sometimes we have to repeat it over and over so that the voices of those who want to wash us away don't drown out our hope.

When Pope John Paul II spoke at Yad Vashem, the holocaust memorial in Jerusalem, he began and ended by quoting from this psalm. He commented, "We are overcome by the echo of the heart-rending laments of so many." But we are not overwhelmed because we know that "evil will not have the last word. Out of the depths of pain and sorrow, the believer's heart cries out: 'I trust in you, O Lord; I say, "You are my God."'"

PSALM 32

Love Covers a Multitude of Sins

David's. An instruction.

¹ The blessings of the one whose rebellion is carried,
   whose offense is covered!
² The blessings of the person for whom Yahweh does not
      count waywardness,
   in whose spirit there is no deceit!
³ When I was silent, my bones wasted away
   with my anguish all day long.
⁴ Because day and night your hand was heavy upon me;
   my strength was sapped [as] in the summer drought. (*Rise*)
⁵ I acknowledged my offense to you;
   I did not cover my waywardness.
   I said, "I will confess my rebellions to Yahweh,"
   and you yourself carried the waywardness of
      my offense.   (*Rise*)

⁶ Because of this everyone who is committed should plead
        with you
    at the time when he is found out.
  Yes, when many waters overwhelm,
    they will not reach him.
⁷ You are a hiding place for me;
    you protect me from trouble,
    you surround me with shouts of rescue.   (*Rise*)

⁸ "I will instruct you, teach you in the way you should go;
    I will offer counsel—my eye is on you."
⁹ Do not be like a horse, like a mule that has no sense,
    whose advance requires curbing with bit and bridle,
    or there is no coming near you.
¹⁰ Many are the pains of the faithless,
    but the person who trusts in Yahweh—
    commitment surrounds him.
¹¹ Rejoice in Yahweh, celebrate, you faithful;
    shout, all you upright of mind.

Yesterday a federal court found six police officers guilty of shooting six citizens in the aftermath of Hurricane Katrina. My wife and I were reflecting about how the rest of us can't simply dissociate ourselves from an event such as the shooting. The police represent us; we commission them to maintain order in the *polis*, the city. The defense argued that we ought to make allowances for mistakes people make in such dangerous situations, for they are having to make split-second, life-and-death decisions. Whether or not this is so, the further offenses involved in orchestrating a systematic cover-up of what happened reduce the sympathy one feels for officers caught up in the horrendous pressures of such a situation. Still, we have to see the officers' failure as also our failure insofar as we owe them our support.

Psalm 32 incorporates some of the Old Testament's key words for thinking about such events in relation to human beings and in relation to God. The first is the word "carry," the literal meaning of the Hebrew word that most often lies behind the word "forgive" in English translations of the Old Testament. When someone does wrong by someone else, the wronged party "carries" the wrongdoing, accepts responsibility for its consequences even though he or she was not responsible for the wrongdoing itself. Instead of seeking redress, the wronged party refuses to let the wrongdoing come between the two people. While it is the state's task to decide whether and how the wrongdoer must be punished, it is the wronged person's job to "carry" the wrongdoing.

The second word is "cover," which can be used in two ways. There is potentially a covering up by the wrongdoer and another covering up by the person who has been wronged. The incident in New Orleans led to an attempt at cover-up, and the psalm expects us to be able to say that we have not been involved in such cover-up. It also speaks of the wronged party as involved in a positive cover-up. The Old Testament often speaks of wrongdoing as causing a stain; murder literally does so because the victim's blood lies there on the ground. One of the New Orleans victims lost a hand in the shooting and had to take the oath by raising her left hand. Suppose she were to use that hand to cover up the blood that flowed from her right hand, in the sense that she refused to draw attention to her loss and ask for vengeance?

The third word is "count." It suggests the image of a court record. When I committed a road-traffic offense a few weeks ago, I paid a fine, but the offense entered my record. My pleading guilty would not affect that process. Personal relationships work a different way. We do not keep a record of the wrongs that other people do to us. Admittedly we cannot assume that someone will act in this way, especially if we attempt to cover things up—hence the psalm's comment about there being no deceit in our spirit. It's not that the relationship works contractually; again, there is a proper difference between how the law works and how personal relationships work. We can't say, "I have come clean; you have to forgive me." But if we do not come clean, we are not entitled to any such hope. Conversely, we can't say, "He hasn't come clean; therefore I need not forgive him." On that side, too, it's not a contractual or legal relationship.

Such is the way human relationships are supposed to work. The psalm's point is that relationships with God work that way. God carries our wrongdoing, taking on responsibility

101

for preventing its coming between us and him. God covers our wrongdoing, puts his hand over it so he can't see it. God declines to count it, refuses to keep a record of it. The Old Testament is the story of God's behaving in this way in relation to Israel, often chastising his people but never finally casting them off. It's the story that comes to a climax when God lets his son be executed. That's the ultimate in taking responsibility for his relationship with us instead of making us carry the responsibility. Of course God's carrying, covering, and not counting work only if we cooperate, if we let them do so. That's the implication of the psalm's testimony. If we try to cover up our waywardness and decline to acknowledge it, then we risk frustrating God's willingness to carry it, cover it, and not count it, and we risk increasing its likely ongoing effect.

PSALM 33

God's Commitment Fills the Earth

[1] Resound, faithful people, in Yahweh;
     praise is fitting for the upright.
[2] Confess Yahweh with the guitar;
     make music for him with the ten-stringed harp.
[3] Sing him a new song;
     do well in playing, with a shout.
[4] Because Yahweh's word is upright,
     and every act of his is done in truthfulness.
[5] He gives himself to faithfulness in exercising authority;
     Yahweh's commitment fills the earth.

[6] By Yahweh's word the heavens were made,
     by the breath of his mouth all their army,
[7] gathering the sea's water as in a dam,
     putting the deeps in storerooms.
[8] All the earth is to be in awe of Yahweh;
     all the world's inhabitants are to revere him.
[9] Because he is the one who spoke, and it happened;
     he is the one who commanded, and it stood up.
[10] Yahweh has foiled the nations' policy,
      frustrated the peoples' intentions.

11 Yahweh's policy stands forever,
       the intentions of his mind for generation after generation.
12 The blessings of the nation for which Yahweh is its God,
       the people he chose as his very own!
13 From the heavens Yahweh has taken note,
       seen all humanity.
14 From the place where he lives he has gazed
       at all the people who live on the earth,
15 the one who shapes their minds, all together,
       who discerns all their actions.
16 There is no king who delivers himself by means of a
          great force;
       a warrior does not rescue himself by means of great
          strength.
17 The horse is a deception for deliverance,
       and with the greatness of his strength he does not escape.

18 There: Yahweh's eye is on people who are in awe of him,
       people who wait for his commitment
19 to rescue them from death
       and keep them alive in famine.
20 Our spirit hopes for Yahweh;
       he is our help and shield.
21 Because in him our heart rejoices;
       because in his holy name we have trusted.
22 May your commitment be over us, Yahweh,
       as we have waited for you.

Yesterday we went to the beach. It was a foolish venture because
it was an August Saturday; I forgot that everyone else would
have the same idea and that the parking would be impossible,
but in the late afternoon we finally sat on the sand in a little
cove and watched huge waves with their white crests pounding
the shore. When we went for a little walk, I assured my wife
that we could leave our blanket; the sea would never come up
that high on the beach. I was right, but only just; a little later, to
general amusement, a giant wave surged over the sand near us
where a couple of small groups of people were settled in what
they thought was a safe place. As we drove home (we spent
more time on the road than at the ocean), my wife commented
that she kept seeing the image of those awe-inspiring waves.

Some Israelites would know about giant waves. The story of Jonah implies some knowledge of them. If you stand on the headland at Jaffa, the port from which Jonah set sail when he was trying to get away from God's call, you can watch waves pounding the rocks in the same way as they do in Europe or in the United States. They are not in themselves an indication that "**Yahweh's commitment** fills the earth." They can sometimes surprise us and even threaten to wash us away (see the comment on Psalm 31). They could make you wonder what has happened to Yahweh's commitment. At the beach, I went to climb on the rocks, but my wife stopped me because she didn't want the lifeguards chasing me. And as we left, they rushed onto the rocks and around the headland, apparently to deal with a crisis that someone had gotten into.

The psalm declines to let such events imperil the truth that God keeps the seas under control. More often than not, if we take note of the patterns to their behavior, they are not a danger to us; we are more a danger to ourselves by assuming we will get away with something we should know is dangerous. The psalm declares that God's act of creation resembled the act of an engineer who constructs a dam to contain waters. Or perhaps more likely, it resembled the humbler act of a shepherd who constructs a little dam with a few stones and some sand to contain the waters of a stream so that they will be still waters that don't frighten the sheep (see Psalm 23). Or it resembled the act of a farmer who constructs a similar dam to hold in some of the winter rains so that they are available for the irrigation of crops during the summer drought. The mighty act of creation that keeps the waters in their place is no more trouble for God than those bits of engineering. Creation is an embodiment of God's commitment to us.

While the psalm talks about the past events of creation, it also talks about the present events of politics and declares that God's commitment operates there, too. Maybe there was a reason beyond their inherent impressiveness that made my wife keep thinking about those waves. As it happens, that beach has traumatic associations for her because of experiences from the distant past. These experiences could have been overwhelming—indeed they have seemed to be overwhelming. But she is

104

not actually overwhelmed. As the psalm puts it, she has waited for God's commitment, looked for it, relied on it, and proved it.

God shows himself **faithful** in exercising **authority** in his present involvement with the people of God, with nations, and with individuals. God's ongoing action of restraining chaos in these other realms is equally as important to us as his past action in ordering creation so that chaos cannot overwhelm order. In Israel's world, as in our own, there was lots of evidence that the world of the nations was out of control, but the psalm declares that it is not so. When the Old Testament speaks of "the nations," it often refers to the imperial power of the day, the superpower—**Assyria, Babylon, Persia**, or **Greece**. It can seem that the superpower's policies are the decisive factor in the world, but the psalm knows that Yahweh's policy is actually the decisive factor. Military might is not what determines events, as any look at modern history also indicates. The key question is whether God has his eye on you. Sometimes that expression has negative connotations ("Every move you make, I'll be watching you"). Sometimes it has positive connotations ("Will you keep an eye on the kids for a minute?"). Here the connotations are positive. God's eye watches, and then God protects and blesses. Whereas it could seem that human government is always on the brink of turning the world into chaos, in fact we are still here, and we still have dry land to live on even though the seas can heave wildly.

PSALM 34

I Will Survive

David's. When he concealed his sanity before Abimelech so that he expelled him, and he went.

¹ I will worship Yahweh all the time;
    his praise will be in my mouth continually.
² In Yahweh my spirit exults itself;
    the lowly should listen and celebrate.
³ Magnify Yahweh with me;
    we will exalt his name together.

⁴ I sought help from Yahweh and he answered me,
    and rescued me from all my terrors.
⁵ People take note of him and become bright;
    their faces need not be shamed.
⁶ This lowly man called, and Yahweh listened,
    and delivered him from all his troubles.
⁷ Yahweh's aide camps around the people
    who are in awe of him and rescues them.
⁸ Taste and see that Yahweh is good—
    the blessings of the man who relies on him!
⁹ Be in awe of Yahweh, you who are his holy ones,
    because there is no lack for people who are in awe of him.
¹⁰ Lions are in want and starve,
    but people who seek help from Yahweh do not lack any
    good thing.

¹¹ Come, children, listen to me;
    I will teach you awe of Yahweh.
¹² Who is the person who relishes life,
    who loves days for seeing good things?
¹³ Keep your tongue from evil,
    your lips from speaking a lie.
¹⁴ Turn from evil and do good;
    seek well-being for people, pursue it.
¹⁵ Yahweh's eyes are on the faithful,
    his ears are to their cry for help.
¹⁶ Yahweh's face is against people who do evil,
    to cut off mention of them from the country.
¹⁷ People cry out, and Yahweh listens,
    and rescues them from all their troubles.
¹⁸ Yahweh is near to the people who are breaking inside,
    and delivers the people who are crushed in spirit.
¹⁹ When the evils that come to the faithful are many,
    Yahweh saves them from them all.
²⁰ He looks after all his bones;
    not one of them breaks.
²¹ Something evil may kill off the faithless person,
    and the opponents of the faithful may suffer
        punishment;
²² Yahweh redeems the life of his servants,
    and all who rely on him do not suffer punishment.

Our preacher yesterday told us how two years ago she had married a man who was soon abusing her. So after a short while she had to decide to leave him, though it was enough time for her to be pregnant. Thus she soon found herself divorced, jobless, and a single parent. You might have thought she would be disillusioned with life and with God, but the text for her sermon came from Philippians 4, where Paul urges people not to worry or be anxious but to rejoice in God; then they will find that God's peace reigns in their hearts. Our preacher is about to be ordained, though her ministerial assignment does not bring a salary with it, so she has to find a job, but she is confident that God will come through for her. In the subsequent discussion, the sermon drew someone else to give her own testimony to the way God had taken her through a similar experience.

Psalm 34 puts onto our lips a testimony of a similar kind. It pictures a person who has gone through terrors—maybe objectively terrifying circumstances, maybe subjectively terrifying fears. It's a lowly, ordinary, powerless person, not someone with wealth or position. It's someone who has had to "cry for help"; the Hebrew word is similar to the word for God's **delivering** someone, so that the word itself hints at the content of the cry. It's someone who has had to **cry out**, a different word, used elsewhere of the Israelites crying out in **Egypt**; that situation is the kind the person now faces, but maybe God will respond as God did then. It's someone who has gone through "troubles"; the psalm uses that word twice. It's a prayer for someone who has been "broken inside" and "crushed in spirit." The pressures on David, who is on the run from Saul, could illustrate that experience.

But it's a person who has survived, and not because (like Gloria Gaynor in the song) she had determined, "I will survive" and has done so even though it took all the strength that she had if she was not to fall apart. She does now hold her head high and has become "somebody new," but not because she was able to summon the resources from inside herself to do so. She has survived because God answered and rescued, God listened and delivered, God listens and rescues, God is near and delivers. This psalm, like others, works with the two-stage understanding of answers to prayer. First God listens and answers, which in itself changes the look on one's face: people look to God, and their faces start to brighten up. Then God rescues and delivers. It's as if God's **aide** who leads God's army camps around the person so that the people who are on the attack are no longer able to reach their intended victim.

The song "I Will Survive" is addressed to the former lover whom the person he jilted refuses to have back. The psalm is addressed to other people who might go through the experience the psalm presupposes. I described previously how another person in our congregation was drawn out to give her own testimony that corresponded to the preacher's. Maybe there were other people in church beset by troubles who were also drawn inwardly to say, "I will also survive," not because they have the resources but because they now believed that God could help them do so.

If it's to happen, the psalm says, you have to turn to God. It also emphasizes that you can't expect to be able to turn to God and plead for rescue unless you have also turned from wrongdoing so as to walk in God's way. Four times the psalm talks about **awe** before God. It's the verb that denotes reverence in relation to God but also doing what God says (some translations have "fear," but that translation gives a false impression). If you want God to protect you from other people, you need to be the kind of person whose own relationships with other people are in order.

This morning I went to visit a man in our congregation who couldn't come to church yesterday because he had a pacemaker fitted last week and had to stay at home. Several conversations with him have issued in stories that make me think. This morning, for example, he told me how he returned home after serving in the Second World War and found that his church's services were full of spiritual life but that the people who were spiritually alive in church were immediately gossiping about their neighbors when they got outside church. It made him give up church for some years. The people who profit from this psalm's promises aren't the kind of people who gossip or give false testimony in order to appropriate someone else's land or property. They are more interested in seeking **well-being** for other people than in doing so for themselves, or more interested in making peace with them than wronging them. They are interested in pursuing peace, in chasing after people's well-being.

PSALM 35

They Hated Me without a Reason; They Will Treat You the Same

David's.

1 Contend with the people who contend with me, Yahweh,
   fight the people who fight me.
2 Take hold of hand shield and body shield,
   and arise as my help.
3 Draw spear and pike to meet my pursuers;
   say to me, "I am your deliverance."
4 They must be disgraced and shamed,
   the people seeking my life.
   They must fall back and be dismayed,
   the people planning evil for me.
5 They must be like chaff before the wind,
   with Yahweh's aide pursuing.
6 Their way must be darkness and slipperiness,
   with Yahweh's aide chasing them.
7 Because without reason they have hidden their net's pit
      for me,
   without reason they dug it for my life.
8 Disaster must come that he does not recognize,
   his own net that he hid must catch him, as disaster may
      it fall on him.

9 But my spirit will rejoice in Yahweh,
   it will be glad at his deliverance.
10 All my bones will say,
      "Yahweh, who is like you,
   one who rescues the lowly person from the one stronger
         than he,
      the lowly and needy person from the robber?"

11 Violent witnesses take their stand,
      people who ask me about what I do not know.

¹² They repay evil for good,
mourning for my spirit.
¹³ But I—when they were sick,
my clothing was sackcloth.
I humbled myself with fasting,
and my plea would return to my heart.
¹⁴ I walked about as if it was my friend, as if it was a brother;
as if I were a mother grieving, I bowed down, gloomy.
¹⁵ But at my stumbling they have rejoiced and gathered,
gathered against me as assailants.
People I did not know have torn at me
and not stopped.
¹⁶ As the most profane twisted mockers,
they have ground their teeth against me.
¹⁷ My Lord, how long until you look?—
restore my life from their devastation,
my dear life from the lions.
¹⁸ I will confess you in the great congregation,
among a mighty people I will praise you.
¹⁹ My lying enemies must not rejoice over me,
the people who are against me without reason who glint
their eyes.
²⁰ Because they do not speak of peace;
they are against the quiet people in the country.
They plan false statements
²¹ and they have opened their mouth wide against me.
They have said, "Hey, hey,
our eye has seen it!"
²² You have seen, Yahweh, do not be silent;
my Lord, do not be distant from me!
²³ Stir yourself, wake up, to make a decision for me,
to contend for me, my God and my Lord!
²⁴ Decide for me in accordance with your faithfulness,
Yahweh my God;
they must not rejoice over me.
²⁵ They must not say inside, "Hey, our desire!"—
they must not say, "We have devoured him!"
²⁶ They must be disgraced and dismayed altogether,
the people who rejoice at evil coming to me.
They must be clothed in disgrace and shame,
the people who act great over me.

²⁷ They must resound and rejoice,
    the people who delight in the faithfulness shown me,
  so that they will say continually,
    "Yahweh is great, the one who delights in the well-being
      of his servant,"
²⁸ and so that my tongue may tell of your faithfulness,
    of your praise all day.

It's amusing that many of the nastier parts of the Old Testament don't seem to raise a problem for Jesus in the way they raise a problem for Western people; it helps us see that our niceness has nothing to do with our being Christian (Jews, Muslims, atheists, and other Western people are nice, too). In John 15 Jesus tells his disciples to expect people to persecute them because, after all, they persecuted him, and he comments that their resistance to him makes them guilty before God in a way they were not previously. In this context he declares that in opposing him and his Father they are fulfilling or filling out what it says in this psalm about hating someone without reason.

In the United States, politics has become more polarized, and the political system, more confrontational as more and more people have fallen below the poverty line. As I write, people in Britain have been rioting in the streets partly because of similar factors. One significance of Psalm 35 for Western readers is to remind us of realities about life for many people in many parts of the world in many epochs of history. It reminds us to bring these realities to God. Psalm 34 speaks about being peacemakers, another theme from the Old Testament that Jesus affirms. Paradoxically, we might infer from Psalm 35 as from other psalms that bringing to God any unjustified, hostile, corrupt treatment we receive from other people may make it easier to resist the temptation to treat other people in the same way as they treat us. Our confidence that God is just and is involved in the world makes it easier to accept that we do not need to take justice into our own hands (as if our justice could ever be as just as God's!).

Jeremiah illustrates this dynamic (see Jeremiah 18; 20; 38). He too speaks of being hated without reason and of people repaying good with evil. He speaks of people hiding snares for his feet and digging a pit to push him into, and his sub-sequent story shows that the latter is not only a metaphor. He too speaks with confidence about the way God will turn things around and see that his persecutors get their comeuppance. And it looks as if his freedom to talk to God about these reali-ties and his conviction that God will take this action are key to his keeping going. Admittedly it is a wavering rather than an unwavering conviction. Maybe that fact raises the question whether the same is true of someone who prays this psalm. It is precisely because you are troubled that you need to speak the way the psalm does. If you were less troubled, you would be praying Psalm 23 or Psalm 27. One of the great things about the Psalter is that it provides examples of prayer that people in all sorts of situations and moods can pray. You don't have to get yourself into a specific situation or mood.

Within this psalm, as within others, there is also room for maneuver about the needs we pray about. The talk of **Yahweh**'s "contending" is legal language, and it would be possible for someone who is falsely accused to use the psalm as a prayer for Yahweh to act as advocate and to mean the language about weaponry more metaphorically. On the other hand, someone who was physically under attack could use battle language more literally. Other psalms show that in the end there may not be much difference between an attack in court and an attack in the street, because a guilty verdict could mean the loss of one's farm and thus one's means of staying alive, if it did not mean actual execution. Either way, the psalm prays for vindication and thereby the reestablishment of honor for oneself, and thus for discredit and shame for one's attackers. Because God will bring the justice, we can let go and get on with our lives rather than having to be constantly trying to even things up between us and other people. Once again, Jesus confirms the psalm's instinct that it is not our business to act against our attackers but that it is appropriate for God to see to their downfall in a way that confirms the moral structure of the universe, for peo-ple get caught by the devices they have tried to use on people who don't deserve them.

Of course it will be possible to pray this way only if one can truly claim (as the psalm does) to have lived with integrity

112

in one's relationships with other people, and specifically with one's attackers. The psalm thus drives us to examine ourselves before we dare pray this way.

PSALM 36
On Living in Two Different Worlds

The leader's. Yahweh's servant's. David's.

1. A rebellious utterance by a faithless person is in my mind;
     there is no awe in relation to God before his eyes.
2. Because he flatters himself in his own eyes,
     in connection with being found out for his waywardness,
     in connection with being repudiated.
3. The words of his mouth are wickedness and deceit;
     he keeps away from being wise, doing good.
4. He plans wickedness on his bed,
     he sets himself on a no-good path,
     he does not reject evil.

5. Yahweh, your commitment is in the heavens,
     your truthfulness reaches to the skies.
6. Your faithfulness is like the majestic mountains,
     your authority is like the great deep.
   Human being and animal you deliver, Yahweh;
7.   how valuable is your commitment.
   Divine beings and human beings rely on
     the shadow of your wings.
8. They feast on the richness of your house,
     you let them drink from your lovely river.
9. Because with you there is a living spring;
     in your light we see light.

10. Continue your commitment to the people who
      acknowledge you,
      your faithfulness to the upright in spirit.
11. The lofty foot must not come on me,
      the hands of faithless people must not make me flee.
12. The people who do wickedness have fallen there,
      they have been thrown down, they cannot get up.

The governor of Texas recently held a prayer rally that aroused the ire of people who believed he was transgressing the boundary between church and state, and it also aroused the fascinated incomprehension of commentators. One remarked that it was a spectacle "that—let's be honest—most of us in the news media don't really get." Praying as a reaction to an awareness of the country's woes seems to suspend disbelief. It doesn't work on the basis of reason. There seems to be a gulf fixed between faith and prayer, on one hand, and the big issues of national life, on the other. Yet (he went on to say), isn't faith involved in more secular responses to the country's woes? Economists have strong views about how to deal with a recession and with debt ceilings, but their views differ, and views on the right and the left are based on faith. We all want there to be an answer, but economics is not really a science, and the jump from problem to solution involves a leap of faith.

Psalm 36 juxtaposes two realities in a way related to that sense of disconnect between a country's woes and the practice of prayer. The psalm's woes are moral ones. There are no-good people in the community who are characterized by rebelliousness against God, by **faithlessness**, by a confidence about leaving God out of account and ignoring God's expectations, by waywardness, by wickedness, by deceit, by secret scheming, and by an assurance that they can get away with such a lifestyle without losing their acceptance in the community.

The other reality is **Yahweh**, whom the no-good person ignores, the God characterized by **commitment**, truthfulness in the sense of reliability and steadfastness, **faithfulness**, **authority** exercised in the making of decisions in the right way, and involvement in **deliverance** on behalf of both human beings and animals. The psalm piles up familiar terms for proper behavior and declares that Yahweh manifests them in spades. It thus draws in sharp colors the contrast between the person it describes by means of a list of familiar correlative terms for human wrongdoing. Then it gives more distinctiveness and individuality to the portrait of God. On one hand, it's not only earthly creatures that rely on God; other heavenly beings do so, too. Further, God's provision operates not merely at survival level; it's luxurious. When you live with God, you enjoy a feast. You live well. Water and light are expressions for blessing. While there is no literal spring on the temple mount, there is provision for your needs flowing from God's presence. When light shines out of God's face, protection and life follow.

The prayer occupying the psalm's last three lines is its means of bringing together these two opposing realties. The psalm's opening talk about faithless people was not mere theory, like much of our discussion of the problem of evil. The rebellious schemers are people whose feet and hands might be directed against the faithful, stamping them down and throwing them out. When you have no way of ensuring that the first reality will not win out (and maybe if you have some way of doing so), you urge God to ensure that the second reality wins out, and with the eyes of faith you see it already happening.

PSALM 37:1–20

The Lowly Will Inherit the Land

David's.

1. Don't vex yourself because of evil people;
     don't fret because of people who do wrong.
2. Because like grass they fade quickly,
     like green plants they wither.

3. Trust in Yahweh and do good,
     dwell in the country and feed on truthfulness.
4. Be appreciative of Yahweh,
     and he will give you the requests of your heart.
5. Commit your way to Yahweh;
     trust in him and he will act.
6. He will bring out faithfulness for you like light,
     a decision for you like midday.
7. Be still before Yahweh
     and wait patiently for him.
   Don't vex yourself at the person who makes his way
        successful,
     at the one who acts on his schemes.
8. Drop anger, abandon rage;
     do not vex yourself, only to do evil.

⁹ Because evil people will be cut off,
    but those who look to Yahweh—they will inherit the
      country.

¹⁰ Yet a little while, and there will be no faithless person;
    you will look at his place, and there will be no one.
¹¹ The lowly—they will enter into possession of the country
    and appreciate great well-being.
¹² The faithless person schemes against the faithful
    and grinds his teeth against him.
¹³ The Lord laughs at him,
    because he has seen that his day will come.
¹⁴ Faithless people have drawn the sword
    and directed their bow,
  to bring down the lowly and needy,
    to slaughter people who are upright in their way.
¹⁵ Their sword will go into their own heart,
    their bows will break.

¹⁶ Better is the little of the faithful
    than the great abundance of the faithless.
¹⁷ Because the arms of the faithless will break,
    but Yahweh upholds the faithful.
¹⁸ Yahweh will acknowledge the days of people who have
     integrity,
    and their own possession will last forever.
¹⁹ They will not be shamed in an evil time
    and in days of famine they will be full.
²⁰ Because the faithless will perish,
    Yahweh's enemies.
  They will come to an end like the most valuable of pastures,
    they will come to an end in smoke.

The day before yesterday, in a demonstration that turned violent, the police station a quarter of a mile from where I lived as a child in Birmingham, England, and a quarter of a mile from my church there, was set on fire. One has a lot of sympathy with the people involved in the demonstrations in England, in the United States, and elsewhere who see the decision makers in their society doing well, like many people who benefit from their governments' policies, while many ordinary people are jobless and/or homeless and have nothing to live with or for. Further, the economic crises of the past three or four years have produced situations and policies that make lives that were only marginally viable into lives that are not viable at all.

In this context, Psalm 37 may be either annoying or encouraging, possibly both at different moments. Suppose you are an ordinary person with no job and no job prospects, aware that members of the government, businessmen, and professors have more fulfilling ways of spending their days and have more money than you do. If that difference is inherently wrong or if the way such people use their opportunities and their money is wrong, the psalm encourages you to remember that they will pay for it in due course. Maybe they won't fade quickly in the sense of immediately, but they will fade suddenly, perhaps at a moment when they look secure.

The psalm urges people not to let themselves be dragged down by them. If they are agents of oppression and means of exercising "institutionalized violence," you demean yourself by giving up faithful living and by joining the faithless. The psalm three times urges people not to "vex themselves," not to rage like a fire over a situation they can't do anything about. The Hebrew word and its related noun are nearly always used of God, and when human beings are raging mad, the implication is that they are usurping God's prerogative. It's not always so; the best day in Saul's life is when God's spirit comes on him so that he turns raging mad and takes some decisive violent action (see 1 Samuel 11). But usually we need to be held back from acting in rage and to trust that God will do so. If we are not too directly affected, it's useful not to have to take responsibility for everything in the world. Our attitude toward our situation is our choice, not something thrust on us from outside by the circumstances. We can decide to stop worrying about other people's sins and focus on our own relationship with God and on doing good works. It could be a relief.

To put it positively, the opposite of vexing oneself or fretting is trusting in God or being appreciative of God. There's a calm about trust, but there's a calm and also a passion about appreciation, which makes being appreciative of God more closely the opposite to vexing or fretting. It honors your

117

energy and offers to direct it. If you are trusting and appreciating and refuse to be dragged down by the people who are pushing you down, then you can see the fruit of doing so. You can live in the country, not be thrust off your land by these people; you can feed on truthfulness; because of God's and/ or your truthfulness, you will have food to eat. Nicely at the center of this first half of the psalm, that promise is one Jesus affirms when he says that the lowly will inherit the country or the earth (both Hebrew and Greek use words that can mean either "country" or "earth").

The psalm doesn't mean that no one should demonstrate or be politically involved. It's a psalm for people who feel powerless and helpless, and it is designed to help them see that being powerless and helpless doesn't mean being hopeless. If they do have scope to assert themselves, it draws their attention to grounds for hope when they do so, and also to the danger they need to watch when they do so.

It's also a psalm for people in government, business leaders, and professors to read so as to overhear what God says to powerless people and work out what they therefore need to do.

PSALM 37:21–40

Did You Have Your Eyes Shut, Then?

21 The faithless person borrows and cannot repay,
   but the faithful person is gracious and gives.
22 Because the people blessed by him will enter into possession of the country,
   but the people slighted by him will be cut off.
23 A man's steps are made firm by Yahweh
   when he delights in his way.
24 When he falls, he is not thrown headlong,
   because Yahweh supports with his hand.

25 I was young, and yes, I am old,
   but I have not seen a faithful person abandoned,
   or his offspring seeking bread.
26 Every day he is gracious and lends,
   and his offspring are a blessing.

27 Turn from evil and do good,
  and dwell forever.
28 Because Yahweh gives himself to the exercise of authority
  and does not abandon people committed to him.
  They are watched over forever,
    but the offspring of the faithless are cut off.
29 Faithful people will enter into possession of the country,
  and dwell for ever and ever.
30 The mouth of the faithful person utters insight,
  and his tongue speaks with authority.
31 His God's teaching is in his mind;
  his steps do not falter.

32 The faithless person watches for the faithful
  and seeks to kill him.
33 Yahweh does not abandon him into his hand
  and does not let him be condemned when they are
    making a decision about him.
34 Look to Yahweh, and keep his way,
  and he will raise you up
  so that you enter into possession of the country.
35 I have seen a faithless man, brutal
  arousing himself like a flourishing native tree,
36 But he passed on—there, he was gone;
  I sought him, and I could not find him.

37 Watch the person of integrity, see the upright person,
  because there is a future for the man of peace.
38 But rebels are destroyed all at once;
  the future of the faithless is cut off.
39 The deliverance of the faithful comes from Yahweh,
  their stronghold in time of trouble.
40 Yahweh helps them and rescues them,
  saves them from the faithless and delivers them,
  because they rely on him.

There's a poem by Jacqueline Osherow in which she imagines a Jewish boy who has learned the Psalms by heart saying them at Auschwitz and puzzling over Psalm 37 ("Psalm 37 at Auschwitz," in *Dead Men's Praise* [New York: Grove Press, 1999], 60–64). How could someone never have seen the faithful begging bread? Is it related to the conviction that they are "nourished by faith" (to adapt her translation of verse 3)? She refers to the way the line is used in the Jewish grace after meals (and thus in the Passover liturgy), and she describes how as a child she would never say it because she knew about Auschwitz and about what had happened to members of her family. Her rabbi told her that the psalm wasn't to be taken historically; it was to be held onto like a dream. Yet the statement is expressed in the past tense, as if it happened. She does love to sing it now. Perhaps it's a kind of confession; the hungry were there, but the psalmist didn't see them. Yet at least it's possible to imagine someone in the line at Auschwitz being able to repeat verse 10. Just a little longer, and the tormenters will be gone. And they were.

Other people have described the statement in the psalm as a vision or a prophecy. Or they have suggested that maybe the person saying the psalm made sure the faithful didn't beg bread by making sure to offer bread to the people who needed it. Or they have wondered whether the psalm belongs in a social context where people in general lived the way the **Torah** says, which would have the same implications. Or perhaps the use of the psalm in thanksgiving prayers after a meal means it gives us the opportunity to express our gratitude for our own experience of being provided for.

Its statement is the kind that Job's friends made and is thus the kind of statement that the book of Job is designed to question. One does not have to go as far as the book of Job to look for statements that conflict with it. The Psalter is full of them. They stand either side of Psalm 37. All Psalm 37 does is affirm particularly concretely the promises in Psalm 1, which recur throughout Scripture. The statement in this psalm is no more untrue than Jesus' promise that people who seek God's reign will have food, drink, and clothing; Jesus says he agrees with Psalm 37.

We can be unimaginative in the way we read the Bible. If we read the Psalms' statements about suffering in a literal way, it will give us an unreal impression of people's experience (go back to Psalm 22:11–18, or read on into Psalm 38). The Bible loves hyperbole; consider the accounts of slaughter in Joshua or the size of the armies in Chronicles. "Everything is possible for the person who believes," says Jesus in Mark 9:23. I don't think so. If the objections to Psalm 37 that we make as Westerners had been made to the psalmist, he or she might just have looked blank. Further, we need to bear in mind that the psalm is present in the Psalter not because things appeared this way to one individual, who might have been avoiding looking facts in the face. It evidently won the approval of the community that put the Psalter together and the community that accepted the Psalter into their Scriptures. The individual and the community knew that a statement like the one in verse 25 was putting vividly and personally the truth about God's care for his people when they are needy. It is a shame if our woodenness makes us miss the psalm's point.

PSALM 38

When Suffering Links to Sin

A composition. David's. For commemoration.

1 Yahweh, do not reprove me in wrath
     or discipline me in rage.
2 Because your arrows have descended on me,
     your hand has descended upon me.
3 There is no wholeness in my body because of your fury;
     there is no well-being in my bones because of my offenses.
4 Because my wayward acts have passed over my head;
     like a heavy burden, they are too heavy for me.
5 My wounds have smelled and festered
     because of my stupidity.
6 I have become low, utterly bowed down;
     all day I have gone about gloomy.
7 Because my loins are full of burning,
     and there is no wholeness in my body.
8 I have become numb, utterly crushed;
     I howl because of the rumbling in my mind.

9 My Lord, all my longings are before you;
     my groaning has not hidden from you.
10 My heart has taken flight, my strength has abandoned me;
     the light in my eyes—they, too, are not with me.

121

¹¹ My friends and neighbors
    stand back from my affliction.
   The people near me have stood at a distance,
¹² and people who seek my life have laid traps.
   People who aim at evil for me have spoken of destruction;
    all day they utter lies.
¹³ But I myself am like a deaf person who cannot hear,
    like a dumb person who cannot open his mouth.
¹⁴ I have become like someone who does not hear;
    there is no reproof in my mouth.
¹⁵ Because I have waited for you, Yahweh;
    you—you will answer, Lord my God.
¹⁶ Because I said, "They must not rejoice in relation to me;
    when my foot faltered, they acted big over me."
¹⁷ Because I am set for stumbling;
    my pain is before me continually.
¹⁸ Because I admit my waywardness,
    I am anxious because of my offenses.
¹⁹ My mortal enemies are strong,
    the people who are against me with falsehood are many.
²⁰ The people who repay evil for good
    attack me for my pursuit of good.
²¹ Do not abandon me, Yahweh;
    my God, do not be distant from me.
²² Hurry to help me,
    my Lord, my deliverance.

A friend of mine recently gave me a moving description of the
Alcoholics Anonymous group to which he belongs. People
go to meetings because they are desperate. They know they
cannot kick their habit on their own. It's more like a disease.
They know they need God's help, and they know that without it they are doomed. Some of them will find that help and
will find spectacular deliverance. Some will not. I write a few
weeks after the death of a great singer, Amy Winehouse, who
made two great albums; in her first and biggest hit, she sang,
"They tried to make me go to rehab, but I said, 'No, no, no.'" She
never managed to escape the effects of her addictions and died
at twenty-seven. Alcoholics eventually realize that they come
to the meetings as people responsible both for the mess they
have gotten into and for the wrong they have done to other

people in getting into that mess, and that they come as people who are simply in deep trouble. They need to repent and accept responsibility for their behavior, but that is not enough; they need help. They need assistance from outside in order to get out of the trouble they are in, but that is not enough; they need to own their responsibility for where they are.

Psalm 38 is an unusual example of a psalm that combines an awareness of sin with an awareness of being in trouble. While many psalms are designed for people experiencing attack, affliction, pain, and suffering, most declare or imply that this trouble is not related to the sufferer's wrongdoing. They don't imply that we should claim to be sinless, but like the story of Job, they imply that the trouble is out of all proportion to the sinfulness that the person shares with other people and is unrelated to any particular wrongdoing for which the trouble could be a specific punishment. It's easier to be able to dissociate sin and suffering. Either I come to God as a sinner and seek forgiveness or I come as someone in trouble and seek deliverance (or I may assume that if I am a sinner, I shouldn't come to God as someone in trouble).

Psalm 38 is for people who know these two are mixed up, as they are for an addict. It's not for someone like the blind man in John 9 to pray, whose blindness was not attributable to his sin. It's a psalm for someone like the disabled man in Mark 2, whose sins Jesus forgives. My friend described it as a great psalm for alcoholics. Like other psalms, it expresses an awareness that God is behind the troubles that have come; it speaks to God about "your arrows," "your hand," "your fury," like other psalms. But it doesn't see these as inexplicable, as other psalms do; it also speaks of drowning in one's waywardness, and it acknowledges one's stupidity—not the lack of brains but the refusal to use them. The psalm makes it OK to acknowledge that we have done something stupid but still appeal to God for help.

It describes my sins as a heavy burden. It doesn't mean that I *feel* burdened by them, nor does it mean they will be a burden that deprives me of eternal life. It means they are a burden in the way they have brought overwhelming trouble to me. The reference to pursuing good, later in the psalm, perhaps implies an ability to claim that one has related to other people in a proper

123

and faithful way; the waywardness lies in relation to God. One might (for instance) be trusting in resources other than God. The psalm expresses an awareness of having been jolted to one's senses in this connection as it speaks of saying nothing and uttering no reproofs. All the complaints are addressed to God, not to other people, specifically the people who are either ignoring the trouble or seeking to increase it.

There is reason for the arrows, the hand, the fury. But they are not merely an expression of punishment. They are "reproof" or "discipline." They are designed to stop me from acting in one way and push me into acting in another way. Often addicts are driven to seek help by an awareness that they are causing disaster not only in their own lives but in those of people near to them, but they have to reach the point of being brought up short (being caught drunk driving or being taken to the emergency room can become a blessing). That is what God seeks in making his hand fall on us as sinners. Maybe God has to make his hand fall on us so heavily that we cry out in pain, "Don't discipline me in rage"— in other words, discipline is all very well, but couldn't you be a bit easier? Answer—no, not if I want to get your attention.

Yet the toughness of God's action doesn't mean the discipline isn't done in love, as the New Testament points out in Hebrews 12. Neither does it mean you can't cry out, "That hurts, please stop!" That cry may indicate that God's purpose is achieved; he has jolted us to our senses. In Western law, a penalty can't be mitigated because the guilty person sees the point and repents. God's action is not punishment of this kind. It is chastisement like that of a parent or a teacher. So people who know they are in trouble for their sins can plead not only for forgiveness but for relief.

PSALM 39

I Am Going to Die

The leader's. Jeduthun's. A composition. David's.

1 I said, "I will keep guard on my ways,
so that I do not offend with my tongue.

124

I will keep a muzzle on my mouth
    as long as a faithless person is in my presence."
² I was dumb, in silence;
    I was quiet, more than it was good.
But as my pain stirred,
³   my mind became heated within me.
While I talked, fire burned;
    I spoke out with my tongue.

⁴ Get me to acknowledge my end, Yahweh—
    the number of my days, what it is.
⁵ Now. You made my days handbreadths;
    my span is as nothing before you.
Yes, every human being, standing firm,
    is simply a breath;   (*Rise*)
⁶   yes, it is as a shadow that someone walks about.
Yes, it is for a breath that people hustle;
    a person may heap up, but not know who is going to
        gather in.
⁷ So now, what have I looked to, my Lord?—
    my hope lies in you.
⁸ Rescue me from all my acts of rebellion,
    do not make me an object of reviling to the rogue.
⁹ I was dumb, I did not open my mouth,
    because you were the one who acted.
¹⁰ Turn away your affliction from me;
    because of the blow of your hand I—I am done.
¹¹ With reproofs for waywardness you have disciplined a man
    and consumed like a moth what he values;
    yes, every human being is a breath.   (*Rise*)
¹² Listen to my plea, Yahweh,
    give ear to my cry for help,
    do not be silent at my weeping.
Because I am a sojourner with you,
    a transient like all my ancestors.
¹³ Look away from me so that I may smile,
    before I go and there is nothing of me.

I didn't think much about dying until my grandson was born, and then the thought came to me that I could die now; I had done my job for the human race's future by fathering a son who had himself fathered a son. I thought about it again three or four years later when I reached sixty—somehow reaching that age brought home my mortality. I thought about it some more another three or four years later when I reached the age my father had been when he died; I was relieved to get past that marker. I thought about it again another three or four years later when I agreed to write the Old Testament for Everyone series: I would look stupid if I made that commitment and then went and died. I thought about it again when my first wife died, for she was totally disabled, and I had always been a bit apprehensive about dying before her because my dying would raise tricky questions about what would happen to her. And then I thought about it again when I met my second wife, who would prefer me not to die too soon. I now have renewed enthusiasm for living to a ripe and irresponsible old age.

We have little control over when we die, and death may come long before we reach sixty or seventy. The middle part of the psalm asks for the willingness to acknowledge that lack of control. It knows we must face up to our mortality. God's life is eternal; our life has a beginning and will have an end. (Of course the psalmist is actually going to enjoy resurrection life, but this will be a surprise—only Jesus' death and resurrection will make it possible.) Compared with God, our life is like something just a few inches long compared with something that is miles long. Or it's as evanescent as a breath; people may look as if they are standing firm and could live forever but suddenly drop dead. Or it's as insubstantial as a shadow; there's nothing solid about it. So the hustling that people do may get them nowhere. They may not live to enjoy what they toil for.

The background to the psalm's reflection on mortality is an experience like the one in Psalm 38. It presupposes the reality of affliction and grief and acknowledges that sometimes these come because we deserve them. The suffering is not chance and not random, and it is not exactly punishment but reproof and discipline that chastise us for our rebellion and waywardness. Presumably the awareness of being rebellious and wayward, and of being under chastisement for this fact, lies behind the failed attempt at silence of which the first part of the psalm speaks. "I'm in enough trouble as it is," the psalmist says; "I'd better not risk getting into more trouble by opening my big mouth to complain at suffering I deserve, especially in the presence of people who will be only too glad to make my complaints a basis for causing me more trouble." But attempts to keep one's mouth shut do not always work.

The content of the speaking out is then maybe the plea in the last part of the psalm rather than merely the reflection on mortality. When we are suffering and are aware that we are going to die, we may need to talk about it, and the psalm doesn't advise us not to talk to other human beings, but it does advise us to talk to God about it. The person in control of when we die is God. Further, like Psalm 38, this psalm doesn't assume that our responsibility for the messes we get into means that we can't talk to God about them. The only person who can do anything about the affliction that comes to us is God; hence the appeal both to rescue and to "look away" in the sense of not looking at us in hostile fashion. We need not indulge in the futile attempt at silence.

The Juduthun mentioned in the psalm's introduction is mentioned in 1 Chronicles as a temple music leader in David's and Solomon's day.

PSALM 40

Praise and Thanksgiving as a Key to Prayer—II

The leader's. David's. A composition.

¹ I had simply looked to Yahweh,
    and he had inclined to me and listened to my cry for help.
² He brought me up from the roaring pit,
    from the overflowing mud.
He set my feet up on a crag,
    he established my steps.
³ He put a new song in my mouth,
    an act of praise to our God.
Many could see it and be in awe,
    and trust in Yahweh.

⁴ The blessings of the man who makes
    Yahweh his trust

127

and has not turned to the arrogant
    or to people who follow what is false!
5 You, Yahweh, my God, have done many things;
    your wonders and your plans for us—
    there is no one to set alongside you.
Were I to declare and speak,
    they are too numerous to recount.

6 Sacrifice and offering you did not want—
    you dug ears for me;
burnt offering and purification offering
    you did not ask for.
7 Then I said, "Now. I have come;
    in a written scroll it is inscribed for me."
8 I wanted to do what you favor, my God;
    your teaching was within my inmost self.
9 I brought the news of your faithfulness
    in the great congregation.
There—I would not close my lips;
    Yahweh, you yourself know.
10 I did not hide your faithfulness within my heart;
    I told of your truthfulness and your deliverance.
I did not conceal your true commitment
    before the great congregation.

11 You, Yahweh, may you not close up
    your compassion from me;
may your true commitment
    protect me continually.
12 Because evils beyond numbering
    have surrounded me.
My wayward acts have caught up with me;
    I have not been able to see.
They are more numerous than the hairs on my head;
    my mind has failed me.
13 Show favor, Yahweh, by rescuing me;
    Yahweh, hurry to be my help.
14 May they be shamed and disgraced altogether,
    the people who seek my life, to destroy it.
May they fall back and be dishonored,
    the people who want evil for me.

¹⁵ May they be desolate because of their shame,
    the people who say to me, "Hey, hey!"
¹⁶ But may they celebrate and be glad in you,
    all the people who seek help from you.
May the people who give themselves to your deliverance
    say continually, "Yahweh is great."
¹⁷ So I am lowly and needy;
    may the Lord take thought for me.
You are my help and my rescuer;
    my God, do not delay.

As usual we had a time of sharing praise and prayer concerns in church yesterday, and as usual I had more success getting people to share prayer concerns than to share reasons for thanksgiving. As far as I remember the only thing anyone was thankful for was waking up and being alive that morning. Being alive is a great gift to give praise for, but it doesn't count as thanksgiving as the Old Testament understands it. Thanksgiving relates to particular blessings that God has given us, as when we talk once a year about harvest thanksgiving or when we get children to write thank-you notes after Christmas. Moreover, in both those cases there is a link between prayer and thanksgiving. We pray for a good harvest, and if we get one, we thank God for answering our prayer. A child asks a grandparent for some vitally important game and writes to say thank-you on receiving it. I have known one or two people keep a prayer journal where they note what they are praying for; they can then look back over the entries and be struck by how many of the prayers have been answered—which encourages further prayer.

Psalm 40 draws attention to the link between thanksgiving and prayer, and it was this link that could be important to our congregation. While prayer needs to lead into thanksgiving, as Psalms such as 18 and 30 indicate, prayer also issues from thanksgiving; the awareness that God has previously answered your prayer encourages you to believe that you can come to God again with your plea for help, and it gives you a basis for leaning on God like a child or a grandchild ("You did it before; you could do it again").

So this prayer psalm spends more than half its time recalling something God did in the past, and you could easily think it is simply a thanksgiving psalm, though maybe its covert agenda as an introduction to a prayer pokes through the first part. There's less detail on the nature of the answer to prayer than appears in some thanksgiving psalms, though it presupposes that death was threatening the person. It stresses how the prayer reached out to **Yahweh** rather than to other people who had themselves turned away from Yahweh and looked to other, false gods. It stresses how the person praying had then given testimony to what the one true God did. "Sacrifice and offering you did not want" presumably implies that these were not all that Yahweh wanted. The psalm goes on to talk about paying attention to a written scroll and to Yahweh's teaching, Yahweh's **torah**, and it would be impossible for someone who had read the Torah to talk in terms of Yahweh's simply not wanting offerings. Rather, Yahweh did not just want offerings. While mere words are cheap, mere offerings are mute; as words need offerings, offerings need words that (in this case) give account to other people of the way God has answered prayer so that they function as testimony. Thus the psalmist can say, "I was not just thankful inside. I was thankful outside. I was not shy. I did not make my sacrifice at a moment when no one else would be there, or sit in the temple quiet when people were there. I gave my testimony to what God had done for me." ("You dug ears for me" in verse 6 may refer to God's making the holes in our head where our ears go.)

It's on that basis that the psalmist can ask God to show compassion and **commitment** once more. As in preceding psalms, all the declarations in the first part do not imply a claim that the trouble that has come was undeserved, but neither does it presuppose that guilt means we cannot plead with God to rescue us. Maybe the implicit irony is that the psalmist had not maintained trust in Yahweh and that the waywardness of which the psalm speaks consists in a turning to other gods; if so, the psalmist has now come back and rejoined the circle of people who seek help from Yahweh rather than from anywhere else.

PSALM 41:1–12

How to Learn from the Poor

The leader's. A composition. David's.

1 The blessings of the one who thinks about the poor person
  whom Yahweh rescues on an evil day!
2 Yahweh guards him and keeps him alive,
  and blesses him in the country,
  and you will not give him to the will of his enemies.
3 Yahweh sustains him on his sickbed;
  his entire bed you have transformed, in his illness.

4 I myself said, "Yahweh, be gracious to me;
  heal me, because I have offended against you."
5 My enemies speak of evil for me:
  "When will he die, and his name perish?
6 If he comes to see [someone],
  he speaks falsehood.
His mind collects wickedness for himself;
  when he goes outside, he speaks [it]."
7 All the people who are against me whisper together
    against me;
  they think up evil against me.
8 "A lethal pestilence besets him; in that he has laid down,
  he will not get up again."
9 Even my friend, whom I trusted, one who eats bread
    with me,
  has magnified himself against me as a cheat.
10 But you, Yahweh, be gracious to me,
  raise me up, and I will be friends with them.

11 Because of this I have acknowledged that you delighted
    in me,
  because my enemy does not shout over me,
12 and I—in my integrity you have upheld me
  and set me before you forever.

As we arrived at church on Sunday, a homeless man named
Alex who sometimes comes to church was sitting in the shade

of the parish hall, drawing on a cigarette as he waited for the time of the service. During the service we read the story of the Canaanite woman who tries to get Jesus to heal her daughter, initially fails, but eventually succeeds. Alex was the one person in the congregation who responded with a gasp or an exclamation at appropriate moments in this astonishing story. When we came to the point in the service when we share prayer needs, Alex asked us to pray that that cigarette we saw him smoking would be his last. Alex was a blessing to me twice on Sunday: in his unmistakable interaction with the Scripture reading and in the simplicity of his prayer.

And just now I have experienced some blessings that have arisen from thinking about this particular poor person. The Hebrew word for "one who thinks" is the same as the word for "instruction" that comes in the introduction to some psalms (including Psalm 42). The psalm is the testimony of a poor person whose experience is designed to be instructive for other people.

There are many homeless people in our city who don't have a testimony to God's rescuing them on an evil day. As it happens, on Sunday we also had a report from someone who had been involved in doing a kind of census of the city's homeless, with a particular concern to identify and help the especially vulnerable; of the six hundred people the team met, two hundred were in such bad health that they will be in danger of not surviving the coming winter. One had just lost a child and had no money to bury it. Yet there are some homeless people with whom our church has contact who can say that God has rescued them on an evil day. The psalm provides a testimony for such a person to share whereby he or she can acknowledge that evil days come but testify that God can rescue you from them. Maybe some of those vulnerable people to whom I just referred will be able to share that testimony.

So the psalm starts with a generalization, then gives most of its space to an account of the way the person prayed when living through that evil day, and finally summarizes the results of the prayer that provide the basis for the generalization. If you are a homeless person who has no desire to live on the streets and wishes you could get medical care, then someone telling you that God rescues, guards, keeps alive, blesses, and sustains may make you just want to roll your eyes or hit the person speaking with you. But if the speaker is someone like you who knows what evil days are like and can talk on the basis of personal experience, your reaction may be different.

The middle part of the psalm, recounting the prayer the poor person prayed on the evil day, begins and ends with an appeal for God's grace. Such appeals often feature in psalms, but here there is a particular reason for this feature; the psalm is yet another acknowledging the sinfulness of the person praying yet still appealing to God to answer the prayer. My wife has described to me how a church she once belonged to encouraged people to make a covenant each year with respect to different aspects of their lives, including prayer. In their covenants about prayer, most people said not only that they didn't know how to pray but also that they were reluctant to pray for X because they felt they had no right to do so because they had done Y. The psalms encourage us not to feel that hesitation.

Many people are poor or homeless because of what other people have done to them or because of "bad luck"—in Israel, maybe their land was poor or they were swindled out of their land by other wealthy or powerful people or they were troubled by sickness. Other poor or homeless people have to accept some responsibility for their predicament—in Israel, maybe it was their laziness as farmers that took them into debt and eventually into the loss of their land. Factors can combine; so the psalm speaks both of personal responsibility and of illness and of the false accusations of other people in the community. Like some other psalms, this testimony also manages to combine an acknowledgment of sin with a claim to integrity. Maybe the psalm refers to an integrity in relation to other people in the community that contrasts with the stance they have taken as the recollected prayer has described it. We don't come to God with a claim to sinlessness, but we need to be able to come to God with a claim to a basic integrity or with as much truthfulness as we can manage.

PSALM 41:13

An Interim Closing Act of Praise

¹³ Yahweh the God of Israel be worshiped,
  from age to age.
  Amen, amen.

The Psalter divides into five books, like the **Torah**, and with Psalm 41 we come to the end of Book One. There is no particular significance in making the transition at this point—it could have come after Psalm 40. The point is simply to mark the Psalter as resembling the Torah. So this act of praise is not actually part of Psalm 41 but is a kind of "Amen" to the first forty-one psalms.

PSALM 42

Where Is Your God?

The leader's. An instruction. The Qorahites'.

¹ Like a deer that strains toward streams of water,
  so my spirit strains toward you, God.
² My spirit is thirsty for God, for the living God;
  when will I come and appear before God?
³ My weeping has become for me my food
  day and night,
while people say to me all day,
  "Where is your God?"

⁴ These things I bring to mind
  as I pour out my spirit within me:
that I shall pass along in the shelter,
  lead people to the house of God,
with a resounding and thankful voice,
  the festive crowd.
⁵ Why do you bow low, my spirit,
  and shudder within me?
Be expectant of God, because I shall yet confess him
  for the deliverance that comes from his face.

⁶ My God, my spirit bows low within me;
      therefore I bring you to mind,
   from Jordan country and the Hermons,
      from Little Mountain.
⁷ Deep is calling to deep
      in the sound of your waterfalls.
   All your breakers and your waves
      have passed over me.
⁸ By day may Yahweh command his commitment,
      and by night may his song be with me.
   A plea to my living God:
⁹ I will say to God, my crag,
      "Why have you put me out of mind,
   why do I go about dark,
      with oppression from an enemy,
¹⁰   with murder in my bones?
   The people watching for me have reviled me,
      as they say to me all day,
      "Where is your God?"
¹¹ Why do you bow low, my spirit,
      and why do you shudder within me?
   Be expectant of God, because I shall yet confess him
      as the deliverance of my face and my God.

There is a poignant movie called *James' Journey to Jerusalem* about a young Zulu who has been designated to be his village's next pastor. If it were the West he would be sent to seminary, but the village decides that the best way to prepare him for his vocation is to send him on a pilgrimage to Jerusalem. He gets to Tel Aviv all right, but from then on the journey turns out to be daunting and fraught with danger, and much of the suspense of the movie relates to the uncertainty about whether he will ever get there. The villagers and James knew there was something significant about Jerusalem, not because it is inherently a particularly beautiful or important location but because of the significance that God had given it. God had agreed to dwell there, and Jesus had died and risen there.

Psalm 42 presupposes that Jerusalem is indeed the place where you meet with God. It dates from before Jesus' dying and rising in Jerusalem; indeed, it provides some of the background to those events. In Gethsemane Jesus echoes the refrain's talk about the spirit's being bowed low, while people's subsequent taunting of Jesus echoes the mocking question "Where is your God?" But it presupposes the same awareness of how important Jerusalem and the temple are. Admittedly its stance toward them is paradoxical. It does not assume that only in Jerusalem can you talk with God, meet with God, or know God is acting to **deliver** you; otherwise there would be no sense in praying when you are somewhere else. Yet it does assume that there is something special about Jerusalem and the temple. God had promised to be there to accept people's offerings and listen to their prayers. So straining toward God isn't merely something inward; it's something outward, involving body and geography.

So the psalm pictures someone far away from Jerusalem and unable to get there. Maybe literally the location is in the far north of the country. The foothills of Mount Hermon where the waters of the Jordan burst from the mountain, the region known as Caesarea Philippi in the Gospels, is as far away from Jerusalem in Israel as you can get (we don't know what "Little Mountain" refers to). The bursting of the waters from the mountain provides an image for the way things can overwhelm us. They are like huge waves crashing over us. The trouble is that they are God's waves. Or maybe their being God's waves is good news; it means they are under God's control.

People who live on Israel's northern borders are always aware of being far away from the temple; they can hardly go there more than once a year at the most. But there can be more than geography stopping you from going to Jerusalem, something such as illness, and it is a circumstance made worse by the mockery of people who perhaps see the sufferer as under God's judgment or who worship a god other than **Yahweh** and mock reliance on Yahweh and Yahweh's apparent inability to heal someone. So the psalm reflects an argument with other people.

It also incorporates an argument with God. Other people's "Where?" is accompanied by the psalmist's "Why?" Yet further, it incorporates an argument within the psalmist that recurs in a slightly different form in the psalm's refrain. It's an odd notion, in a way, the notion of arguing with oneself. It implies that human beings are designed to be people who are divided within themselves. They are not simply to give in to their (proper) sadness, fears, or temptations. They are to do battle with themselves. If they can come to the temple and pray when they are under attack, then their friends or a priest or a prophet may be able to minister God's word to them and encourage them. When you are cut off in the way this psalm presupposes, you have to do your encouraging for yourself.

PSALM 43

When Life Continues to Be Darkness

1 Decide for me, God,
      contend for my cause.
   From a nation that is not committed,
      from a deceitful and wicked individual,
         rescue me.
2 Because you are God my stronghold;
      why have you rejected me?
   Why do I go about dark,
      with oppression from an enemy?
3 Send your light and your truthfulness;
      they will lead me.
   They will bring me to your holy mountain,
      to your great dwelling,
4 so that I can come to God's altar,
      to the God in whom I rejoice joyfully,
   and confess you with the guitar,
      God, my God.
5 Why do you bow low, my spirit,
      and why do you shudder within me?
   Be expectant of God, because I shall yet confess him
      as the deliverance of my face and my God.

I've just been reading a Darfuri refugee's account of how he came to be in a camp in Chad. As a farmer in Sudan he was tortured by the application of a clothes iron to his back, his legs, his hands, and his head because the members of one of the militias had determined to take over his land. So that is how he "lost his life" in Sudan, as he put it. Despite the pain he was in, he walked the three hundred miles to the border between Sudan and Chad, thanking God that he was able to get there but was told initially that the refugee camp was closed. "Life seems to be darkness to me," he said.

It's all very well to argue with yourself, but the argument may not work, and when this happens, you probably shouldn't feel guilty. It looks as if it doesn't work in Psalms 42 and 43, at least not instantly. The refrain at the end of Psalm 43 is the same as the one that recurs in Psalm 42, so evidently the two psalms belong closely together. The same point is suggested by the fact that Psalm 43 has no introduction, unlike most of the psalms that precede and follow. The line about going about dark and gloomy also recurs from Psalm 42. Maybe one psalm with three stanzas was separated into two so that they could more easily be used separately, or maybe Psalm 43 was written separately to take further the point in Psalm 42.

Again, then, the psalm voices a plea for God to take up the sufferer's cause in relation to the community and/or the individual who is causing the suffering and expresses dreams of the freedom to come to the temple. Psalm 43 goes beyond Psalm 42 in actually pleading for that freedom (rather oddly, you might think, for while Psalm 42 announced the intention to plead with God, it never got around to an actual prayer for God to act). As well as the plea for God to take the suppliant's side, there is the neat plea for God to send out his light and his truthfulness to bring the suppliant to the temple. It's as if God is the king who is to send some **aides** to make sure the suppliant can get to the palace, offering the protection that will be needed for the journey that people are keen to oppose. It's a terrible deprivation to be unable to join the community in its worship; rejoicing on one's own is not the same, because proper rejoicing is a matter of celebration and needs to be done with others. Getting to Jerusalem will be like coming in from the cold.

The psalm has a comprehensive vision of the worship it will be possible to offer there. It will take place in the real presence of God because the temple is the place where God dwells and the place where the community gathers. It is not like a church, empty and quiet except for an hour or two each week; it is instead a vibrant and bustling place where people gather every day to worship, pray, and give thanks for what God has done for them. The worship will involve the freedom to make a sacrificial offering at the **altar** as an expression of commitment and thanksgiving and to give testimony to other people to God's **deliverance**. It will involve joy and music.

So verse 4 would make a great ending to the psalm. But then that refrain again follows. The psalm lives for the future, but it also lives in the present, and while there is a sense in which hope transforms the present, there is another sense in which it leaves the present unchanged. When life continues to be darkness, you aren't expected to pretend that things are otherwise.

One other feature of these two psalms deserves mention. It's illustrated by the phrase "God, my God" in Psalm 43. In most psalms, there are many occurrences of the **name** of God, **Yahweh**. In most psalms you would find the psalmist saying, "Yahweh, my God" rather than "God, my God." In Psalms 42 to 83, there are very few occurrences of that name. Either the original psalmists avoided it, or revisers removed most of the occurrences. The background might be the same as the instinct that eventually led many Jews to avoid using the name of Yahweh—maybe reverence, maybe a sense that this odd name gave other peoples the impression that Israel's God was simply Israel's national God, whereas Israel knew that Yahweh was *the* God.

PSALM 44

Wake Up, God!

The leader's. The Qorahites'. An instruction.

¹ God, we have heard with our ears,
     our ancestors have told us,
   about the deed you did in their days,
     in past days,
² you yourself with your own hand.
   You dispossessed nations and planted them;
     you brought calamity on peoples
       and spread them out.

3 Because it was not by their sword that they entered into
         possession of the country,
      it was not their arm that delivered them,
   but your hand and your arm,
      and the light of your face,
      because you favored them.

4 You are the one who is my king, God;
      command deliverance for Jacob!
5 Through you we charge at our foes,
      by your name we tread down our attackers.
6 Because it is not in my bow that I trust;
      my sword does not deliver me.
7 Because you have delivered us from our foes
      and shamed our opponents.
8 God is the one whom we praise every day;
      your name we will confess forever.

9 Yet you have rejected and disgraced us,
      and you do not go out with our armies.
10 You turn us back from the foe
      and our opponents have plundered us at will.
11 You make us like sheep for food
      and you have scattered us among the nations.
12 You sell your people for nothing;
      you did not go high at their price.
13 You make us an object of reviling to our neighbors,
      scorn and derision to the people around us.
14 You make us an object lesson among the nations,
      something to shake the head at among the peoples.
15 Every day my disgrace is in front of me;
      the shame of my face has covered me,
16 at the voice of the person reviling and taunting,
      at the presence of the enemy exacting redress.

17 All this has come upon us
      and we have not put you out of mind;
      we have not been false to your covenant.
18 Our heart has not turned back;
      our steps have not deviated from your path,
19 that you should have crushed us into the place of jackals
      and covered us over with deathly darkness.

²⁰ If we had put our God's name out of mind
    and spread our hands to a foreign god,
²¹ would God not search this out,
    because he knows the secrets of the heart?
²² Rather, it is because of you that we have been slain every day;
    we have been thought of as sheep for slaughter.

²³ Rise up, why do you sleep, Lord?—
    wake up, do not reject forever!
²⁴ Why do you hide your face,
    put our lowliness and oppression out of mind?
²⁵ Because our whole being bows down in the dirt,
    our heart clings to the ground.
²⁶ Get up as our help,
    redeem us for the sake of your commitment!

In connection with Psalm 20 I've mentioned that our church has just had to accept that we could no longer afford to pay the salary of a pastor. I mentioned this to one of my sons in England, who expressed surprise that such a thing could happen, surmising that it could hardly happen in the Church of England. The system of financing and paying salaries there is more centralized. In England, however, financial factors can mean that a minister who leaves may not be replaced; the church may have to share a minister with the next parish. In the United States and in Britain, there are churches that grow and new churches that start up; all is not doom and gloom. But the position of many local churches is discouraging. Our instinct is then to blame ourselves or to blame sociological factors.

Like us, Israelites could look to the past, reflect on how much better things were then, and wonder why. In contrast to our reaction, however, Psalm 44's reaction is to infer that God has abandoned us and to ask why he has done so. It sets the stage for asking that question by recalling how things once were and by declaring a trust in God based on how God formerly related to the people. It does so at such length and so unequivocally that by the time you get to the end of the first section of the psalm, you could think it was a psalm of praise or a psalm of trust. Indeed, when church lectionaries set this psalm for use in a service, they often simply choose the first section and use it as a psalm of praise.

Such selective use of Scripture is not exactly wrong, but it misses the point of this particular psalm, in which the recollection is simply the starting point for asking why things have changed so much. When God gave Old Testament Israel its country, the crucial factor was not the nation's military strength. As they told the story, sometimes the walls of a city simply fell down. The Israelites didn't even fight. And in the present they continue to trust God rather than trust their fighting ability.

But in their experience and in their lifetime, things don't work out the way they did for their ancestors. In different contexts there were historical and political explanations why this was so, explanations tied up with Middle Eastern politics. The psalm ignores such considerations in the conviction that God is not bound by them. If God gets the credit when things go well, God gets asked the questions when they go badly. In contrast, Christians often tell God what needs to be fixed in our political situation rather than just asking for **deliverance** or asking God, "Why are *you* doing this?" Failing to accuse God implies a failure to acknowledge who is really in charge, who really has power.

One can imagine that the psalm belongs in a context where the community gathers in the temple to bring its situation before God with fasting and prayer. The move from "we" to "I" during the psalm perhaps indicates that the king or another leader takes part in the use of this psalm on such an occasion.

As well as declining to blame the change in the people's experience on sociological or political factors, the psalm declines to assume that it is the people's own fault. There are psalms as well as prayers outside the Psalter that do so; it is not that Israel cannot imagine being at fault. It is that it can imagine situations when suffering comes to it through no fault of its own. The implication of the third section of the psalm is that people have not turned to other gods since trouble came to Israel, but the section eventually makes clear that the people can also say that neither had they turned to other gods before the trouble came. It is because of God that they are in the mess they are in. Paul picks up that line in Romans 8 and tweaks it; he and his friends,

142

too, are in a mess because of God, because they give their lives to seeking to serve God.

It transpires that the recollection, the protest, and the apologia all prepare the way for an extraordinary challenge in the last paragraph, a challenge to God to wake up. In 1 Kings 18, Elijah dared Israelites who worshiped **Canaanite** gods to come to a competition to see whose God answered prayer, and when the Canaanite gods fail to respond, Elijah hypothesizes that they may be asleep. Here the psalm turns the accusation onto Israel's own God. In prayer, nothing is barred as a means of provoking God to respond.

PSALM 45

The Marriage Challenge

The leader's. On Lilies [perhaps a tune]. The Qorahites'. An instruction. A love song.

¹ My mind stirs with a fine message;
    I am speaking my poem to a king,
    my tongue is the pen of a speedy scribe.

² You are the most handsome of human beings;
    grace is poured onto your lips—
    therefore God has blessed you forever.
³ Fasten your sword onto your side, warrior,
    with your honor and majesty,
⁴   and with your majesty win.
  Ride in the cause of truthfulness and faithful lowliness,
    so that your right hand directs you to awe-inspiring
      deeds.
⁵ Your arrows are sharpened;
    peoples are beneath you.
  [Your arrows] fall in the heart of the king's enemies;
⁶   your throne, God's, is forever and ever.
  Your royal scepter is an upright scepter;
⁷   you give yourself to faithfulness and you oppose
      faithlessness.
  Therefore God, your God, has anointed you
    with celebratory oil beyond your peers.

⁸ All your clothes are myrrh, aloes, and cassia;
   from your great ivory palace strings entertain you.
⁹ The great princess stands in your jewels,
   the queen at your right hand in gold of Ophir.

¹⁰ Listen, young lady, look, incline your ear;
   put out of mind your people, your father's household.
¹¹ The king will desire your beauty;
   since he is your lord, bow low to him.
¹² The city of Tyre will seek your favor with a gift,
   the richest of the people ¹³with all wealth.

To the inside, the princess, with her gold embroidery,
   her dress ¹⁴of colored cloth, will be taken to the king,
The girls behind her, her friends,
   will be brought to you.
¹⁵ They will be taken with joyful celebration;
   they will come into the king's palace.
¹⁶ In place of your ancestors will be your sons;
   you will appoint them as leaders throughout the country.
¹⁷ I will commemorate your name through all generations;
   therefore peoples will confess you forever and ever.

When you're young and you get married, you have to get your parents' approval, but when you're old and you get married, you have to get your children's approval. So I was nervous about telling my sons that I was getting married again eighteen months after their mother died and was therefore deeply moved at their joy and enthusiasm. I was also nervous about meeting my prospective stepdaughter, but that was fine too. And Kathleen was nervous about meeting her two stepsons at our wedding thanksgiving service in London, but I knew it would be fine. It had been different when I married my first wife, Ann, against her parents' wishes. They disapproved of me because I was such an ungentlemanly young man and also because I was a pastor and because I was taking away their daughter; for years she had to battle to be independent of them. When you get married, you have to be prepared to leave your father and mother, and maybe your son and daughter.

144

It's the same if you are a princess, only more so, and probably for extra reasons. The higher you are in the power structure or the class system, the less freedom you may have about whom you marry. In traditional societies, too, marriage isn't merely a private matter between two individuals. It brings about new relationships between two families in the village. Further, while marriage creates a new unit, it's not exactly a new family that comes into being, certainly not until the couple have children of their own. The new married couple is a subunit within a larger family, which in most societies means the bride joins the groom's family. For the relationship to work, as well as for the larger community or the political relationships to work, the bride has to be prepared to put her old family out of mind and enter with enthusiasm into this new web of relationships. No doubt there is a sense in which the groom has to do so, too; his relationship with his family changes. Maybe that consideration lies behind the comment in Genesis 2 that marriage requires a man to leave his father and mother and form a new unit with his wife. In a patriarchal society, marriage means that a woman bows to her husband's authority instead of to her father's. There is again some contrast with Genesis 1–2, where there is no suggestion that a husband has authority over his wife, but the psalm is dealing with the reality of life in the world outside Eden, where the question wasn't whether you submitted to some man but rather to which man you submitted.

Both groom and bride look terrific on this grand occasion. The issue that the psalm raises for the man is different from the one it raises for the woman, though he too needs to look to the future and not to the past as he thinks about his family. Possibly this love song (as the introduction calls it) was designed for ordinary couples to use, their wedding being an occasion when they are king and queen for a day. Whether that is so or not, the psalm actually speaks in terms of a royal wedding, and the challenge to the groom relates to his exercise of power in the world. In effect he sits on God's throne, the psalm says; he reigns on God's behalf, as God's vice-regent in Jerusalem. Maybe one could argue that any leader does so. As king he has power to wield. He needs to wield it in the way God wields power—with truthfulness, **faithfulness**, lowliness, and uprightness—and to oppose **faithlessness**. In connection with marriage, too, a woman will find it easier to submit to a man with such qualities. They are a visionary combination that lays a daunting challenge before a leader or a groom, or before a bride in a more egalitarian society.

PSALM 46

Be Still and Know That I Am God

The leader's. The Qorahites'. On Secrets [perhaps a tune]. A song.

¹ God is for us refuge and strength,
  a help in troubles, readily available.
² Therefore we are not afraid when the earth shakes,
  when mountains topple into the middle of the seas.
³ They may rage and foam,
  the mountains may quake when it lifts up high.   (*Rise*)

⁴ A river with its streams rejoices God's city,
  the holy place where the great dwelling of the One on
    High is.
⁵ God being in its midst, it will not topple;
  God helps it as morning arrives.
⁶ Nations rage, kingdoms totter;
  when he gives his voice, earth dissolves.
⁷ Yahweh Armies is with us;
  Jacob's God is a tower for us.   (*Rise*)

⁸ Go and look at the deeds of Yahweh,
  who brought about great destruction in the earth,
⁹ halting battles to the ends of the earth,
  when he shatters the bow and snaps the spear,
  burns chariots in the fire.
¹⁰ "Stop, and acknowledge that I am God;
  I will be high among the nations,
  I will be high in the earth."
¹¹ Yahweh Armies is with us;
  Jacob's God is a tower for us.   (*Rise*)

For nearly a thousand years, most of what is now Germany, Austria, Switzerland, the Netherlands, Belgium, and other areas comprised the Holy Roman Empire. It had a legislative assembly confusingly called a diet, which in 1521 met at a German city called Worms (hence the even more confusing title the Diet of Worms) to consider the pope's condemnation of the teachings of Martin Luther (not to be confused with Martin Luther King Jr., as sometimes happens). Luther had published views on the nature of the Christian faith and the authority of the church that conflicted with the church's official teaching. The Edict of Worms declared that Luther should be arrested and punished. Whereas the pope had taken words from Psalm 74 as the title of his encyclical about Luther, "Arise, Lord, and Defend Your Cause," Luther, threatened with execution, took his motto from Psalm 46 and wrote the hymn "A Mighty Fortress is Our God," which he based on the psalm. Nowadays his hymn is less controversial and even appears in some Roman Catholic hymnbooks.

Luther proved the psalm to be true. He could indeed say that in his time the earth was shaking and nations were raging; they were raging at him. Partly as a result of controversies he stirred up, they came to be shaking in another sense. Over the next century the unity and central power of the empire steadily weakened. Anyone who was in a position to stand back and wonder about where this political ferment might lead would have a right to be fearful for the future. It was a time like the opening decades of the twenty-first century. Indeed, a prayer letter I just received from an organization concerned for Christian witness in the Middle East in its current turmoil used the opening of Isaiah 46 as its epigraph.

Israel often lived in such times of turmoil. If you live in an earthquake or tsunami region, you will appreciate the promise that you can find God in the midst of such an event. In the psalm, these are images for the tumult of the nations. The way the psalm speaks is reminiscent of the first part of the book of Isaiah, when the nations that were raging were the nations of the **Assyrian** empire. They caused devastation in Israel on more than one occasion, but they never managed to take Jerusalem. For **Yahweh**'s own city, Yahweh indeed proved to be a refuge and strength, a help in troubles, readily available. The

King James Version translates that last phrase "a very present help in trouble." More literally, the Hebrew says God is "much to be found," easy to find. You just have to turn to him, Isaiah said. He is **Yahweh Armies**.

The nations were uncomfortably like a tsunami threatening to overwhelm Israel, but like Isaiah the psalm reminds people that Jerusalem has another watercourse in its midst. There's an irony about this comment, because the city's position on a mountain ridge means that a wide and deep river is exactly what Jerusalem does not have. It does have a stream gushing out of a spring, which the psalm turns into a picture of the way God looks after his city. This being God's city, it will not fall to the Assyrians or anyone else (unless God wants to yield it to some attacker out of annoyance with its people, which later God does more than once). The moment of greatest danger is dawn, when an enemy army will attack; but God helps it as morning comes.

If you don't believe me, the psalm says, go and look. Have the walls of Jerusalem been breached? No. Did God devastate the Assyrian army? Yes. You can read the story in Isaiah 36–37. World peace will come, the psalm says, by God's stopping nations from making war in order to extend their empires. We use the challenge "Be still and know that I am God" as an invitation to stop rushing around, to be quiet and center on God, which is an invitation we do need. In the psalm, it is a challenge to great nations to stop thinking that they are so great, to stop thinking they can do what they like in the world, and in particular to stop thinking they can do what they like with God's people and God's city. It's another way of envisaging the coming of world peace. Israel did not experience its arrival, and neither do we, but little experiences of God's winning the battle give grounds for believing that God will ultimately do so.

PSALM 47

The Outrageous Confession

The leader's. The Qorahites'. A composition.

1 All you peoples, clap hands,
   shout to God with a resounding voice.

148

² Because Yahweh, the One on High, is awe-inspiring,
    the great king over all the earth.
³ He subdues peoples under us,
    nations under our feet.
⁴ He chooses our own possession for us,
    the height of Jacob which he loves.   (*Rise*)
⁵ God has gone up with a shout,
    Yahweh with the sound of a horn.
⁶ Make music to God, make music;
    make music to our king, make music.
⁷ Because God is king of all the earth;
    make music with understanding.
⁸ God has become king over the nations;
    God has sat on his holy throne.
⁹ The lords of the peoples have gathered,
    the people of Abraham's God.
Because the shields of the earth belong to God;
    he has gone up very high.

In church yesterday we made our usual outrageous confessions, such as the declaration that Jesus is Lord. They are outrageous because the day's news seems to belie them. Dozens of people have died in an attack on a mosque in Pakistan. Car bombs have exploded outside a British cultural relations center in Kabul. In the United States, many people with cancer cannot get the drugs they need, partly because the drug companies don't make enough profit out of making them. Radiation has been discovered in rice near Tokyo. Scores of people have been killed in antigovernment demonstrations in Syria. Jesus is Lord?

When Israel declared that **Yahweh** is God, that its God is king of all the earth, it made its equivalently outrageous confession, and when it challenged all the peoples of the earth to join that declaration, its confession was the more outrageous. How could it make such a confession? Psalm 47 compares and contrasts with Psalm 46. The content of that preceding psalm suggested a link with Israel's history in the time when people were composing and singing the psalms, a time such as that of Isaiah. It didn't belong to long-gone history (though it would be long-gone for later worshipers). You could go and look at

149

the walls and gates of Jerusalem for the evidence that God had kept the city safe.

In contrast, Psalm 47 looks back to the events that made Israel Israel—that is, it refers to Yahweh's original subduing of the country's inhabitants and his gift to Israel of its mountain country, which Yahweh loves. Israel settled in this mountain country on God's coat tails as God made his ascent there like a warrior with a shout and with the sound of the horn signaling the moment for advance. So Israel's outrageous statement is that Yahweh is "the great king over all the earth." The title is one the king of **Assyria** claimed (it comes in the story in Isaiah 36–37 about the Assyrian attempt to take Jerusalem, to which I referred in connection with Psalm 46). It would be a plausible claim. But Psalm 47 says, with great chutzpah, "You know who is the real great king of all the earth? I will tell you."

The second half of the psalm follows the pattern of the opening half—first there is an exhortation to acknowledge God, then there are the reasons, the substance of the praise. It is the regular way a psalm of praise works. Like Psalms 30 or 42, the psalm cannot be satisfied with saying something once; it says it twice. Like the repetitions within a line, however, the second half of the psalm does more than merely repeat the first half; it pushes things further. So the renewed exhortation adds music to the shouts and hand claps of the first exhortation. It adds the emphasis that *the* king is *our* king. The substance of the praise then refers to God's sitting on his throne, which takes us beyond the taking of the country to the building of the Jerusalem temple. It is here that Israel would gather to sing this psalm. The reason that Israel could make these outrageous confessions would be that Israel knows the story of Yahweh's taking hold of this country and taking up his throne there. This achievement makes it possible to believe that Yahweh is king when the day's news seems to belie it—just as our knowledge of the Jesus story makes it possible to declare that Jesus is Lord when the day's news seems to belie it.

The description of the nations' leaders, their lords or shields, gathering to acknowledge Abraham's God is an act of imagination, but it is a vision whose fulfillment is guaranteed by what this God has done already. At the beginning of Israel's story, people such as the Gibeonites were compelled to make this acknowledgment of Abraham's God; they are a first stage in a process that will eventually come to completion. Once again the psalm shows how Israel knew that Yahweh's involvement with Israel was not focused merely on Israel for its own sake. Precisely because Yahweh is the king of all the earth, Israel's faith involves an interest in the whole world. The lords of the peoples gather as the people of Abraham's God or with the people of Abraham's God (the terse sentence doesn't make clear which is the right translation, but it makes little difference). The point is not merely that they should be "saved" but that they should recognize God as God. Analogously, what God has done with and through Jesus is the guarantee that the world will recognize that Jesus is Lord.

PSALM 48

Is This the City?

A song. A composition. The Qorahites'.

1. Yahweh is great, and much to be praised,
     in our God's city.
   His holy mountain ²is a beauty of a height,
     the greatest joy in all the earth.
   The heights of Zaphon are Mount Zion,
     the great king's town.
3. In its citadels God has caused himself
     to be acknowledged as a tower.
4. Because there—the kings assembled,
     passed over together.
5. When they saw, they were stunned,
     they were terrified, they panicked.
6. Trembling took hold of them there,
     writhing like a woman in labor.
7. With an east wind
     you break up Tarshish ships.
8. As we have heard, so have we seen,
     in the city of Yahweh Armies,
   in the city of our God,
     which God will establish forever.   (*Rise*)

⁹ God, we have reflected on your commitment,
   within your palace.
¹⁰ God, like your name, so your praise
   reaches to the ends of the earth.
   Your right hand is full of faithfulness;
¹¹   Mount Zion will celebrate.
   The cities of Judah will rejoice
   for the sake of your decisions.
¹² Go around Zion, circle it,
   count its towers.
¹³ Set your mind on its rampart,
   tour its citadels,
   so that you can recount to a future age
¹⁴   that this is God,
   our God forever and ever—
   he will direct us against death.

When my first wife and I moved to the United States, people would ask what I would miss about England, to which I would answer not fish and chips or even Indian food but proximity to France and to Israel. Since the move I haven't been to Israel, partly because it's a long way, partly because Ann's being in a wheelchair made it too complicated, but also partly because the political situation (especially the building of the wall separating Palestinian areas from Jewish areas) made the situation there so grievous that I didn't want to face it. But my new wife and I have been discussing the possibility of spending some time in Jerusalem next year. It seems time to face facts. More important, being in Jerusalem brings home the having-happenedness of Jewish and Christian faith. That faith is not a collection of theological ideas or behavioral principles but the story of something that happened in a particular location at a particular time.

We have noted in connection with Psalms 42 and 46 how it is thus important that Jerusalem is a real place. Psalm 48 again exhorts people to go and have a good look at the city. It starts from the city's natural impressiveness and beauty. In reality, Jerusalem is just a little spur off a ridge, not as high as the hills around, such as the Mount of Olives. It became beautiful through the building done there out of the cream stone quarried from underneath it. The psalm calls it "a beauty of a height" not because of its natural or humanly manufactured beauty but because **Yahweh** made it his home. Far to the north, on the boundary of Syria and Turkey, is Mount Zaphon, twice as high as Mount **Zion** and the place where **Canaanites** located the home of the **Master**. I'll tell you where the real Mount Zaphon is, the real mountain home of God, says the psalm. It's little Mount Zion. It's typical of God to go for an insignificant little mountain in an insignificant location (Israel was an insignificant little people; David, an insignificant little boy; and Nazareth, an insignificant little village). It becomes significant through God's actions there.

"The great king" is a significant title as it was in Psalm 47 but here perhaps for a religious reason as well a political one. The Master could be called the king of the gods. "I'll tell you who the real king of the gods is," the psalm says. The enigmatic closing phrase about Yahweh's directing the people against death maybe has a background in setting Yahweh over against the Master, because the Canaanites told a story about the Master being overcome by Death and needing to be brought back to life.

The psalm focuses on the political. It recalls how foreign forces tried to take Jerusalem and failed. They were as impressive as Tarshish ships, big ocean-going merchant vessels, but even Tarshish ships are vulnerable to a gale from the east. The impressive foreign forces turned out to be vulnerable. "I came, I saw, I conquered," Julius Caesar once said about one of his campaigns. "They came, they saw, they fled," Calvin tartly observes in his comments on the psalm.

If you can go and look at the city, the story is not merely one you hear about from your parents or grandparents or a priest recounting it in a service in the temple. You can go and look. The medieval city of Jerusalem, the "Old City," is surrounded by walls that do not follow the lie of the walls of Old Testament times, but they give you the right impression of what it would be like to go around the city after it had been besieged and to note the good shape its citadels and walls are in. **Yahweh Armies** is the people's tower, but Yahweh operates by preserving the city's own defenses. Once again, Yahweh's activity in Jerusalem is not merely good news for Israel and bad news for its attackers. It is to be the means of Yahweh's coming to be praised through the world. Week to week, Jews, Christians, and Muslims praise God and make mention of Jerusalem not only in Jerusalem but to the ends of the earth.

But eventually Yahweh let the city of Jerusalem fall, and Lamentations 2 then pictures passersby snidely asking, "Is this the city that was called a beauty of a height, the greatest joy in all the earth?" In decades where Jerusalem has been divided and been a place of conflict rather than concord, we echo the same question. Psalm 48 reminds us of God's intention for this city and gives us reason for hope.

PSALM 49

Death Catches You When You Don't Expect It To

The leader's. The Qorahites'. A composition.

¹ Listen to this, all you peoples;
     give heed, all you inhabitants of the world,
² both ordinary people and important people,
     wealthy and needy together.
³ My mouth will utter insight,
     the talk that comes from my mind will be understanding.
⁴ I will incline my ear to a lesson,
     I will resolve my question to the guitar.

⁵ Why should I be afraid in evil days,
     when my assailants' waywardness surrounds me,
⁶ people who trust in their wealth
     and boast in their great riches?
⁷ Huh. It definitely cannot redeem someone;
     it cannot give God his ransom.
⁸ The redemption of his life would be expensive;
     it would be insufficient forever,
⁹ so that he should live on forever,
     not see the pit.
¹⁰ Because one can see that people of insight die,
     the foolish and stupid person perish together.
     They leave their wealth to others,

11   whereas their inward thought is that their home will
         be forever,
     their dwelling to all generations;
         they had called lands by their name.
12 A human being does not abide in honor;
         he is like cattle that perish.
13 This is the way things are for them, the people
         characterized by foolishness,
         and after them the people who favor their talk.   (*Rise*)
14 Like sheep they have headed for Sheol;
         death shepherds them.
     The upright have dominion over them at morning,
         and their form is for wasting by Sheol,
         away from its lofty home.
15 Yet God will redeem my life from the hand of Sheol,
         because he will take me.   (*Rise*)

16 Do not be afraid when someone becomes rich,
         when the splendor of his house becomes great,
17 because when he dies he does not take it all;
         his splendor does not go down after him.
18 Even if he blesses himself in his lifetime,
         and they recognize you that you do well for yourself,
19 he goes to the company of his ancestors;
         never does he see the light.
20 A human being in honor
         but who does not have insight is like cattle that perish.

We recently buried the second-oldest member of our congregation, who until she faded away quickly at the end had regularly attended church. We drove quite a way to the cemetery, and I wondered why, until I discovered that her husband was buried there. We were going to lay her beside him. Yesterday I was visiting the oldest member of our congregation, who is ninety-six. Until recently she was at church most weeks, but she has been unable to be there because of a sore on her leg. She hopes to be back in a week or two, but she is looking frailer, and I wondered whether I will soon be conducting her funeral. You can live on into your nineties, but eventually death is going to get you. When I got home, I heard about the death of a former fellow pastor, about the same age as I am, who had been in good health the last time I saw him but had suddenly become ill and died. You may not live on into your nineties. Death may get you before then.

The psalm's point is that it is God who controls when this happens. It's tempting to think that the money to cover a comprehensive health plan is the decisive factor in determining how long you live, and/or that discipline over diet and keeping fit are decisive factors. They are influential, but we are always hearing stories about people who try to make sure they have everything going for them but then get struck down. The psalm invites us to set this fact in the context of God's involvement in the world. Someone with a boss who has a great health plan but who doesn't pay the more lowly employees enough for them to afford one has a right to feel some resentment, but that's when you have to remind yourself that it's not the ultimate factor in determining what happens. However much money you spend on your plan, it can't be enough to buy a longer life, nor can it alter the fact that eventually you are going to die. It doesn't make any difference how wealthy you are or how clever you are.

When you're young or middle-aged, you probably don't think much about death, and as a result you live as if you think you will live forever, even though in theory you know that is not the case. When the psalm characterizes well-to-do people as thinking that their nice homes will be theirs forever, I don't imagine it implies this is their conscious assumption—it's more the implication of the attitude they take to their homes. The same assumption is implicit in the instinct to other forms of accumulation, like land (or books, in my case, or CDs—you can name your own accumulation of choice). It's stupid, the psalm says, and this stupidity is shared by people who would like to emulate those well-to-do people.

But the psalm isn't talking about the general stupidity of behaving as if you think you will live forever. It's talking about people who combine wealth with an instinct to trample on others (of course wealth often issues from an instinct to trample on others rather than hard work or creativity or good luck). The Old Testament's ideal is to combine wealth with generosity to the needy. Combining wealth and trampling on others

156

is real stupidity, the Old Testament assumes. People affected by this attitude are people who find death shepherding them before their time. In contrast, the upright find God delivering them at morning—as in Psalm 46, dawn is the moment of greatest danger. Yesterday the foolish, wealthy person rules. Today the wealthy person has passed, and the upright person rules. Threatened by the possibility of death, the people with no resource but God can prove God's capacity to deliver them from ending up in **Sheol** before their time. The psalmist knows it doesn't always work but wants people to trust in the reality of God's involvement in the world, which means it often works.

PSALM 50

Keep It Simple

A composition. Asaph's.

¹ God, Yahweh God, has spoken,
   and called the earth
   from the rising of the sun to its going down.
² From Zion, the fullness of beauty,
   God has shone out;
³   our God comes and cannot be silent.
Fire devours in front of him,
   and around him it has stormed greatly.
⁴ He calls to the heavens above,
   and to the earth for a decision about his people.
⁵ "Gather to me the people committed to me,
   the people who sealed a covenant with me over
      a sacrifice."
⁶ The heavens have told of his faithfulness,
   because he is a God who exercises authority.

⁷ "Listen, my people, and I will speak;
   Israel, and I will testify against you—
   I am God, your God.
⁸ About your sacrifices I do not reprove you,
   and your burnt offerings are continually before me.
⁹ I would not take a bull from your house,
   goats from your pens.

¹⁰ Because every animal in the forest is mine,
        the cattle on a thousand mountains.
¹¹ I know every bird in the mountains,
        and every creature of the wild is with me.
¹² If I were hungry, I would not say so to you,
        because the world and what fills it is mine.
¹³ Do I eat the flesh of buffalo
        or drink the blood of goats?
¹⁴ Sacrifice a thank-offering to God,
        fulfill your promises to the One on High.
¹⁵ Call me on the day of trouble;
        I will rescue you, then you will honor me."

¹⁶ But to the faithless person, God has said:
        "What is your business in recounting my laws
        and taking my covenant on your lips,
¹⁷ when you are one who is against discipline
        and throws my words behind you?
¹⁸ If you have seen a thief, you have favored him,
        and your life has been with adulterers.
¹⁹ You have given your mouth to evil;
        you harness your tongue to deceit.
²⁰ You sit speaking against your brother,
        with your mother's son you find fault.
²¹ These things you have done and I have been silent;
        you have thought I really was like you.
   I reprove you and lay it out in front of you;
²²   do consider this, you who put God out of mind,
        lest I tear you apart and there is no one to rescue.

²³ The person who sacrifices a thank-offering honors me,
        and the person who directs his way—
        I show him God's deliverance."

It's kind of complicated being a church. It was brought home to me yesterday when for the first time I took the bunch of church keys that I recently inherited to go for a meeting with a couple whose baby we are going to baptize. There are fifteen keys. I never found the right one to open the front gate, but we were able to use the back gate, so we were OK. At first I thought I couldn't find the right key to the church building, but the lock was simply stiff. Only by accident did I then discover how to turn on the lights and the fountain in the grounds. Then there is the copier, and the Web site, and the mail (who would have thought that a church got so much junk mail?). . . .

Maybe being a church should be simpler. Psalm 50 closes with God's declaring that there are just two or three things that matter. To begin at the end, there is the experience of God's **deliverance**. The trouble with it is that we are not able to control it. Ordinary Israelites had much less control of their lives than Western Christians, which in an odd way put them in an easier position. They couldn't exercise much control over their destinies. Politically, they were more in the position of a nation in the two-thirds world than of a Western power. Economically, they were dependent on the weather more than Western people are. Medically, when they got sick, there wasn't much they could do but cast themselves on God. But in a strange way, being out of control may be good, because God's deliverance is more reliable than human control. Time and again we discover that human control doesn't work in the realm of politics or economics or medicine, but this experience is inclined to make us try harder rather than cast ourselves on God.

You can do so with confidence (the psalm's last line adds) if you are people who direct their way. The psalm is interested in people's control of their lives but in a different sense from the one I was just describing. Indeed, we may make excuses for not exercising moral control of our lives ("It's hard for me to resist working too hard or being cynical or overeating or watching too much television or buying more clothes"). God expects us to do so. It's hard, but it's not very complicated. The psalm pictures people who are committed in their participation in worship. They say all the right things there, but their attitudes outside worship don't correspond to their words. It's as if they are throwing away God's words like the wrapping on a sandwich. They don't care what they say about other people. In another sense, whereas we may think of tolerance as a virtue, God sees it as a vice. Only if there is moral direction to your life can you expect to see God's deliverance. Beware when God doesn't have mercy on you by rebuking you, the psalm adds; God's silence when you are in the wrong is itself a frightening judgment.

When you do see God's deliverance, the appropriate response is to bring a thank-offering. The last line of the psalm starts here. A thank-offering is the sacrifice that naturally accompanies a thanksgiving psalm. When we want to express appreciation to someone, we often make that a reason for making a gift and not merely saying thank-you. The Old Testament assumes the same is true in relationships with God. Mere words are cheap. Sometimes people brought thank-offerings simply because God had answered a prayer, maybe for healing or protection from attack. Sometimes in the course of praying, a psalm will envisage bringing an offering when the prayer has been answered, so some thank-offerings are the fulfillment of such promises—hence the reference to fulfilling promises in this psalm.

So a relationship with God is a simple affair, the psalm says. You live an upright life; you get into trouble; you call on God; God rescues you; you bring a thank-offering. The trouble is that people made it much more demanding. They made huge offerings to God, as if size matters, as if we are bribing God. People who didn't live upright lives tried to compensate by making big offerings; even upright people might think that they had to make big offerings. What does that instinct imply about how you think of God? the psalm asks. Keep it simple.

Asaph was one of the leaders of the music in temple worship appointed by David, according to 1 Chronicles 16 and 25. Chronicles often mentions the descendants of Asaph in this connection, and the reference to Asaph in Psalm 50 may allude to this Asaphite choir, as "David" can refer to the Davidic kings in general.

PSALM 51

Teach Me to Repent

The leader's. A composition. David's. When Nathan the prophet came to him as he had come to Bathsheba.

¹ Be gracious to me, God,
　　in accordance with your commitment.
　In accordance with the greatness of your compassion
　　wipe away my rebellions.

² Wash me thoroughly from my waywardness,
  cleanse me from my offense.
³ Because I do acknowledge my rebellions;
  my shortcoming is in front of me all the time.
⁴ Against you alone have I offended
  and done what is evil in your eyes,
  so that you are faithful in your speaking,
  in the clear in your making decisions.
⁵ On one hand, in waywardness I was birthed,
  in shortcoming my mother conceived me.
⁶ On the other, you delight in truthfulness in hidden places;
  in the secret place you make me acknowledge insight.
⁷ Remove my shortcoming with hyssop so I am clean,
  wash me so I am whiter than snow.
⁸ Let me listen to joy and celebration;
  may the bones you have crushed rejoice.
⁹ Hide your face from my shortcomings,
  wipe away all my wayward acts.

¹⁰ Create for me a clean mind, God;
   renew a firm spirit within me.
¹¹ Don't throw me out of your presence;
   don't take your holy spirit away from me.
¹² Give back to me the joy of being delivered by you;
   may your generous spirit sustain me.

¹³ I will teach rebels your ways,
   and offenders will return to you.
¹⁴ Rescue me from shed blood, God,
   the God who delivers me;
   my tongue will resound concerning your faithfulness.
¹⁵ My Lord, open my lips,
   and my mouth will tell of your praise.
¹⁶ Because you would not delight in a sacrifice, were I to
      give it;
   you would not favor a burnt offering.
¹⁷ Godly sacrifices are a broken spirit;
   a broken, crushed mind, God, you would not despise.

¹⁸ Do good to Zion by your favor;
   build up Jerusalem's walls.

¹⁹ Then you will delight in faithful sacrifices,
    burnt offering and whole offering;
    then people will take bulls up onto your altar.

John Donne was a seventeenth-century priest, love poet, and member of parliament. He also wrote a series of "Holy Sonnets" (found in *The Oxford Book of English Verse*, ed. Christopher Ricks [New York: Oxford University Press, 1999], 117). In one he imagines resurrection day, then recalls how the coming of that day will mean it is too late to ask for forgiveness. So he concludes by saying to God,

Here on this lowly ground,
teach me how to repent, for that's as good
as if Thou hadst seal'd my pardon with Thy blood.

One could ask whether Donne is right that teaching us to repent is as good as dying for us; if God hadn't been prepared to give his son for us, our repenting would get us nowhere. But he is surely right to imply the converse; if God does give his son for us but does not also teach us to repent, then his giving would get us nowhere. And we need to be taught to repent. It doesn't come naturally, partly because we are usually busy making excuses to ourselves for what we have done or not done.

The introduction to Psalm 51 gives the psalm a link with David's repentance over the Bathsheba affair, but the link with **David's story** raises the same questions as arise in connection with Psalm 18. "Against you alone have I offended"? If David said those words, then God has more to do in teaching David the meaning of repentance. "Create for me a clean mind, God; renew a firm spirit within me"? If David prayed that prayer, it seems that God did not grant it, because David's story as father and as king unravels from the time of the Bathsheba and Uriah affair onwards. Apparently it is possible for God to put away sin in the sense of not responding to it in active wrath, yet it does not mean that God intervenes to halt the consequences of what we started by our wrongful deeds. Our violation of the commandments can still tear the fabric of society in a way that isn't easily fixed, even if individuals are healed. As the commandment puts it, the sins of the parents are visited on the children.

So the introduction's encouragement to set the psalm and David's story alongside each other is illuminating in the way it raises questions about David. If the prayer was for him to pray as someone who needed to repent, then there are ways in which it does illustrate how he needed to pray. But in light of what we know from the rest of Scripture, we can infer something of God's negative reaction as well as God's positive reaction. Like other psalms, it drives us to examine ourselves and not simply assume that our discernment about ourselves is genuine discernment.

Starting from the other end of the psalm offers some complementary insights. The plea to God to build up Jerusalem's walls also doesn't fit very well with David's day, when they were intact. It suggests a time between Jeremiah's day (when they were demolished by the **Babylonians**) and Nehemiah's day (when they were rebuilt with the help of the **Persians**). Religiously speaking, they were demolished because of the attitude **Judah** had been taking to **Yahweh** for a century or more—its trust in politics rather than in Yahweh and its turning to other gods rather than to Yahweh. In that context, the confession "Against you alone have I offended" makes sense. The "I" of the psalm might be the ordinary Israelite, as when churches that say a creed may use one that says, "I believe" when it is the whole congregation that says it. Or it might be the leader of the community, someone like Zerubbabel or Nehemiah.

In that situation, offering sacrifices to God does not get you anywhere. Sacrifices can deal with small problems of uncleanness but not serious sin; and sacrifices that express praise and commitment are nonsense when your relationship with God has broken down. When your wife has caught you being unfaithful, a gift of flowers or even a new car is not going to get you anywhere. It's the same with God. All you can do when you have committed serious sin is cast yourself on God's grace as someone who is crushed and broken by the price you have paid for your wrongdoing—as the Jerusalem community was in the **exile**. Then, if God forgives you and answers the prayers that come in the psalm, and does see to the city's rebuilding, you can recommence your regular life of worship, in which sacrifice has its proper place as an expression of praise and commitment.

In Psalm 51, then, the people of God casts itself on God's mercy and compassion. It recognizes how sin has characterized its life from its earliest beginnings at Sinai or in the church's early years as the New Testament describes them. It acknowledges that it can't get away with saying one thing in public but doing something different in private. It knows that it cannot complain at God's treatment of it and that its life is forfeit. It needs God to transform it. Then it will be in a position to tell the world about Yahweh's grace.

It looks as if God answered the psalm's prayer as prayed by Judah. The temple and the walls did get rebuilt, the community over the succeeding centuries did show more signs of being indwelt by God's spirit, and it was in a position to share what it knew about God in surrounding countries so that there were Jewish congregations attracting Gentile believers widely spread by Roman times.

PSALM 52

How to Stand Tall—I

The leader's. An instruction. David's. When Doeg the Edomite came and told Saul, "David came to Ahimelech's house."

1. Why do you exult in evil, warrior?—
     God's commitment holds every day.
2. Your tongue plans evil,
       like a sharpened razor,
       you who are acting with deceit.
3. You give yourself to evil rather than good,
       to lying rather than faithful words.   (*Rise*)
4. You give yourself to all destructive words,
       you deceitful tongue.
5. Now God will tear you down forever,
       break you and pull you from your tent,
       uproot you from the land of the living.   (*Rise*)
6. The faithful people will see and be in awe,
       and will laugh at him:

⁷ "There is the man who did not make God his stronghold,
⁸   but trusted in the greatness of his wealth,
      found strength in his destructiveness."

⁹ But I am like a thriving olive tree
      in God's house;
   I have trusted in God's commitment
      forever and ever.
   I will confess you forever
      because you have acted.
   I will look to your name, because it is good,
      in front of the people committed to you.

The dedication of the Martin Luther King Jr. Memorial was scheduled this weekend in Washington (but a threatened hurricane has caused a delay in this event). Inevitably, perhaps, there's some difference of opinion about whether it is the right sort of memorial or whether any memorial of this kind is an appropriate commemoration of this man. What strikes me as I think about Psalm 52 is that Dr. King was someone who knew he was confronted by people who planned and did evil against him and other African Americans, but he stood tall when threatened by them. Somehow he managed to be realistic about the danger that threatened him and also trust in God.

So I can imagine him saying Psalm 52, among many other psalms, as he faced the calling that had been placed on him. The people who opposed him were Christians, as he was, and they were not people who thought themselves as exulting in evil; they thought they were being faithful to their Christian commitment. The Hebrew word for "evil" is like the English word "bad"—it can denote actions that are morally bad but also events that are calamitous and painful. In this latter sense God can be involved in "evil"; God sometimes makes bad things happen. Dr. King's opponents knew that they were planning disaster for him; they did not think they were planning moral evil, yet it is what they were doing. In the same way, the man in the psalm who exults in evil likely doesn't think he is rejoicing in moral evil; he had ways of convincing himself that what he was doing was right.

As is the case with Psalm 51, there is a bit of overlap between the psalm and the episode in **David's story** to which the introduction refers (1 Samuel 21–22). Although the portrait of the "warrior" only partially fits Doeg (indeed, one might wonder if the warrior is Saul), the description of the trusting attitude that closes the psalm fits David. In this connection we can see Psalm 52 as a psalm for someone in David's position to pray—someone like Dr. King. The psalm piles up descriptions of the particular warrior it is concerned about, one who exults in evil, plans evil, gives himself to evil. He can tell the kind of deceitful lies that destroy someone; he has the kind of resources that will buy someone's downfall. Yet it does so in order to pour scorn on him. He takes no account of God's **commitment**, of God's willingness to act on behalf of the faithful. Those realities mean that the person confronted by this dangerous threat can stand tall and look forward to the moment when the **faithful** who identify with him will see, be in awe, and laugh.

You might question whether a man like Ahimelech, who was slain by Doeg, or like Dr. King, who was assassinated, resembles a thriving olive tree in God's house, but if you quiz them about this on resurrection day, they may say that their trust in a commitment by God that would last forever was vindicated and that this would still be the case even if there were no resurrection day (Ahimelech didn't even know this day was going to come). In front of the people committed to God's way Dr. King looked to God's **name** because it is good. His testimony, combined with the assassination that might seem to disprove the psalm, contributed to the process whereby God tore evil people down and whereby the faithful came to see, be in awe, and laugh.

PSALM 53

There Is No God Here

The leader's. On Pipe [perhaps a tune]. An instruction. David's.

[1] The scoundrel has said to himself,
   "There is no God here."
People have been destructive and loathsome in wrongdoing;
   there is no one doing good here.

166

² God has looked out from the heavens at human beings,
    to see if there is someone of understanding,
    someone who inquires of God.
³ The whole of it has turned away,
    altogether they are foul.
  There is no one doing good,
    there is not even one.
⁴ Do they not acknowledge, the wrongdoers,
    who eat up my people as they eat food,
    when they do not call God?
⁵ There, they have totally panicked,
    when there was no panic.
  Because God has scattered the bones of your besieger;
    you are shamed, because God has rejected them.
⁶ If only there were deliverance for Israel from Zion,
    when God restores his people's fortune.
    Jacob will rejoice, Israel will celebrate.

Yesterday, my wife and I walked through crowds of people
whose faces seemed to say, "There is no God here." They were
crowds walking up and down the pier at Santa Monica among
the stands selling ice cream and sunhats and hotdogs. They
should have been enjoying themselves; they were on holiday.
Yet their faces were blank or bored or disappointed. There was
no contact between the people on the pier; they stared ahead as
if they were the only ones there. There was a sadness or a dead-
ness about their eyes. Grieving over the experience of being
among them as we walked along the sand, my wife said she felt
as if she should set up a prayer stall alongside all the other stalls
on the pier, inviting people to have her pray for them. Perhaps
we will return and do so.

The psalm speaks about people who live as if there is no
God here. The people it has in mind are also people with no
understanding, people who do not (yet) inquire of God, people
who do not call God (the bold expression almost suggests the
idea of summoning God like a boss summoning an employee).
Worse, they are people who have made the logical inference
that in our moral lives we can live as if God is not present. They
become not only people over whose faces one grieves but people who count as scoundrels. They are people with no moral

commitments. The conviction that "there is no God here" generates a situation in which "there is no one doing good here." They are ruthless in the way they indulge themselves, not worrying that the way they eat means they are consuming the lives of other people.

Translations have them declaring that "there is no God," which makes them sound like atheists, but they are not exactly denying that God exists. They are rather denying that God is involved in the world. God is far away in heaven, letting human beings do what they like. God doesn't care what happens. It is perhaps a more cynical, more hopeless conviction than believing that God simply does not exist (which perhaps links with the fact that many people who are atheists in the Western sense are people who do a lot of good).

In a way you can't blame people for doubting if God is involved in the world, whether it leads them to the bleakness we saw in people on the pier or to the moral destructiveness of which the psalm speaks. As we walked along the beach, an airplane flew past, trailing an advertisement. God's involvement in the world is not trailed past in that obvious way. One can miss God's involvement. The psalm declares that God actually does look out from the heavens at what is happening in the world. The psalmist knows that the God who looks is also the God who acts, and he imagines that God has already put the wicked down. Yet the psalm also lives with the reality of a situation in which the community needs God to take action to restore it, and it wistfully expresses the wish that the moment for this action might come. It is an indirect form of prayer that might, in its understatement, get God's attention as effectively as a direct prayer.

PSALM 54

How to Stand Tall—II

The leader's. With strings. An instruction. David's. When the Ziphites came and told Saul, "Actually, David is hiding with us."

1 God, deliver me by your name,
     by your might decide for me.

² God, listen to my plea,
   give ear to the words of my mouth.
³ Because aliens have risen up against me,
   terrifying people have sought my life,
   people who have not put God in front of them.   (*Rise*)
⁴ There—God is my helper,
   the Lord is the very sustainer of my life.
⁵ May he make the evil come back to the people who are
       watching for me—
   in your truthfulness wipe them out.
⁶ With a voluntary offering I will sacrifice to you,
   I will confess your name, Yahweh, because it is good.
⁷ Because it has rescued me from every trouble,
   and my eye has looked at my enemies.

I found myself thinking and talking about Martin Luther King Jr. again yesterday (see the comment on Psalm 52), the day set for the dedication of his memorial and the anniversary of his "I Have a Dream" speech. It fit neatly with the Scriptures that were set for our reading in church. We began with the call of Moses, whom Dr. King resembled in being called to a role for which he had no personal desire; he expected to lead the quiet life of an academic and pastor, like me. The Gospel passage related Jesus' warning to his disciples that people who followed him were going to have to take up their own cross just as he did, which was certainly true of Dr. King. The epistle from Romans 12 spoke of love and a refusal to take redress; leave that to God. Such action heaps coals on your enemies' heads, says Paul, quoting Proverbs 25. Maybe the image refers to God's punishment; maybe it means people come to see the error of their ways.

Like Psalm 52, Psalm 54 has an introduction that connects it to a situation when David had to leave redress to God. The somewhat comical double story comes in 1 Samuel 23 and 26. Actually David didn't *have* to leave redress to God; he had several opportunities to kill Saul, but he didn't take them. So Psalm 54 imagines how someone like David might pray in a situation of that kind, to help us see how to pray then.

In many respects, the psalm is simply a standard way of praying in any situation of pressure. There are three elements to the actual prayer: "Listen to me"; "Rescue me"; "Put my attackers down." We have noted that Western people can be offended by the last element in the prayer, though the New Testament incorporates similar prayers. One way they have something to teach us is that they take seriously the extent to which the world is skewed when people attack one another; such actions can't be left there spoiling the world. In this sense the human desire for justice is quite appropriate. Another implication of such prayers is that realigning the situation when it is skewed by such wrongdoing is not our business. We talk to God about it, then leave it to God, which is quite a test of faith. We are fortunate that we don't have to figure out what should happen to the people we judge as "evil." We might be wrong about how evil they are, and we don't want to become like them in becoming mean as we take revenge. Further, as Westerners we may think we are nice, and as Christians we may think we are supposed to become even nicer, even though we are secretly watching all kinds of TV where we can agree with the putting down of the bad guy, whether in a drama or on the evening news.

Apart from the prayer itself, the psalm comprises a statement of trust in God and a promise to give God the appropriate recognition and praise when God has acted. The final line comprises a further statement of confidence and trust as it imagines the prayer as being not merely answered by God's having determined to act but by God's having actually acted in such a way that one can see it.

PSALM 55

Throwing Things onto God

The leader's. With strings. An instruction. David's.

1 God, give ear to my plea,
     do not hide from my prayer for grace.
2 Pay heed to me and answer me;
     I am frantic in my lament, and I reel
3 at the voice of the enemy,
     in the face of the pressure of the faithless,

because they bring down evil upon me,
    and in anger harass me.
4 My mind whirls within me,
    deathly terrors have fallen upon me,
5 fear and trembling come into me,
    horror has enveloped me.
6 I said, "If only I had wings;
    like a pigeon I could fly and find rest."
7 Yes, I would go far away in flight,
    I would lodge in the wilderness.   (*Rise*)
8 I would hurry to my haven,
    from the sweeping wind, from the tempest.
9 Lord, swallow up, divide their speech,
    because I have seen violence and contention
      in the city.
10 Day and night they go around it on the walls,
    while wickedness and trouble are inside it.
11 Destruction is within it;
    oppression and deceit do not leave its square.
12 Because it is not an enemy that reviles me,
    which I could bear,
or my opponent that has acted big over me,
    from whom I could hide,
13 but you, a person of my kind,
    my companion, someone I knew,
14 together we would enjoy fellowship
    as we walked in the throng into God's house.

15 Great desolation on them,
    they will go down to Sheol alive,
because there is great evil in their sojourning place, in the
    midst of them.
16 Because I call to God,
    Yahweh will deliver me.
17 Evening and morning and noon
    I lament, and I reel,
    but he has listened to my voice.
18 He has redeemed my life in safety from my encounter,
    because many indeed were with me.
19 God listens and puts them down,
    the one who sits [enthroned] of old,   (*Rise*)

the one in whom there are no changes—
    but they have no awe of God.

20 He has reached out his hand against his friends,
    he has violated his covenant.
21 The butter in his mouth was smooth,
    but encounter was in his mind.
His words were softer than oil,
    but they were unsheathed swords.

22 Throw onto Yahweh what is given you,
    and he himself will sustain you.
He will never let
    the faithful person fall down.
23 God, you yourself will bring them down,
    to the deepest pit,
The murderous and deceitful people
    will not have half their days,
    but I—I will trust in you.

A therapist friend of mine has described to me the process she goes through after spending a day listening to clients, who unburden themselves of their hurts, sufferings, and sins. It seems that these burdens have to go somewhere, a little like the demons that Jesus allows to enter some pigs. They cannot simply disappear into thin air; if they could, perhaps the presence of a therapist would be unnecessary. So listening requires the therapist to take them into herself, at least momentarily. But a mere human being can't simply absorb into herself the hurts, sufferings, and sins of all her clients. So my friend stops at a roadside rest area at the brow of a hill on the way home, sits in the car, and passes them over to God.

    She is doing what the end of Psalm 55 recommends when it speaks of throwing things onto **Yahweh**. Maybe the action is more hostile than is implied by "throwing onto." Maybe the idea is that you can throw things *at* Yahweh, like a child behaving aggressively toward a parent. Parents can cope with that experience; presumably God can also do so. Either way, what you are throwing is "what is given you." In other words, the psalm describes the experience of attack and pressure, of people's wicked harassment, of deceit and betrayal, as God's gift, though not a very nice one. After all, God allows it to happen, and at the moment it is happening God is doing nothing about it. You are in a position like the therapist's, except that she voluntarily agrees to receive what her clients "give" her. It is important that she does not try to keep hold of the burden of what she is given. She has to hold it for the duration of the time with her client, but then she needs to pass it onto God, like a hot potato. God can then sustain her in her work and make it possible for her to begin again the next day. The psalm likewise implies that if we throw people's threats and deceits onto God, God can both sustain us in our inner being and protect us from the implementation of the threats and the success of the deceit. It offers more clues to standing tall.

Those statements near the end of the psalm are quite something, given the extreme nature of the statements near its beginning. The psalm offers us a form of prayer in which protest can move toward confidence, and it gives another illustration of how the Psalter provides ways to pray for people in all degrees of need (another indication of the importance of getting to know the Psalter so as to be able to help people use it in a way that corresponds to where they are). Suppose you are frantic; you howl and reel; your mind whirls; fear and trembling overwhelm you; horror envelops you (literally, horror is "clothing" you; it's totally covering you). You watch birds flitting at the threat of danger from a human being with a sling, and you wish you were in a position to do the same. Maybe your danger is no greater than that of which other psalms speak; maybe you are simply easier to scare. It doesn't matter. This psalm provides a way for you to pray.

The psalm has a distinctive way of describing God as "the one in whom there are no changes." The Old Testament often affirms that God can have a change of mind, but it doesn't thereby imply that God is fickle or unreliable. God has a change of mind in interaction with the way we relate to God and to life. It is usually a change that involves God's not bringing trouble that he has threatened to bring. But the psalm asserts that God's consistency can be relied on.

There are two further distinctive features about the situation the psalm protests. First, the violence and oppression characterize the entire city, and second, as they affect the psalmist, they come at the hand of people the psalmist ought to have been able to trust. One might see a link between these features. Community life depends on people being able to trust one another, but when people's words cannot be trusted, it not only affects interpersonal relationships but undermines the life of the city as a whole. Or one could reverse this dynamic: when unprincipled people undermine the city's life, individuals cease to be able to trust one another. The psalm directly confronts the friend who has become a deceiver: "It was you, someone I thought was my friend!" Perhaps the former friend is present only in the psalmist's imagination; perhaps the psalm imagines the community gathered in worship and envisages directly confronting this person.

When a woman is raped, it is often by someone she thought was a friend or by a relative, and this psalm has been seen as one particularly appropriate for a victim of rape or other sexual abuse, to whom it gives voice when voice is denied.

PSALM 56

I Whistle a Happy Tune

The leader's. On the Silent Pigeon of Far-off Places [perhaps a tune]. David's. An inscription. When the Philistines captured him in Gath.

1 Be gracious to me, God, because someone has hounded me;
      all day long a fighter oppresses me.
2 The people watching me have hounded me all day long,
      because those fighting me from a lofty position are many.
3 On the day I am afraid,
      I do trust in you.
4 In God whose word I praise,
      in God I have trusted.
      I am not afraid: what can flesh do to me?
5 All day long they pervert my words;
      all their plans against me are for evil.
6 They stir up strife, they lie in ambush, those people,
      they watch my steps, as if they are looking for my life.

174

7 For their wickedness carry them off,
       in anger put the peoples down, God.
8 You have recorded my lamenting, you yourself,
       you have put my tears into your flask;
       yes, they are in your record.
9 Then my enemies will turn back on the day I call;
       I know this, because God is mine.
10 In God whose word I praise,
       in Yahweh whose word I praise,
11 in God I have trusted, I am not afraid:
       what can a human being do to me?

12 Because my promises are binding upon me, God,
       I will render thank-offerings to you,
13 Because you have saved my life from death,
       yes, my foot from tripping up,
   so that I might walk about before God,
       in the light of life.

During the past few days people on the East Coast of the United States have been living through Hurricane Irene, which the media report to be among the top ten most costly disasters in U.S. history. As the Rock River rose on Sunday morning in Williamsville, Vermont, firefighters went from door to door telling people they had hours, maybe minutes, to get out of their houses, which were in danger of being flooded by the river's waters. Some houses were fine; some were partly washed away; at least one was totally engulfed. On a normal Sunday morning many of the eight hundred residents of the village would be preparing to go to church. What were they thinking this Sunday morning?

Psalm 56 interweaves talk of fear and of trust in a way that might look contradictory but reflects the way things are in such a crisis. When we speak of people involved in acts of bravery, we sometimes speak of them as fearless, but people who are fearless are probably stupid, and their action involves neither courage nor trust in God. Fear is a God-created human instinct that encourages us to avoid danger; fear led many sensible people to evacuate their homes as Hurricane Irene approached. It is when a person undertakes an act of bravery in circumstances of which they are properly fearful that they show courage. And

175

it is in such circumstances that the question of trust in God arises. In **David's story** there are two incidents set in Gath, in 1 Samuel 21–22 and 27–29, though neither refers to his being captured by the **Philistines**.

The psalm may speak paradoxically about these dynamics, but it speaks appropriately. Within a couple of lines it says, "On the day I am afraid I trust in you" and "I am not afraid: what can flesh do to me?" Maybe it means "When I am afraid, I start trusting, and I stop being afraid." But maybe it implies that we can be afraid and not afraid at the same time. We are afraid because that is the rational response to the danger that assails us. But we are not afraid in the sense of being overwhelmed or paralyzed by fear (there is a book called *Feel the Fear and Do It Anyway*). Either way, trust in God is the antidote to fear, because the reality of God is bigger than the reality of the object that causes us fear.

It is not merely trust that is the answer. In the musical *The King and I* Anna sings, "Whenever I feel afraid, I whistle a happy tune, so no one will suspect I'm afraid," and she finds that as well as fooling other people, she fools herself: "The happiness in the tune convinces me that I'm not afraid." So you can be as brave as you pretend you are while whistling a happy tune. That dynamic is not to be despised, but it is not the psalm's dynamic. Here, it is important that the trust has an object and the bravery thus has a basis.

The key to a trust with a foundation lies in the line "In God whose word I praise, in God I have trusted," which recurs later in the psalm. Typically, the "refrain" recurs with variation; Western convention likes identical refrains, but the Psalms like repetition with variation. When they talk about "God's word" they regularly refer either to God's commands or to God's promises (although Scripture is a repository of God's commands and promises, it does not refer to itself as God's word). When they refer to trust, the reference will to be God's promises. The psalm could thus be encouraging us to think of trust in God's general promises about looking after his people (promises we thus need to be familiar with so that we can recall them in a crisis), or of trust in a specific promise God has given us. Either way, these become the object of praise. Praise for God's promise or trust in God's promise makes it possible to overcome fear; either we stop being fearful or we stand tall even though we are fearful. We thus prove that trust is what gives substance to the things we hope for (as Hebrews 11 puts it). It brings home the reality of things (such as God's deliverance of us) even though these things are in the future rather than presently actual.

Trust also brings home the reality of things that are present and actual but invisible (as Hebrews 11 also declares) and give us a basis for rest. I can't *see* that God sits there in heaven with a record of my lament playing or with a flask containing my tears sitting before him, but I know this is the real situation. And as I know that God will fulfill his word to me, I commit myself to fulfilling my promise to God, that I will come back with a thank-offering when he has rescued me. I then can recommence my secure, ordinary life before God.

PSALM 57

Remembering Makes All the Difference

The leader's. Do not Destroy [perhaps a tune]. David's. An inscription. When he fled from Saul into the cave.

¹ Be gracious to me, God, be gracious to me,
     because my life relies on you.
   And in the shadow of your wings
     I shall rely until destruction passes.
² I will call to God, the One on High,
     to God who is going to bring it to an end for me.
³ May he send from the heavens and deliver me,
     as he reviles the one who persecutes me.   (*Rise*)
   May God send his commitment
     and his truthfulness ⁴to my life.
   I shall lie down among lions—
     devouring human beings,
   their teeth a pike and arrows,
     their tongue a sharp sword.
⁵ Rise above the heavens, God,
     with your honor over all the earth.

177

⁶ People fixed a net for my feet;
    my life was bowing down.
  They dug a pit in front of me;
    they fell right into it.   (*Rise*)
⁷ My mind is fixed,
    God, my mind is fixed.
  I will sing and make music;
⁸   wake up, my heart.
  Wake up harp and guitar;
    I shall wake up the dawn.
⁹ I will confess you among the peoples, my Lord,
    I will make music for you among the nations.
¹⁰ Because your commitment is as great
    as the heavens, your truthfulness as the skies.
¹¹ Rise above the heavens, God,
    with your honor over all the earth.

I've been thinking about memory. As a result of a comment by a student, I found myself reflecting on the fact that we don't think much about the link between memory and our life with God—our ethics and our spirituality—though there are lots of books about the psychology of memory. I did come across the statement that "Remember" is the most frequent command in the Bible, though my wife's response was that she thought "Don't be afraid" was the most frequent command in the Bible. Then we realized that these two might be connected. One key to avoiding fear is to remember.

Psalm 57 implies as much. It lives in the present, the future, and the past. The negative reality of the present is destruction, persecution, humans being devoured (maybe lions are devouring humans, or perhaps humans are "devouring" other humans like lions), and people who are capable of doing terrible things by their words (e.g., lying in such a way as to bring disaster or death to a person). The positive aspect of the present is the reality of God, of God's **commitment** and God's truthfulness, and thus the possibility of relying on God and of having a mind that is made up. Such an attitude merges into an attitude to the future. I'm intent on lying down among these lions; I'm not afraid of them. God will bring an end to this crisis. Indeed, I'm looking forward to the moment when I can praise God with such enthusiasm that I shall need to wake my heart, my instruments, and the dawn itself, which was looking forward to another moment or two of sleep but has to face my impatience.

One key to having such an attitude to the future is the recollection of the past expressed at the beginning of the psalm's second half. "I've been this way before," the psalmist notes. People attacked me and then fell by means of the trap they set. They tried to bring disaster upon me by telling lies, but the elders at the city gate saw through their deceit, and the attackers paid for it. Because they fixed a net and got caught in it, my mind can be fixed. Remembering the past is key to living in the present and having hope for the future. It doesn't make prayer unnecessary; it does make it possible. The psalm begins with a prayer for God's grace and closes each half with a prayer for God to rise above the heavens and for God's honor to be over all the earth. That repeated prayer links with the psalmist's commitment to confess God among the nations because his commitment and truthfulness are as great as the heavens. God is great on earth and in the heavens; God's action will provide a demonstration of that fact. Confessing that this is so enables people who say or sing the psalm to go through the same process of recollection and encouragement vicariously. When they've become familiar with the way the psalm works, they can profit from the experience it relates if they go through such an experience themselves.

The reference to **David's story** in the psalm's introduction suggests allusion to the incidents in 1 Samuel 21–22 and 24.

PSALM 58

A Challenge to the Principalities and Powers

The leader's. Do not Destroy [perhaps a tune]. David's. An instruction.

¹ You gods, do you really speak faithfully,
  exercise authority for human beings uprightly?
² No, with your mind you devise acts of wrongdoing in
    the country;
  you deal out violence with your hands.

³ Faithless people go astray from the womb;
  people who speak lies are wayward from birth.
⁴ Their poison is like snake poison,
  like a deaf viper that blocks its ear,
⁵ so that it does not listen to the voice of the charmers,
  the expert weaver of spells.

⁶ God, smash the teeth in their mouth;
  break the fangs of the lions, Yahweh.
⁷ They should vanish like waters when they go away;
  when one aims his arrows, so should they dry up.
⁸ Like a snail that vanishes as it goes,
  like a woman's stillbirth, they should not see the sun.
⁹ Before your pots sense the thorn,
  like a living person, so should fury whirl them off.
¹⁰ The faithful person will celebrate when he sees redress,
  when he bathes his feet in the blood of the faithless.
¹¹ Someone will say, "Yes, there is fruit for the faithful,
  yes, there are gods exercising authority in the country."

A New Year event called the Rose Parade passes our house, and this year the organizers were in a state of panic about possible demonstrations designed to disturb it and make waves on TV. Here as in European cities and a number of Middle Eastern countries, people who lack proper jobs and/or housing and/or food or who sympathize with others in that position perceive people in power, who have jobs, housing, and food, as responsible for others' lack and/or as colluding with the one percent of the population who are doing really, really well. Power and prosperity accompany one another, and so do powerlessness and neediness, whether the people in power were democratically elected or rule as unelected autocrats. Admittedly the protesters may exaggerate the extent to which the people in power are in a position to do something about their needs, and they may underestimate the forces that constrain rulers of goodwill who do care about their people. When the New Testament talks about these dynamics, it sometimes refers to powers and authorities (principalities and powers, in the King James Version) in a way that might suggest that there is something supernatural about them. This fits our sense that the dynamics of order and disorder in our world seem more than merely human.

Psalm 58 makes the same assumption, or at least manifests the same ambiguity. I have assumed it addresses "gods," though some translations take the word to denote powerful human rulers. Either way, the psalm recognizes that political affairs keep questions about power separate from questions about uprightness and faithfulness. Either it recognizes what the protesters see, that their rulers do not rule in a way that gives priority to integrity and concern for their people, or it recognizes such characteristics at a further level to reality. There are supernatural forces working through human rulers, supernatural forces that are cynical about uprightness and faithfulness.

People concerned for the state of their society, then, need to recognize that the forces working against human well-being are more than merely human. It makes prayer vital to working out a concern for society, prayer that recognizes these realities. The psalm begins by addressing the forces themselves, so it is at that point more an act of prophecy than a prayer, a little like Jesus' prophetic acts when he tells a bad spirit to get out from an individual. Yet it goes on to address God, who overhears the challenge to the forces and is challenged to do something about them.

The prayer is a prayer for desperate people, for powerless people threatened by powerful people who are as dangerous as deadly snakes that will not listen to anyone who tries to stop them from using their poisonous potential. They are as threatening as lions, whose potential victims need them simply to disappear. The victims do not aim to exact justice, but they know that God exacts justice, and they look forward to the relief that will come when God does so. Then the cosmic entities that rule the earth under God will operate in accordance with who God is, not in accordance with their own interests.

While the desperate victims have a right to feel such a longing, the privileged—who are the majority of those reading this psalm—also have a responsibility to share such a longing and to pray this way. And in case we ever become desperate, we had better be familiar with its dynamic so that we can call on it when we need it.

PSALM 59

How to Be Immoderate

The leader's. Do Not Destroy [perhaps a tune]. David's. An instruction. When Saul sent and watched his house in order to kill him.

¹ Save me from my enemies, my God;
    do set me on high above the people who rise up against me.
² Rescue me from those who do wickedness,
    deliver me from murderous people.
³ Because there: they lie in wait for my life;
    strong people stir up strife against me.
  Not for my rebellion, not for my offenses, Yahweh,
⁴   and not for my waywardness, do they run and take
      their stand.
  Stir yourself to meet me, and look,
⁵   yes, you, Yahweh God Armies, God of Israel.
  Wake up to attend to all the nations;
    do not show grace to any of the wicked betrayers.   (*Rise*)
⁶ They come back in the evening,
    they howl like a dog as they go around the city.
⁷ There, they bellow with their mouth,
    with swords on their lips,
    because who is listening?

⁸ But you, Yahweh, laugh at them,
    you are amused at all the nations.
⁹ My strength, I watch for you,
    because God is my tower.
¹⁰ The God committed to me will join me,
    God will enable me to look at the people who are
      watching for me.
¹¹ Do not slay them, in case my people are unmindful;
    by your might, make them wander.
  Put them down, Lord our shield,
¹²   for the offense of their mouth, the word on their lips.
  so that they are caught in their majesty
    and by the oath and the lie they proclaim.
¹³ Put an end to them in wrath,
    put an end to them so they are no more,

so that people may acknowledge that God rules in Jacob,
  to the ends of the earth.   (*Rise*)

¹⁴ They come back in the evening,
    they howl like a dog as they go around the city.
¹⁵ Those people—they wander about for food;
    if they are not full they stay the night.
¹⁶ But I—I will sing of your strength,
    I will resound in the morning at your commitment.
  Because you have become my tower,
    a haven on the way when I was in trouble.
¹⁷ My strength, to you I will make music,
    because God is my tower,
    the God committed to me.

People just down our street are incensed. There's an affordable
housing project whose residents are incensed because it has
become a base for drug dealers and a locus of conflicts between
local gangs. City officials and city police are incensed because
they have put a lot of energy into trying to clean up the area
and have failed. There's a small supermarket and liquor store
(with bullet-proof glass around the cashier's desk) where I have
occasionally shopped; its owners are incensed because they feel
they are being scapegoated by the police in connection with the
drug use, fighting, and marketing of pirate DVDs in its parking lot, not to say prostitution. Other people who live in the
area are incensed because the police have failed to get on top of
the situation. There is something scary about a situation where
there is so much anger being expressed.

    There is a lot of anger in Psalm 59. It's a psalm for some-
one who is incensed and who is the victim of people who are
incensed (like David in 1 Samuel 19). The latter are "murderous people"—literally, "people of bloods" or "people of bloodshed." They lie in wait in order to fulfill their intent, but they
also run to take their stand—the tension between these two
descriptions already signals that we need to work with the way
the psalm speaks in powerful metaphors. They are like dogs
that howl and bellow. They have swords in their mouths; they
fulfill their murderous intent by false accusations that have the

potential to mean death for the people they attack. They might do so directly, by causing them to be found guilty for some wrongdoing to which a death penalty attaches; words such as *rebellion*, *offense*, and *waywardness* might imply praying to other gods. Or they might do so indirectly by swindling them out of their farms and their livelihoods and thus ultimately out of their lives. Such is the effectiveness of "the oath and the lie they proclaim." The description of them as foreigners also makes one think of a situation like that of Nehemiah, who is under pressure from people from other communities in Jerusalem and who gets pretty incensed.

Maybe they aren't incensed. Maybe they are quite cool. Or maybe they are indeed incensed because they believe in the truth of their accusations. In turn, the accused person is incensed because the accusations are both false and dangerous, and they are dangerous likely not just for him but also for his family. And he doesn't merely want to be rescued from these accusers. He wants them to be put down. Merely rescuing him doesn't do justice to the enormity of their wrongdoing. Then there is that chilling plea that they should be put down but kept around—a quick death is too good for them and stops them from being an object lesson to other people. In other words, it's possible to see the death penalty as a deterrent, but it's also possible to see a deterrent value in not executing people. Yet without worrying about consistency, the psalmist goes on to urge God to put them to death. He knows that God gets incensed at the kind of wrongdoing to which he is being subjected, and he wants God to express his wrath.

How free the Psalms invite people to be in their prayers when they are helpless and in grave danger!

PSALM 60

How to Deal with Unfulfilled Promises

The leader's. On The Lily of Testimony [perhaps a tune]. An inscription. David's. For teaching. When he fought Aram Naharaim and Aram Zobah, and Joab came back and hit Edom in Salt Valley, twelve thousand men.

PSALM 60   How to Deal with Unfulfilled Promises

1 God, you have rejected us,
       broken us, been angry—turn to us!
2 You have shaken the country, torn it open—
       mend its splits, because it has collapsed.
3 You have made your people see hardship,
       you have made us drink wine that caused us to stagger.
4 You have given people who are in awe of you
       a banner to flee to because of the bow.   (*Rise*)
5 So that your beloved people may be rescued,
       deliver with your right hand, answer me.

6 God spoke by his holiness:
       "I will exult as I allocate Shechem
       and measure out the Vale of Sukkot.
7 Gilead will be mine, Manasseh will be mine,
       Ephraim will be my helmet, Judah my scepter,
8 Moab will be my washbasin,
       against Edom I will throw my shoe.
   Raise a shout against me, Philistia!—
9   who will bring me to the fortified city,
       who will lead me to Edom?"

10 So have you yourself not rejected us, God?—
       you do not go out with our armies, God.
11 Give us help against the adversary,
       given that human deliverance is futile.
12 Through God we will act with might;
       he is the one who will trample on our adversaries.

Yesterday in church the Gospel reading from Matthew 18 included Jesus' promise that where two people agree on anything, our heavenly Father will do it for them. Yet lots of people have the experience of God's not doing something that they and their friends have agreed to pray for. We could have read Jesus' promise that people who seek God's kingdom will have food and clothing and reflected that it doesn't always work out that way.

Psalm 60 starts from the experience of God's promises not being fulfilled in people's experience. The promise is contained in the middle of the psalm. It goes back to the time before Israel arrived in **Canaan**. As the Old Testament tells the story, the

185

people came there from **Egypt** with implausible promises from God ringing in their ears. The lines at the center of the psalm sum them up poetically (in other words, there is not a promise using these actual words in Exodus or Joshua, but the psalm sums up the implications of God's promises in vivid images). When you make a promise, you may swear by something or someone bigger than yourself, such as the temple, but Hebrews 6 notes that God has the problem that there is nothing or no one bigger to swear by, so God swears by himself, or in the case of Psalm 60:6 "by his holiness." In effect God says, "If I do not do what I say here, then I do not deserve to be regarded as the Holy One." They are very solemn promises.

God then speaks as the warrior who intends to take control of Canaan. Shechem is the biggest city in Canaan, the city where Joshua and the Israelite clans indeed celebrated **Yahweh's** taking control of the country (Jerusalem was an unimportant little town until David made it his capital). Sukkot is on the other side of the Jordan, in the area that is not strictly part of Canaan but in which some of the clans settled. So Shechem and Sukkot suggest the country as a whole, which Yahweh intends to allocate to the Israelite clans. Gilead and Manasseh also suggest the areas east of the Jordan—Gilead is the name of a major part of the area, while Manasseh was the major clan group represented there. **Ephraim** and **Judah** then stand for the areas west of the Jordan. They became the foremost clans in the north and the south, giving their names to the two countries into which Israel divided after Solomon's day. In the psalm's imagery, these two clans are the armory God will use in taking control of the country.

There's then a big contrast between God's lordship over these countries and peoples and God's way of describing Moab, Edom, and **Philistia**. God has nothing against those peoples. If they just mind their own business, they will get along fine. God has no designs on the territory of Moab and Edom. The Philistines raise a different question in that they are not long-standing occupants of land in this region like Moab and Edom but rather Johnny-come-lately Europeans from across the Mediterranean. They will be wise not to start competing with Yahweh for possession of Canaan. Don't even think about it,

God says to Moab, Edom, and Philistia, because if you do. . . .
They did, but by David's day they had all been put in their place.

The trouble is that things didn't stay that way, and at various points over succeeding centuries Moab, Edom, and Philistia were quite capable of threatening the possession of the country by Yahweh's people. David had to take on each of these peoples (see the introduction to the psalm and the stories in 2 Samuel 8 and 10); hence the protest in the first section of the psalm. After its complaint, the point about referring to God's promise is to challenge God about not keeping it. So the last section reiterates the protest but doesn't stop there. It goes on to challenge God to act in accordance with the promise. It acknowledges that the people are helpless without God. It also indicates how the mere fact that God has not fulfilled his promise today does not stop people from believing that God might fulfill it tomorrow.

PSALM 61

How to Pray with Your Leader

The leader's. On a stringed instrument. David's.

1 Listen to the noise I make, God,
      heed my plea.
2 From the end of the earth I call to you,
      while my heart flags.
   To a crag that rises high above me
      may you lead me,
3 because you have been a refuge for me,
      a strong tower in the face of the enemy.

4 I shall dwell in your tent forever,
      I shall rely on the shelter of your wings.   (*Rise*)
5 Because you, God, have listened to my promises;
      you gave their possession to the people who hold your
         name in awe.
6 You will add days to the days of the king;
      his years will be like one generation after another.
7 He will dwell forever before God;
      appoint commitment and truthfulness so that they may
         guard him.

187

8 Thus I shall make music to your name forever
   in fulfilling my promises day by day.

During a recent presidential election, a spoof organization
called the American Institute of Mentality published the find-
ings of a research project on the question "Why would anyone run for president?" Their conclusion was that presidential
candidates fit into two categories. Either you are a saint, a
person without concern for yourself who wants to be president in order to help the people of the United States, or, more
often, you are a pathological narcissist who has no concern
for other people, is worried about physical appearance, and
requires constant adulation (it was odd that the report didn't
talk about a lust for power). It's strange that we insist on elect-
ing someone who *wants* to be president. That would seem to
be a disqualification.

A strength of monarchy is that it is less likely to generate leaders who want to be leaders. It also makes one feel sympathetic
toward people who by accident of birth find themselves in the
demanding and dangerous position of king or queen, at least
in contexts where monarchs had actual power and where being
commander-in-chief required you to go out in battle. It's no accident that many of the prayer psalms are for the monarch to pray.
Psalm 61 signals that it is such a psalm by its reference to the
king. In other words, the king is referring to himself and to kings
like him; it is not that an ordinary citizen is suddenly making
reference to the king.

It is the king, then, who needs to pray the urgent prayer that
occupies the first part of the psalm. We can easily enough imagine him **crying** out in this importunate fashion as he goes out
to fulfill the military responsibility that comes to him because
he was born in the wrong family and not because he stood
out at military academy. The psalm invites him to be pushed
into relying on God and to believe that God has listened to his
prayers and the commitments he expressed in them and that
God has indeed granted his people possession of their country
(so the people they are fighting will not succeed in depriving
them of it). It invites him to live in hope in the midst of danger,
in the knowledge that he can live in God's tent: in other words,

even when he is far away from the temple, out there on the battlefield, he is not far away from God's presence. He can pray for God's **commitment** and truthfulness to protect him.

We can leave aside the fact that some psalms are written for the king to pray so that we can use them for ourselves as ordinary people, but we may then miss one of the reasons that they are important: they push us into praying for our leaders. We then say such psalms with our leaders in mind.

PSALM 62

Silence toward God

The leader's. On Jeduthun. A composition. David's.

1 Yes, toward God my spirit is silent;
     from him my deliverance comes.
2 Yes, he is my crag and my deliverance,
     my tower; I shall not fall down for long.
3 How long will you attack a person,
     commit murder, all of you?
   Like a bent wall, a fence that has been pulled down—
4   yes, they have planned to pull him down from his
         high position.
   They favor deception,
     they bless with their mouth, but inside they slight. (*Rise*)

5 Yes, be silent toward God my spirit;
     from him my hope comes.
6 Yes, he is my crag, my deliverance,
     my tower; I shall not fall down.
7 On God rests my deliverance and my honor;
     my strong rock, my refuge, is God in person.
8 Trust in him at all times, you people;
     pour out your heart before him;
     God is our refuge.   (*Rise*)

9 Yes, human beings are emptiness,
     people are a deception.
10 Going up on scales,
      those people are less than a breath, altogether.

PSALM 62   Silence toward God

Do not trust in extortion,
   do not put empty hopes in robbery;
   resources—when they bear fruit,
   do not give them your heart.
[12] God spoke of one thing, two things that I heard:
   that God has strength, and you, my Lord, have
      commitment,
   that you yourself recompense a person
   in accordance with his action.

A friend of mine has gone on a month's silent retreat (he is answering e-mails, which seems a bit like cheating, but then maybe so is reading or listening to talks). He needs to know what is to be the next stage in his life and his service of God, and he wants to listen to God in the quiet. Another friend of mine recently went on a two-week silent retreat to undertake the exercises devised by Ignatius of Loyola to help us in discerning where we are with God. I quite believe that people need such times of extended silence to get the noise of life out of their ears, but I am nevertheless struck by the fact that there is virtually no encouragement to silence in the Scriptures—hence our need to give a new meaning to a verse such as the one in Psalm 46: "Be still and know that I am God."

Psalm 62 clearly has an ideal of silence, but its logic is different from the one in Western spirituality and the one in Psalm 46. Here silence toward God is an expression of trust in God. That attitude also means that Psalm 62 contrasts sharply with other prayers in the Psalter. In many of these, people are consistently noisy and protesting in their praying, though prayers in which trust is a more dominant feature than protest are closer to Psalm 62 in their ethos. Once again the Psalter extends the range of ways in which it invites people to pray. Often it sets before us the possibility of being more outspoken and noisy in our prayer; here it sets before us the opposite possibility. There are no rules of prayer except to start where you are but also to be open to a new freedom that you have not yet embraced.

The psalm does not presuppose that trust may be easier because the situation is not too pressing. It presupposes the plight of a person under pressure from people who are quite

190

willing to commit murder. The reference to deception likely implies that as usual this situation need not mean that they will be physically attacking their victim; rather they will be taking legal or diplomatic action that could ultimately bring about his death. While pretending to be his supporters, behind the scenes they are dismissing him and plotting his downfall. At the moment he is in a high position (again we can think of someone like Nehemiah), but he is as vulnerable as a wall or a fence that someone has begun to demolish. It is as well that he has Someone higher than himself as a rock on which to take refuge.

So he is in a high position but looks vulnerable; his attackers look like impressive people but actually are vulnerable. He is not really vulnerable because he has that refuge to protect him. They are indeed vulnerable, for their appearance of strength is misleading. Humanly speaking, they may indeed have muscle, influence, and resources on their side, but because it is only human muscle, influence, and resources, it is deceptive and empty. They are using deception, but they are actually the victims of self-deception.

The psalm talks about being silent toward God, and it practices what it preaches for much of the way. Initially it addresses the attackers. The second time it speaks of silence, the psalmist is addressing himself. He is allowing for the internal argument that a relationship with God often involves. The declaration of trust implied by the opening statement about silence is part of what the psalm affirms; it also knows about the effort involved in maintaining that affirmation.

Most of the second part of the psalm, however, addresses other people in the community, people who might be on the psalmist's side or ought to be on his side but need their trust and courage emboldened. They need to be encouraged not to join the attackers in believing that the key to success in life is accumulating resources. Only in the last verse does the psalm break its silence toward God, though still with the intention that other people should hear. To God belong both strength and **commitment**—the capacity to support someone who looks vulnerable and the willingness to do so. That is not merely a theoretical matter. God is involved in the world. God sees that people get what they deserve. In case we are inclined

PSALM 63 The God Present in Jerusalem Is Also Present in the Wilderness

to wonder whether this is really so, Jesus reaffirms it twice, in Revelation 2 and 22.

PSALM 63

The God Present in Jerusalem Is Also Present in the Wilderness

A composition. David's. When he was in the wilderness of Judah.

¹ God, you are my God; I exert myself to reach you,
    my whole person thirsts for you.
  My body aches for you,
    in a dry, faint country without water.
² In the sanctuary I have surely seen you,
    beholding your power and your honor.
³ Because your commitment is better than life;
    my lips will glorify you.
⁴ I will surely worship you throughout my life;
    in your name I will lift up my hands.

⁵ As with richness and juiciness my life will be full,
    and with resounding lips my mouth will give praise.
⁶ When I am mindful of you on my bed,
    I talk of you during the [night] watches.
⁷ Because you have been my help,
    and in the shade of your wings I will resound.
⁸ My whole person has clung to you;
    your right hand has supported me.
⁹ But those people, who seek to destroy my life,
    will go into the depths of the earth.
¹⁰ The people who hurl someone onto the edges of the sword
    will be the prey of jackals.
¹¹ But the king—he will rejoice in God;
    everyone who swears by him will exult,
      because the mouth of people who speak falsehood is
        stopped up.

When I came to the United States, I didn't know that Jesus is a common Hispanic name, nor did I know that Jesus is pronounced "Heysus" in Spanish, which reduces the confusion.

192

The difference in pronunciation is key to our favorite song by a singer we went to hear last night: "Jesus Lives in Juarez, Mexico." Juarez is twin city to El Paso, Texas; they sit either side of the Rio Grande. There was once easy movement between the two cities, but not nowadays. It's not easy for Mexicans who want to get into the United States for work, and in a different way it's not so easy for U.S. citizens aware of Juarez's recent reputation as the murder capital of the world—not least because of its key place in connection with drug trafficking. In the song, the Mexican Jesus tells the storyteller of the tough side to being a migrant worker, driven on by both faith and desperation. Yet there's a gentleness, peace, and grace about this Jesus that conveys something to the storyteller with his own different neediness. Jesus lives in Juarez, Mexico.

The psalmists are like storytellers, sometimes directly relating their own experience, sometimes composing texts that will enable other people to say what they want to say (like the writers of modern hymns and prayers). The person for whom Psalm 63 was written was in a position a little like the Jesus of Juarez. Like a number of psalms, it pictures the people who will pray it as living in the murder capital of their own world. Often they too are trapped somewhere other than where they want to be. Like many people, Jesus of Juarez is caught in a double entrapment. The options are either the poverty and danger of life in Juarez or the isolation and hardship of menial work in "el Norte," "the north." Yet the storyteller senses that Jesus of Juarez lives in the company of Jesus of Nazareth, which stops his entrapment from being a prison. Something similar is the psalm's vision for the person who prays it: the hope that although he lives in a murder capital, he will live there in the company of **Yahweh**.

As is the case with Psalm 62, the eventual reference to the king in the last line suggests that it is a psalm for the king to pray (so another image for psalmists is that they are like presidential speech writers). The king prays simply for himself for the bulk of the psalm, but in the last line sets himself in the line of kings to whom God is committed. The introduction invites us to make a link with the stories about David in 1 Samuel 22–25 and/or 2 Samuel 15–17; in both contexts David is cut off from Jerusalem or Bethlehem and trapped in the wilderness. Like Jesus of Juarez, the person in the psalm is able to live with the frustration and the ache of present circumstances because the God present in Jerusalem is also the God present in the wilderness. Like other psalms, Psalm 63 lives with the apparent contradiction between God's being specially accessible in the temple where people can bring their offerings to God's palace as they bring their pleas to God, and God's not being confined to this palace but present and accessible throughout his country and outside it.

The preciousness of being in God's city and God's palace means that the king could not be satisfied with being cut off from there. For his encouragement, he looks both backward and forward. He looks back to times when he has seen God there and beheld God's power and honor. Maybe he is referring to what he has seen with the eyes of faith as the story of God's acts was recounted there. Maybe he is referring to seeing the covenant chest in the temple, over which Yahweh sat invisibly enthroned, or seeing other symbols of God's presence and activity (Israelites often made visible images of God despite the fact that these were forbidden, but presumably that is not what the psalm has in mind). He also looks back to times when God has proved to be **deliverer**, protector, and supporter. As well as looking back, he looks forward to being involved in such worship again, and he looks forward with the conviction that God's **commitment** does not change; he will experience deliverance, protection, and support once more.

PSALM 64

When the Knock Comes to Your Door

The leader's. A composition. David's.

1 Listen to my voice, God, as I lament,
   may you guard my life from the enemy's terror.
2 May you hide me from the group of evil people,
   from the crowd of wicked people,
3 people who have whetted their tongue like a sword,
   who have directed their cruel word like their arrow,

194

⁴ to shoot from hiding at the person of integrity—
   they shoot at him suddenly and without fear.
⁵ They take hold of an evil word for themselves,
   they proclaim it as they hide traps.
   They have said, "Who will see them?"
⁶   as they plot wickedness.
   "We have completed a plot that is well plotted;
   the inner thinking of a person and his mind are deep."

⁷ But God has shot them with an arrow;
   suddenly their blows have come.
⁸ They made it fall down on themselves with their tongue;
   all who look at them shake their head.
⁹ Everyone was in awe;
   they have proclaimed God's act,
   they have perceived his deed.
¹⁰ The faithful person rejoices in Yahweh
   and relies on him;
   all the upright of heart exult.

I was just checking the U.S. State Department's current travel warnings, a list of places where "long-term, protracted conditions that make a country dangerous or unstable lead the State Department to recommend that Americans avoid or consider the risk of travel to that country." The countries are listed according to the date when they were placed on the list, but all are within the last few months. Near the top is Chad, where my stepdaughter and her husband will be going in a few weeks on one of their recurrent trips in connection with working on behalf of Darfuri refugees. Farther down is Israel, where my wife and I are planning to go next year, and after that is the Philippines, where we are going in a few weeks. Even farther down is Mexico, where we were just now contemplating a few days' vacation.

In any of these countries there are millions of ordinary, honorable people. While our visits there may put us in slightly more danger than driving on the L.A. freeways, these millions of people live all their lives in danger of being caught in the crossfire between different gangs or factions or militias, or between criminals and police or army. They may find themselves under pressure to join one group or another, pressure that may include threats against their children as well as against their own lives; neutrality is not an option.

In such a context, you are pushed back to prayer, to trust in God, and to recollection. The psalm pushes us into praying for people who live all the time in those countries that the State Department suggests may be too dangerous to visit, and it helps us see how to pray. Suppose it is not the first time you have gone through this experience, or suppose it has happened to someone within your family or someone else in your neighborhood. Suppose you are able to recall the miraculous way that these other people escaped the fate with which they were threatened. You know about the way the assailants got caught by their own plots. You heard the story, and you know the way people crossed themselves or fell on their knees in astonishment and praise to God.

All you can do when you know the knock may come to your front door is to recall that event and to rejoice in God and turn to him and rely on him, and then beg him to listen and protect and hide you. You know that sometimes people who turn to God get murdered nevertheless. You also know that sometimes God does rescue and protect, and you plead that this may be such an occasion.

PSALM 65

The God of Atonement and the God of the Harvest

The leader's. A composition. David's. A song.

1 To you silence is praise,
      God in Zion.
   To you a promise is fulfilled,
2   the one who listens to a plea.
   All flesh come to you
3   with their wayward acts.
   Whereas our rebellions would have been too strong for me,
      you yourself expiate them.
4 The blessings of the person you choose and bring near,
      so that he dwells in your courtyards!

May we be full with the good things of your house,
    your holy palace.
5 Answer us with awe-inspiring deeds in faithfulness,
    God who delivers us!
Object of trust for all the ends of the earth
    and the distant sea,
6 who founded the mountains by his strength,
    who is girded with might,
7 who stills the roaring of the seas,
    the roaring of their waves,
    yes, the tumult of the peoples,
8 the people who live at the furthest points are in awe at
    your signs;
    you make the entry points of morning and evening
    resound.

9 You have attended to the earth and watered it;
    you greatly enrich it.
God's channel is full of water;
    you prepare their grain,
    because in this way you prepare it.
10 Saturating its furrows, smoothing its ridges,
    you soften it with rains,
    you bless its growth.
11 You have crowned the year with your good things;
    your cart tracks flow with richness.
12 The pastures of the wilderness flow,
    the hills gird on joy.
13 The meadows put on flocks,
    the vales wrap on wheat,
    they shout, and sing too.

A lively but respectable-looking student was telling me her life story. She had reacted against a Christian upbringing while she was at college and (among other things) had become involved with drugs and with a guy who was abusive. As is the nature of such relationships, it seemed impossible to get away with simply terminating the relationship or walking out on him, but as the situation got worse she was even more burdened by the fact that she was in this mess because she had turned her back on her Christian upbringing. It was as if God could have gotten her out of her mess, but she had wandered so far that there was no way to get back. She did, however, reach out desperately to God, and God did rescue her.

The line "whereas our rebellions would have been too strong for me, you yourself expiate them" made me think of her. In the Old Testament, it is Israel's job to expiate the stain that comes from contact with things that clash with God's nature. There are things of that kind that have nothing to do with morals; a classic example is contact with a dead body. Death is alien to God's nature, so you cannot rush into God's presence in the temple when you have just been involved in preparing a body for burial. There needs at least to be time for the stain to wear off, but in the case of some such stains, one deals with it by means of an offering. God declares that the blood of an animal has a mysterious power to absorb the stain, almost like detergent absorbing the stain on a garment.

Moral wrongdoing, acts of rebellion against God, also bring a stain. They mark us as people whose being is incompatible with God, but you can't remove the stain of moral wrongdoing by making an offering. All you can do is cast yourself on God's mercy. In effect that is what the psalm implies when it speaks of God's expiating our sin. Yes, our rebellions would have been too strong for us. As I write, there have been rebellions against the government in a number of Middle Eastern states, and in a series of cases they have succeeded in overthrowing the governments. What if the government succeeds in resisting, and the rebels eventually have to give in? Supposing they then throw themselves on the government's mercy? There is little chance of the government saying, "OK, go home, and behave yourselves in the future." In effect, that is what God does to rebels. Whereas expiating sin is what human beings have to do if they are to come into God's presence, here (as occasionally elsewhere in the Old Testament), God becomes the one who expiates. Usually people come to God with a sacrifice. This psalm pictures us coming to God with our wayward acts. It is a scandalous, senseless idea, one that expresses something of God's mercy.

No wonder the psalm starts by declaring that silence can be praise. It makes a counterintuitive observation about silence that is comparable with the observation that opens Psalm 62. The Psalms expect praise to be noisy, but this psalm assumes the complementary awareness that God's actions can be dumbfounding. The fact that God listens to the pleas of wayward rebels and expiates the stain left behind by their wrongdoing leaves you simply speechless.

The rest of the psalm only adds to the dumbfounding nature of God. God does not simply decline to take your life for your rebellion; God's act of expiation leaves you squeaky clean so that God can welcome you into his home to enjoy the fullness of it rather than sending you off home with your tail between your legs. That's what it like when God chooses you and brings you near.

Not that God is exclusive, as if having determined to choose particular people and not being interested in others. God's nature as creator of the whole world means all earth's ends can put their trust in him. He provides for the entire world (the entry points of morning and evening are the far-off points where dawn starts and where night starts—that is, the far east and the far west).

The vivid portrayal of the harvest makes one wonder whether this is a psalm that belongs at harvest time. If so, in some contexts the people who sang it would also be observing the Day of Atonement or Expiation, which comes in September or October. This collocation would link well with the psalm's collocation of expiation and harvest. **Yahweh** is the God of forgiveness and the God of the harvest.

PSALM 66

When You Feel Vulnerable and Threatened

The leader's. A song. A composition.

¹ Shout for Yahweh, all the earth,
² make music for the honor of his name!
Make his praise honorable,

³   say to God, "How awe-inspiring are your acts!
At the greatness of your strength
    your enemies wither before you.
⁴ All the earth bow down to you,
    they make music to you,
    make music to your name!"   (*Rise*)

⁵ Come and see the deeds of God,
    the one held in awe for his activity in relation to human
        beings.
⁶ He turned the sea into dry land
    so they could cross the river on foot.
There let us rejoice in him,
⁷   the one who rules forever by his might!
His eyes watch the nations; the rebels—
    they should not rise up against him.   (*Rise*)
⁸ Peoples, worship our God,
    let the sound of his praise be heard,
⁹ the one who places us in life,
    and does not give our foot to faltering.
¹⁰ Because you have tried us, God,
    refined us as silver is refined.
¹¹ You let us come into a net,
    put a constraint on our hips.
¹² You let people ride at our head,
    we have come into fire and water—
    but you have brought us out into flourishing.

¹³ I will come into your house with burnt offerings,
    I will fulfill my promises to you,
¹⁴ the ones my lips uttered,
    that my mouth spoke in my trouble.
¹⁵ As burnt offerings I will offer up fatlings to you,
    with the smell of rams;
    I will make ready bulls with goats.   (*Rise*)
¹⁶ Come listen and I will tell, all you who are in awe
        of God,
    what he has done for me.
¹⁷ To him with my mouth I called;
    he was extolled by my tongue.

¹⁸ If I could have seen wickedness in my heart,
   my Lord would not listen.
¹⁹ In fact God listened,
   paid heed to the sound of my plea.
²⁰ God be worshiped,
   the one who did not turn away my plea
   or his commitment from me!

Today is the anniversary of the September 11 attacks on the United States. For some reason it has reminded me of the first time I visited the United States, during the first Gulf War in 1990. The plane was half empty, which seemed odd, and I was able to stretch out across several seats in order to sleep. I eventually discovered that people from the United States were not flying across the Atlantic because the entire Eastern Hemisphere seemed a dangerous place; it felt safer to stay in the Western Hemisphere. That sense of being safe at home was an assumption shattered by the September 11 attacks. The United States joined the rest of the world in being aware that there is no such thing as security from attack; all countries are vulnerable.

Psalm 66 has some suggestive implications for such an awareness. Admittedly, it speaks of the experience of a much smaller people, but on September 11 the United States had its own experience of another people being able to constrain us, take control of us, and take us through fire (literally) and water. And as I write, we can't really say we have emerged from that experience into one of flourishing of the kind we previously knew.

The middle section of the psalm describes how little Israel went through that experience of control and constraint, fire (again literally) and water, but the psalm issues from a time when it has come out the other side and is flourishing. It can now look back and see that it was being tested or refined. Such a crisis shows whom you can really trust, where your security lies, and whom you recognize to be in control of the world. Crises reveal character.

The first section looks behind that moment of deliverance to an earlier moment, back at the beginning of Israel's story, when God brought the people through the Reed Sea and dealt with the army pursuing them. An implication is that when the nation goes through another experience of threat and vulnerability, it needs to think back to that original act of deliverance, which set the pattern it can expect to see repeated. The people's life as a whole has a place within God's wider purpose, and God can be expected to behave consistently in connection with the pursuit of this purpose.

Both these first two sections of the psalm invite the whole world to come and worship the God of Israel. There is no mechanism whereby the world hears the invitation (Israel sings the psalm, but could the world hear it?). In due course there were such mechanisms when the Old Testament was translated into Greek, but initially the invitation is figurative; in Old Testament times, only Israel hears it. For Israel, the figure's importance is to remind the people of the broader significance of its God and of its God's involvement with it. The pattern of God's acts with Israel is designed to be a pattern that benefits other peoples, not one that excludes them. A country such as the United States or Britain (readers in other parts of the world can substitute the name of their country here) is not God's chosen people, but if it is vulnerable and fearful, it can turn to God and claim the pattern for itself.

The psalm's last section then indicates that the same way of thinking applies to the individual (though the size of the offerings may indicate that the psalm directly has in mind a leader such as a king or governor). Here, instead of an exhortation to other peoples to praise God, the section begins with an act of commitment to praise God for an individual experience like those described in the first two sections that came to the people as a whole. The way God has acted in relation to the people provides individuals with a basis for looking to God to deliver them when they are in trouble. Then, whereas Israel's job is to give testimony to the entire world regarding God's acts of deliverance, the individual's job is to give testimony to the entire people. The warning recognition that you can't expect to **cry** out to God for help if you can look with equanimity at waywardness in your own heart applies to individuals as it does to nations.

202

PSALM 67

Bless Us, and Enable Other Peoples to See for Themselves

The leader's. With strings. A composition. A song.

¹ May God be gracious to us and bless us,
    may he shine his face with us,   (*Rise*)
² for the acknowledging of your way in the earth,
    your deliverance in all the nations.
³ May peoples confess you, God,
    may peoples confess you, all of them,
⁴   may countries rejoice and resound,
  because you exercise authority over peoples with uprightness,
    you guide nations in the earth.   (*Rise*)
⁵ May peoples confess you, God,
    may peoples confess you, all of them.
⁶ As earth has given its produce,
    may God, our God, bless us.
⁷ May God bless us,
    may all the ends of earth be in awe of him.

"God bless America." The fact that this weekend has been characterized by commemorations of September 11 has made that
plea once more resound. Now, the Old Testament is inclined to
make a distinction between blessing and deliverance. Deliverance is what God does when you are in a mess and you need
rescuing; it is an occasional thing. Blessing is what God does
on a more regular basis, making the land, its animals, and its
people fruitful. After September 11, then, I have been inclined
to think that the appropriate prayer is "God deliver America"
or "God protect America."

Psalm 67, however, sets me straight because it forms an
exception to that rule about distinguishing deliverance and
blessing, or it at least affirms that they are indeed related. Near
the end, its background becomes clear: the earth has produced
its harvest. A traditional society cannot assume that this year's
harvest implies fruitfulness next year. There are no such guar-
antees. The success of this year's harvest does not ensure that
there will be rain in the right quantities at the right moments
over the next nine months or safeguard against blight and

locust. Paradoxically, perhaps, this year's blessing makes people pray more earnestly for next year's blessing. It will be an expression of God's grace, and it will issue from God's face beaming out to them. It will be a fulfillment of the blessing that God commissioned priests to declare to the people (see Numbers 6).

That link between this year's harvest and next year's is thus not so surprising. More striking is the connection between both of these and the recognition of God by the world. On one hand, the prayer that God will bless Israel's harvest links with the blessing uttered by Aaron in Numbers 6. On the other, the prayer that this blessing of Israel will lead the ends of the earth to revere God links with the blessing given to Abraham, that all the world will pray to be blessed as Abraham is blessed (Genesis 12). The idea is that the world will see God's "way," the pattern of God's acting in relation to Israel.

The psalm goes on to make that further connection between deliverance and blessing. God's *blessing* will lead to the people's acknowledging God's *deliverance*. These two realities are related because they are aspects of the activities of the same God in relation to the same people. God's delivering Israel and God's blessing Israel are designed to lead to God's being recognized. It will not be mere grudging recognition of God's activity. Nations will rejoice because God does not guide and exercise **authority** over Israel only; the pattern of God's dealing with his people is again designed to be the pattern of God's dealing with the whole world. You can pray for God's blessing on the harvest with more conviction or persuasiveness when you point out that you are not seeking merely to benefit yourself but to benefit other people and to bring honor to God.

PSALM 68:1–18

Father of the Fatherless, Protector of the Widow

The leader's. David's. A composition. A song.

1   When God arises, his enemies scatter,
       his opponents flee before him.
2   You disperse them like smoke dispersing,
       like wax melting before fire.

The faithless perish before God,
3   and the faithful celebrate.
They exult before God,
    they rejoice with gladness.

4 Sing to God,
    make music to his name.
Lift up the one who rides on the clouds—
    his name is Yah—
    and exult before him.
5 Father for orphans, overseer for widows,
    is God in his holy dwelling.
6 God enables people who are alone to live at home,
    brings out prisoners in chains,
    yet rebels dwell in parched land.

7 God, when you went out before your people,
    when you marched through the wilderness,   (*Rise*)
8 earth shook, yes, heavens poured,
    before God, the one of Sinai,
    before God, the God of Israel.
9 You shed generous rain, God;
    your own possession, it was languishing—
    you yourself provided for it.
10 Your dwelling—they have lived in it;
    you provide for the lowly with your goodness, God.

11 The Lord gives the word;
    the women bringing the news are a great army.
12 Kings of armies flee, flee;
    the young girls of the house share the spoil,
13   though they stay among the sheepfolds,
    the wings of a dove covered in silver,
    its pinions in pure gold.
14 When Shadday scatters kings there,
    it snows on Salmon.
15 Mount Bashan is a mighty mountain,
    Mount Bashan is a many-peaked mountain.
16 Why do you keep watch, mountains, peaks,
    on the mountain that God desired as his dwelling?—
    yes, Yahweh will dwell there forever.

¹⁷ God's chariotry were myriads,
    thousands doubled;
    the Lord was among them at Sinai in holiness.
¹⁸ You went up on high,
    you took captives, to receive gifts among people,
    yes, rebels,
        to dwell as Yah God.

In conversations with people who have inquired about getting married or having children baptized in our church, I have been struck anew by how many are children without fathers or mothers without husbands. I think of a boy whose father is in prison and will stay there for a long time, of a girl whose father isn't sure he wants to marry her mother, of two children whose father disappeared and who are looked after by their mother and grandmother. Mothers without husbands may prefer it that way to being married to a man who is abusive or not sure whether he wants to be married, or they may not have thought about the issues. But there will be an aloneness and a vulnerability about their position.

For children without fathers and for mothers without husbands, it is a significant declaration that God is also their overseer. The Hebrew word for overseer or protector or leader is a variant on the one for someone who exercises authority. My wife brought up her daughter on her own for many years; her comment is that God was indeed both their father and overseer, protector, or leader. In the context of the psalm, the children need not be small children. The problem for orphans and widows is a vulnerability of a practical kind. The only viable way to live is in the context of a family because families control land and thus food, and families are headed by their senior male. So an adult orphan is as vulnerable as a widow. Both are dependent on the community's benevolence (which also means that when parents aren't married and/or don't take responsibility for their children, it affects other people) or on its willingness and capacity to employ someone as a day laborer or its unwillingness to employ women for anything but sex. In tough times, neither the benevolence nor the work may be forthcoming. So orphans and widows are pushed back into reliance on God.

This praise psalm reassures them that there is a basis for such reliance. It moves between talking about what God has done and what God consistently does, with the implication that the former is the basis for believing in the latter even when it doesn't look true. Much of the latter part of the verses printed above talks in the past tense, and it rather looks like an account of the way God brought the people to their land in the first place. It's pictured not as a journey that they took, with God guiding from heaven. It's a journey that God took, with Israel accompanying or following. God won great victories in taking control of the land and then in taking control of Jerusalem in particular as the earthly place to have as a dwelling. The psalm pictures an impressive mountain area like Bashan, puzzled and rather hostile over God's preference for that not-very-impressive hill. It pictures the activity of the men involved in the battle and that of the women who look after the flocks in the meantime, who lead the celebration of the victory, and who join in sharing out its spoils (some of the details of the picture are puzzling). God made the rain fall that was essential to the land's being one that could be lived in and lived off of.

But the psalm starts in the present, with a declaration that God's aggressive activity does not merely belong to the past. God still acts against the **faithless** and on behalf of vulnerable people like the orphan and widow. God is described by a series of **names**. There is that regular term for "God" and the familiar name **Yahweh.** In addition, there is the name Yah, which appears within an expression such as "hallelujah"—it may be an earlier version of the name of which Yahweh is then an elaboration. There is the name Shadday, also one with an archaic ring (it comes most often in Genesis and Job). It is similar to the verb "destroy," and that connotation would fit here. God's aggressive power is part of the good news for the fatherless and the widow because another need they have is protection, the kind exercised by a father or leader. One factor that could destroy families and in effect turn people into orphans and widows was the imprisonment of their father or husband, maybe on a spurious basis in connection with someone's scheme to take over the family's land. God is one who releases people from prison and restores their homes to them.

PSALM 68:19–35

Neither Militarist nor Pacifist

¹⁹ The Lord be worshiped, day by day;
   the God who is our deliverer supports us.   *(Rise)*
²⁰ God is for us a God of deliverance;
   to Yahweh God belong departures to death.
²¹ Yes, God smashes his enemies' head,
   the hairy crown of the one who walks about in his
      great guilt.
²² The Lord said, "I will bring them back from Bashan,
   I will bring them back from the depths of the sea,
²³ so that your feet may smash in blood;
   your dogs' tongue—its share may be from your
      enemies."

²⁴ People saw your journeyings, God,
   the journeyings of my God, my king, into the sanctuary.
²⁵ Singers came first, then string players,
   amidst girls playing tambourines.
²⁶ In the great congregation worship God,
   [worship] Yahweh, you from Israel's fountain.
²⁷ There was little Benjamin, ruling them,
   Judah's leaders, their noisy crowd,
leaders of Zebulun, leaders of Naphtali:
²⁸   your God commanded strength for you.
Be strong, God, you who acted for us
²⁹   from your palace; up to Jerusalem
   kings will bring you tribute.
³⁰ Blast the creature in the reeds,
   the assembly of strong ones among the bullocks,
      the peoples.
Trampling on those who love silver,
   you scattered peoples who delight in confrontations.
³¹ Envoys will come from Egypt,
   Sudan will run with its hands to God.

³² Kingdoms of the earth, sing to God,
   make music to the Lord,   *(Rise)*
³³ to the one who rides on the highest heavens of old—
   there, he gives out his voice, a strong voice.

³⁴ Give strength to God,
  whose majesty is over Israel,
  his strength in the skies.
³⁵ God, you are to be held in awe in your most holy place,
  the one who is the God of Israel.
He gives strength and great might to his people;
  God be worshiped.

On the anniversary of the September 11 attacks, I read an article by a Pakistani titled "Why Do They Hate Us So Much?" It picked up a question people in the United States asked after those attacks but reversed it in light of convictions it attributes to people in Pakistan and Afghanistan today who wonder why countries such as the United States and Britain so hate them. They infer the hatred from the policies we implement in those countries, policies that we believe are ultimately in their interests but that are hard for them to see that way. It was then only a day later that the Taliban launched a devastating attack on supposedly secure United States and NATO buildings in Kabul.

In the modern age it is tempting to suspect that hatred begets only hatred and that violence begets only violence. The psalm does not make that inference (nor do other parts of the Old Testament or the New Testament), though it does leave the hatred and violence to God (again, like most of both the Old and the New Testaments). So in this psalm there are people who are designated as God's opponents: faithless people, rebels, kings with armies, guilty people, strong people, and people who love silver and delight in military confrontation (that is, they are happy to make war in order to gain resources). Then there is God, who enables prisoners to be freed and homeless people to have somewhere to live by scattering these opponents, smashing their heads, blasting them, trampling on them, or making it impossible for them to escape by fleeing to the far east or the far depths (Bashan or the sea)—thus proving to be the one who can decide when people depart to death. And there are the faithful, who are not involved in the violence (they are too lowly and feeble to be able to do anything): instead, they celebrate and exult; they sing to God and exalt him. Their only army is an army of girls singing about what God has done and sharing in the gains of the battle that God has won. The psalm's picture recalls the story of when "Joshua fit the battle of Jericho," when Joshua did not actually fight but simply commissioned a worship band. The allusiveness of the psalm as a whole reflects how it tells the story of **Yahweh**'s conquering the land in a way that removes most of the details about places and people and thus suggests that those events do not merely belong to the past but point to a pattern that can be repeated in the worshipers' time.

Again the psalm parallels other parts of the Old Testament and the New Testament in indicating that the faithful are not expected to be unmoved by the downfall of God's opponents and their oppressors. They are expected to rejoice, and they are expected to worship. Indeed, they are expected to slosh about in the blood of the people God takes to their death and to rejoice in their dogs' being able to lap it up. Maybe the psalm assumes that Israel has an army of warriors as well as an army of singers, but if so, this army is practically invisible. The victory is not won by a superior military power but by a ragtag force that would get nowhere if God did not do a miracle. The psalm affirms that God is not one you can mess with and affirms that God's action in defeating his enemies and liberating the people they have oppressed is the kind of action that will lead to the nations' acknowledging God.

The battle the psalm describes thus ignores key principles of just war. The psalm turns inside out our attitude to war whether we are militarists or pacifists. It doesn't give any powerful people a basis for making war, but neither does it give the citizens of a powerful people a basis for saying that war is inherently wrong. Instead, it urges God to act against the powerful on behalf of the weak.

PSALM 69:1–18

Passion Means Persecution

The leader's. On Lilies [perhaps a tune]. David's.

1 Deliver me, God,
    because the waters have come up to my neck.

210

² I have sunk in a deep flood;
  there is no foothold.
I have come into torrents of water;
  a deluge has overwhelmed me.
³ I have become weary with calling,
  my throat has become dry.
My eyes have failed,
  waiting for my God.
⁴ They are more than the hairs on my head,
  the people who are against me without reason.
Many are the people who are trying to put an end to me,
  my enemies, with deception.
That which I have not stolen,
  then I must restore.
⁵ God, you yourself know my stupidity;
  my guilty deeds are not hidden from you.
⁶ The people who look to you must not be shamed because
    of me,
  Lord Yahweh Armies.
The people who seek help from you must not be humiliated
    because of me,
  God of Israel.
⁷ Because it is on account of you that I have borne reviling,
  that humiliation has covered my face.
⁸ I have become a stranger to my relatives,
  an alien to my mother's children.

⁹ Because my passion for your house has consumed me;
  the words of reviling with which people have reviled you
    have fallen on me.
¹⁰ I wept with fasting myself,
  and it became an object of reviling for me.
¹¹ I made sack my clothing,
  and I became a joke to them.
¹² The people who sit at the gate talk about me;
  [I became] the drinkers' song.

¹³ But I—my plea to you, Yahweh,
  is a time of favor.
God, in the greatness of your commitment answer me,
  in the truthfulness of your deliverance.

14 Rescue me from the mud;
 I must not sink.
May I be rescued from my enemies,
 from the torrents of water.
15 The deluge of water must not overwhelm me,
 the flood must not swallow me,
 the pit must not close its mouth over me.
16 Answer me, Yahweh, because your commitment is good;
 in accordance with the greatness of your compassion
  turn to me.
17 Do not hide your face from your servant,
 because I am in trouble—hurry, answer me.
18 Draw near to me, restore me;
 because of my enemies, redeem me.

I dreamed last night that I was being taken to court for preaching. The question "If you were prosecuted for being a Christian, would there be enough evidence to convict you?" is a cliché, but it's a clever and thought-provoking one. When my wife recently drew my attention to a sensible article about the Christian faith in a British journal, it struck me that it would be harder to find such an article in a journal in the United States because of the intensity of the culture wars (the faults are on both sides). Both atheists/agnostics and Christians (or Jews or Muslims) can feel that they are being persecuted or treated with prejudice.

My dream may have been triggered by the fact that I had begun to think about Psalm 69 and about the idea that passion for God's house had consumed someone. The phrase has a different meaning in the psalm from the one it has in John 2 where the disciples see it embodied in Jesus. When Jesus bullwhips people who are selling animals for worshipers to sacrifice in the temple, talk of being consumed by a passion for God's house indicates the strength of his own feelings. In the psalm, passion for God's house has brought trouble or persecution to the person who feels that passion, though this idea comes to apply to Jesus, too (Jesus quotes the psalm in John 15).

One could imagine the psalm being prayed by someone such as Jeremiah or Nehemiah. Through much of Old Testament times, Israelites took a free attitude to the worship they could offer in the temple, following their own hearts in this respect;

for instance, they found it helpful to have an image of God to aid their worship (such as the gold bullock they made at Sinai). Prophets such as Jeremiah took a much more restricted and restricting view of the worship that people could legitimately offer. Campaigning for their more restrictive view naturally met opposition, and the opposition was not merely a matter of debate and argument. The temple was commonly under the control of authorities who were in a position to ban worshipers who opposed the restrictive line of such campaigners, and they could use their power to exclude people from worship, harass them, or worse.

One could draw a comparison with what Protestants and Catholics did to one another in the sixteenth and seventeenth centuries. In the Western church we sometimes talk about worship wars, conflict between people who like different styles of worship. In much of Israelite and Christian history, worship wars had much more serious connotations. We will be glad that we do not live in such centuries. Yet the difference also draws attention to the trivial basis for our conflicts. In those centuries, people were energized over the question of what kind of worship is appropriate to who God is. What kind of worship honors God? Our question is what kind of worship suits us.

So the psalm is for someone who has sought to be faithful to God in connection with that kind of question and who is consequently threatened by lynching or execution. People's disregard of God spills over into a disregard of those who speak up for God, whose grief at what is done in God's name makes them a joke. The reference to deception and false charges presumably indicates that these are ways of providing a more legal-looking basis for taking action against the object of people's wrath, while the reference to stupidity and guilt indicates that the psalm is making no claim to sinlessness, only to an attitude of faithfulness to **Yahweh** and a willingness to stand up for such faithfulness. One might have thought that God would honor this faithfulness; there are many declarations in the Psalms and elsewhere that God would do so. But at the moment there is no sign of things working out that way. And God's holding back is likely to mean not only the discrediting (or worse) of this individual but also the shaming of people who took the same stance.

213

PSALM 69:19–35

Trusting God with Your Anger

19 You yourself know my reviling,
  my shame, my humiliation.
All the people watching for me are before you;
20   reviling has broken my spirit, and I am ailing.
I have looked for someone to sympathize but there is
    no one,
  for comforters but I have not found any.
21 People have put poison in my food,
  for my thirst they have given me vinegar to drink.
22 May their table become a trap before them,
  a snare for their allies.
23 May their eyes go dark so they cannot see,
  may their loins shudder continually.
24 Pour out your wrath on them;
  may your angry burning overtake them.
25 May their encampment become desolate,
  may there be no one living in their tents.
26 Because you—the person you hit, they have persecuted,
  and the suffering of the people you struck, they have
    heralded.
27 Put waywardness onto their waywardness;
  may they not come to your faithfulness.
28 May they be erased from the scroll of living people;
  may they not be written down with the faithful.
29 When I am lowly and suffering,
  may your deliverance keep me safe, God.

30 I will praise God's name with a song,
  I will magnify it with thanksgiving.
31 It will please Yahweh more than an ox,
  a bull with horns and divided hoofs.
32 Lowly people have seen and celebrated;
  you who seek help from God—may your spirit revive.
33 Because Yahweh is going to listen to the needy
  and not despise his captives.
34 May heavens and earth praise him,
  seas and everything that moves in them.
35 Because God will deliver Zion
  and build Judah's cities.

People will live there and possess it,
36   the offspring of his servants will hold it,
people who give themselves to his name will dwell in it.

In a day or two I am to lecture on the Psalms and our spirituality, and I shall talk about the way psalms are designed to feed and shape our praise, prayer, and thanksgiving. Last night as I was finalizing the lecture, I realized I had made a mistake; I had included nothing about the violent and angry side to the psalms. I recalled a previous occasion when I gave such a lecture and said nothing about that feature of them, and this anger was the first issue someone raised in the question time afterward. What struck me on that occasion was that this person was an unhappy-looking, heavy pastor who (I immediately thought this but didn't say it) looked like someone who had turned his anger in on himself. I once heard another professor comment on how we also express our anger in other outward ways, such as in sports or in the way we drive.

I don't know whether the author of Psalm 69 was aware that denying your anger is not much better than expressing it toward other people (whether or not they are the people who provoke it), or whether denying your anger and turning it in on yourself is a bourgeois Western practice for which the Psalms do not need to make allowance. Whether or not that is so, I imagine that it is part of the Psalms' significance for Western people who are involved in such denial, and I can imagine that the fact of people denying their anger was one reason God was happy to have Psalm 69 in his book. Likewise I don't know whether it was part of the author's thinking that expressing to God your anger about your oppressors and your desire for them to be put down was a preferable alternative to taking action against them yourself or to turning it in on yourself. Whatever is the answer, it fits within the attitude that appears within the Psalms and elsewhere in the Old Testament that Israel's vocation is to trust God to take action on its behalf when it is in trouble (occasions such as God's commissioning Israel to fight the **Canaanites** are the exception rather than the rule). So I can imagine that this is another reason that God was happy to have Psalm 69 in his book.

215

There is a related point about the significance of the psalm that the author likely did have in mind. It closes its prayer for the oppressors' punishment with a renewed prayer for **deliverance**. The association of these two is a common feature of the Psalms. They are the two sides of a coin. The reason for urging God to put down the oppressors is that it will take them off their victim's back. The victim knows that God is inclined to be merciful and needs God not to be merciful to these people. (Of course if they give up their waywardness it would be a different story.)

While in one way the prayer's forcefulness is the psalm's most striking feature, it should not overshadow the remarkable nature of the closing verses. As happens in other psalms, the agonizing of the suffering and the urgency of the plea give way to declarations of confidence and anticipation of praise. Nothing has changed in the victim's experience, yet pouring oneself out to God and knowing that God has listened means that everything has changed. The two closing lines set this person's needs and deliverance in the broader context of God's involvement with Israel as a whole, which makes particular sense if the person praying the psalm is a representative figure such as a king or governor. If it is an ordinary individual, the closing lines imply a further reason for hope and a further basis of appeal to **Yahweh**, and they also constitute a reminder that the individual's deliverance will be designed to serve God's wider purpose with Israel.

You could say that Psalm 69 is one of the New Testament's favorites; John quotes the first half twice, and the second half is also quoted twice, in Acts 2 and Romans 11. Evidently the New Testament was also glad that God was happy to have it in his book.

PSALM 70

On Telling God What to Do

The leader's. David's. For commemoration.

[1] God, to save me, Yahweh,
      to my help, hurry!

² They should be shamed and reviled,
    the people who seek my life.
  They should turn around and be disgraced,
    the people who want misfortune for me.
³ They should turn back because of their shameful
        deceptiveness,
    the people who say, "Huh! Huh!"
⁴ They should be glad and rejoice in you,
    all the people who seek help from you.
  They should say continually, "God be great,"
    the people dedicated to your deliverance.
⁵ But I am lowly and needy—
    God, hurry to me.
  You are my help and my rescuer,
    Yahweh, do not delay!

As usual, this Sunday morning in church we prayed that the
church might be one, that it might faithfully preach the gospel
to the ends of the earth, that there might be justice and peace
on the earth, and that the world might be freed from poverty
and famine. And as usual we prayed for some specific needs
of our congregation and community: for a lady who would
be there every week but has been in pain with her back and
legs, we prayed that she would find relief; and for a family who
were just marking the six months' anniversary of the death of
their father and husband, we prayed that they might find comfort. These prayers are very unlike the prayers in the Psalms,
which spend more time than we do in telling God how awful
things are and less time than we do in making suggestions to
God concerning what to do about it. In general I assume their
example suggests insights about how we might rework our way
of praying.

   Psalm 70 is thus unusual in the way it concentrates on making pleas; in this respect it is more like our prayers. The only
direct description of circumstances comes in the phrase "I
am lowly and needy," though the portrayal of the people who
are causing trouble fills out the picture. Maybe there's a link
between the fact that the psalm is more like our prayers in this
respect and the fact that for centuries the opening line of the

psalm was part of the opening prayer in the daily worship of the Western church: "O God make speed to save us; O Lord, make haste to help us" (the version that appears in the English *Book of Common Prayer*).

Another unusual feature of Psalm 70 is the fact that this whole psalm also forms the last part of Psalm 40, in a slightly variant form. It could evidently function on its own but also function in that other way. It's not the only instance of psalm material being used twice in the Psalter—Psalms 14 and 53 are also examples. Maybe that use of the psalm's opening in Christian worship follows its use in Jewish worship; possibly the verses that constitute Psalm 70 had already been separated from Psalm 40 for use in worship on their own.

What Psalm 70 makes clear in its own right is that when you are in a state of panic and all you want to do is urge God to take action, you can do so. The jerkiness of the psalm's opening vividly indicates the urgency of the need. It's sometimes said that God's answer to prayer may be "Yes," "No," or "Wait," and that we must be submissive to God's timing. While in the end we have no alternative to submitting to God's timing, the beginning and end of the psalm indicate that it is fine to tell God to hurry and not to delay, and indeed for this request to be the framing note of a prayer. When you are in a desperate situation, when people are trying to kill you, you don't have to hesitate to tell God that you need action and you need it now. When the going gets tough, the tough get praying, and this is a way they can pray.

God, the psalm presupposes, ought to recognize that the psalmist's situation is one in which people can be divided into two groups. There are people who want the worst for the psalmist, and there are people who have no alternative but to look to God for **deliverance.** God ought to give the first group reason to be ashamed and give the second group reason to celebrate.

PSALM 71

From Birth through Youth to Middle Age and Old Age

¹ I have relied on you, Yahweh;
   I must not be shamed, ever.

218

² In your faithfulness save me, rescue me,
   incline your ear to me, deliver me.
³ Be for me a crag,
   a shelter to which I can always come,
   which you have commanded as my deliverance,
   because you are my cliff, my fastness.
⁴ My God, rescue me from the hand of the faithless,
   from the grip of the wrongdoer and robber.
⁵ Because you have been my hope, my Lord Yahweh,
   the one whom I have trusted from my youth.
⁶ On you I have depended from birth,
   from my mother's womb.
   You have been my support;
   my praise has always been of you.
⁷ I have been a sign for many people,
   as you have been my strong refuge.
⁸ My mouth is full of your praise,
   of your glory all day long.

⁹ Don't cast me off for my old age,
   when my strength fails, don't abandon me.
¹⁰ Because my enemies have said of me,
   and the people who watch for my life have planned
      together:
¹¹ "Since God has abandoned him,
   chase him, seize him,
   because there is no one to save him."

¹² God, do not be far from me;
   my God, hurry to my help.
¹³ They should be shamed and waste away,
   the people who attack my life.
   They should dress themselves in reviling and disgrace,
   the people who seek misfortune for me.
¹⁴ But I—I will hope always,
   and add to all your praise.
¹⁵ My mouth—it will proclaim your faithfulness,
   your deliverance all day long.
   Because I do not know how to write,
¹⁶   I will come with the mighty acts of my Lord Yahweh,
   I will commemorate your faithfulness, yours alone.

¹⁷ God, you have taught me from my youth,
   and until now I proclaim your wonders.
¹⁸ So even until my old age and gray hair,
   God, do not abandon me,
   until I proclaim your strength to [this] generation,
   your might to everyone who is to come,
¹⁹   and your faithfulness, God, on high.
   You who have done great things, God—
   who is like you?
²⁰ You who have let me see troubles, many and hard,
   will revive me again
   and from the depths of the earth
   bring me up again.
²¹ You will grant me much greatness
   and turn to comfort me.
²² And I myself will confess you with the harp
   for your truthfulness, God,
   I will make music for you with the guitar,
   holy one of Israel.
²³ My lips will resound when I make music for you,
   and my whole being, which you have redeemed.
²⁴ Yes, my tongue will talk of your faithfulness all day long,
   because they have been shamed and reviled,
   the people who sought my misfortune.

Several people in our church are in their eighties or nineties, and yesterday several things made me think about the life-long nature of their following Christ. The Gospel passage was Jesus' story about laborers getting the same pay whether they had worked for the whole day or had worked just an hour. One of these senior members was already at church when I arrived for the first service, feeling as if he was a bit drunk because his blood pressure was low. Another wasn't there at all because she is suffering with her back and legs, so we took communion to her after the second service. A third was a bit put out because she had missed last week and I had not brought her communion during the week. They are three people who remind me of the men in Jesus' parable who have been laboring all day long. These three continue to be confident that God will be faithful to them to the end, but they have to deal with the frailty of old age.

In Psalm 71, the expressions "all day long" and "forever" and "always" recur, along with phrases that suggest the psalm's use by someone with youth to look back on and with fears about what old age could bring. As in other psalms, the pressure arises not from physical frailty but from other people's threats, but it raises similar questions to those raised by physical frailty. The psalm looks back to the way God has been the object of hope and trust since one's youth as the friends to whom I referred are able to do; one of them sometimes talks about the way God was his trust when he was drafted into the navy and served in submarines not long after Pearl Harbor. Since youth God has been the object of the praise to which the psalm refers; God has been the psalmist's teacher; and God's faithfulness has been a sign to other people that they can take the risk of trusting in God. Maybe it's possible to be more afraid of the future when you are getting older than you are when you are young and full of confidence. But the psalm seems to presuppose that there can be good reason for greater fear as years pass. Maybe there are people who want to pull others down when they are now (say) responsible for the affairs of a family and in control of its estate. Maybe you don't have the strength to stand firm or fight back that you had when you were younger. Maybe you have had reverses that enable people to infer that God has already abandoned you, and it makes you worry lest they be right. So the psalm starts with a "forever": "Don't ever abandon me."

Three times, then, the psalm talks in terms of "always" (no psalm makes more use of this word). In the past, "my praise has always been of you." In the present, I need you to be "a shelter to which I can always come." In the future, "I will hope always." Giving praise to **Yahweh** "always" indicates not having worshiped other deities or looked to other resources; it means one can now look to Yahweh for shelter and keep hope for the future. Three times, too, the psalm speaks of what is true "all day long." Looking back to the past, "my mouth is full of your praise, of your glory all day long." In the future in light of the way God will continue to protect and rescue, "my mouth will proclaim your faithfulness, your **deliverance** all day long" and "my tongue will talk of your **faithfulness** all day long" (no passage of the Old Testament talks more about God's faithfulness).

221

One can imagine people rolling their eyes at someone who wants to praise God all day long. No doubt there is some hyperbole here, but the psalmist isn't worried about people rolling their eyes.

PSALM 72:1–17

How to Pray for the Government

Solomon's.

1 God, give the king your decisions,
    the royal son your faithfulness.
2 May he govern your people with faithfulness,
    your lowly ones with your decision.
3 May the mountains bear well-being for the people,
    and the hills, in faithfulness.
4 May he decide for the lowly among the people,
    deliver the needy, crush the extortioner.
5 May they be in awe of you while the sun shines
    and before the moon, generation after generation.
6 May he come down like rain on mowed grass,
    like downpours, an overflowing on the earth.
7 May the faithful person flourish in his days,
    and [may there be] abundance of well-being, until the
        moon is no more.
8 May he dictate from sea to sea,
    from the river to the ends of the earth.
9 May wildcats kneel before him,
    may his enemies lick the dust.
10 May the kings of Tarshish and foreign coasts
    bring an offering.
 May the kings of Sheba and Seba
    present a gift.
11 May all kings bow down to him,
    all nations serve him.
12 Because he saves the needy person crying for deliverance
    and the lowly person who has no helper.
13 May he have pity on the poor and needy,
    so that he saves the lives of needy people.

¹⁴ From viciousness and from violence
    may he restore their life.
¹⁵ May he live and be given
    gold from Sheba.
May pleas be said for him always;
    all day long may people pray for blessing for him.
¹⁶ May there be an abundance of grain in the country,
    on the tops of the mountains.
May his fruit shake like Lebanon,
    may people thrive from the city like the grass in the
        country.
¹⁷ May his name be forever;
    before the sun may his name have offspring,
so that people may pray to be blessed through him;
    may all nations count him fortunate.

The phrase "It's the economy, stupid," played a key role in Bill Clinton's 1992 presidential campaign. Most people are not really interested in foreign policy or other such important issues but in whether they are feeling financially prosperous, or at least secure. This is the basis on which they evaluate their government. The phrase also encapsulates much of the dynamic of the popular uprisings in Arab states (and demonstrations in Europe) in 2011. Ordinary people want to put down their dictators not so much for the sake of introducing a democratic system but because they want jobs. And in the United States that same year, forty-six million people were living below the official poverty line.

Psalm 72 believes that "it's the economy, stupid," but it does so on a less cynical basis than might be implied by that phrase. It recognizes that it is indeed the responsibility of governments, whether monarchies, dictatorships, or democracies, to see that a quarter of their citizenry are not living below the poverty line. And while the social system will need safety nets for some of them, in urbanized societies that means more people having jobs than is currently the case in many countries. The psalm is covertly a political statement along those lines to the government. It is appealing to imagine the king showing up at worship in the temple and hearing this psalm sung by the temple choirs, and particularly to think of the psalm as written for Solomon (this is the only psalm that refers to him). The Old Testament story portrays him as the most economically successful of the kings but also as someone who puts many people to tough conscript labor, so it is nice to imagine him feeling embarrassed at the way he betrays the Old Testament's vision for kingship.

There are several interwoven elements in the vision laid before the king (the king and the royal son are two ways of describing the same person). First, it involves the exercise of **authority** or making **decisions** with **faithfulness** in relation to God and to the people. Governance is thus concerned with the good of the people as a whole. If this governance has a concern for particular groups, it is not for the people who are wealthy and powerful, who include the members of the government themselves (and who can look after themselves), but for the lowly, the needy, and the poor and for their protection from the vicious, the violent, and the extortioner who find ways of robbing them of their crops and animals. In practice, it is often people who have power who are thus able to extort, so that there is a further bite to the psalm's words about what people in power are supposed to do. Sandwiched in the midst of this emphasis is the reference to the land's producing **well-being** as an expression of God's faithfulness, with the implication that the government's giving priority to faithfulness and a concern for the lowly will issue in God's ensuring that prosperity follows for the country as a whole. The faithful will flourish. Both in his governing with faithfulness and in his opening up the possibility of this prosperity, the king will be like rain on the land. Also alongside this emphasis is the note about people revering God through the ages; the exercise of authority in faithfulness will be an expression of obedience to God.

Foreign policy, the vision implies, will then look after itself in the same way as the flourishing of the crops. A king who works with these priorities will experience the fulfillment of promises such as those in Psalm 2 about the way the God of Israel will rule the world by means of the king of Israel. Thus the promise to Abraham will be fulfilled; foreign peoples will see the way God blesses him and will pray for similar blessings.

224

Indirectly, then, the psalm lays before the government God's vision for how it should work and makes promises about where implementing the right priorities will lead. But directly the psalm is a prayer, and it comes in a book of prayers and praises. What it directly does is set an agenda for our praying for the government, an activity that may be even more important than advocating for the poor, the needy, and the lowly.

PSALM 72:18–20

Another Interim Closing Act of Praise

18 Yahweh God, the God of Israel be worshiped,
        the one who alone does wonders.
19 His honorable name be worshiped forever;
        may the entire earth be filled with his honor. Amen, amen.

20 The pleas of David, son of Jesse, end.

As the last verse of Psalm 41 is actually the close of Book One of the Psalter, the closing verses of Psalm 72 are not part of this psalm but are an act of worship at the end of Book Two of the Psalter, a little like the "Glory be to the Father . . ." that some churches use after saying an individual psalm. They are a kind of "Amen" to the whole of Book Two, particularly appropriate if we didn't like any of them.

The note about David's pleas being ended presumably refers to a specific collection of David psalms (nearly all of Psalms 51–72 are David psalms); in the Psalter as a whole, there are more David psalms to come (Psalms 86; 138–45).

GLOSSARY

aide

A supernatural agent through whom God may appear and work in the world. Standard English translations refer to them as "angels," but this term suggests ethereal winged figures wearing diaphanous white dresses. Aides are humanlike figures; hence it possible to give them hospitality without realizing who they are (Hebrews 13). They have no wings, hence their need of a stairway or ramp between heaven and earth (Genesis 28). They appear in order to act or speak on God's behalf and represent God so completely that they can speak as if they *are* God (Genesis 22). They are involved in dynamic, forceful action in the world (Psalms 34 and 35). They bring the reality of God's presence, action, and voice without bringing such a real presence that it would electrocute mere mortals or shatter their hearing.

altar

A structure for offering a sacrifice (the word comes from the word for sacrifice), made of earth or stone. An altar might be relatively small, like a table, and the person making the offering would stand in front of it. Or it might be higher and larger, like a platform, and the person making the offering would climb onto it.

Assyria

Assyria was the first great Middle Eastern superpower, which spread its empire westward into Syria-Palestine in the eighth century. It first made **Ephraim** part of its empire, then when Ephraim kept trying to assert independence, Assyria invaded Ephraim, destroyed its capital at Samaria, transported its people, and settled people from other parts of its empire in their place. Assyria also invaded **Judah** and devastated much of the country, but it did not take Jerusalem. Prophets such as Amos and Isaiah describe how **Yahweh** was thus using Assyria as a means of disciplining Israel.

authority

People such as Eli, Samuel, Samuel's sons, and the kings "exercise authority" over Israel and for Israel. The Hebrew word for someone who exercises such authority, *shopet*, is traditionally translated *judge*, but such leadership is wider than this term implies. In the book called Judges, these leaders are people who have no official position like the later kings, but who arise and exercise initiative in a way that brings the people **deliverance** from the trouble they get into. Likewise it is a king's job to exercise authority in accordance with **faithfulness** to God and people. Exercising authority means making decisions and acting decisively on behalf of people in need and of people wronged by others. Thus speaking of God as judge implies good news (unless you are a major wrongdoer).

Babylon

A minor power in the context of Israel's early history, in the time of Jeremiah Babylon took over the position of superpower from **Assyria** and kept it for nearly a century until conquered by **Persia**. Prophets such as Jeremiah describe how **Yahweh** was using Babylon as a means of disciplining **Judah**. Its creation stories, law codes, and more philosophical writings help us understand aspects of the Old Testament's equivalent writings, while its astrological religion also forms background to aspects of polemic in the prophets.

Canaan, Canaanites

As the biblical terms for the land of Israel as a whole and for its indigenous peoples, "Canaanites" is not so much the name for a particular ethnic group as a shorthand term for all the peoples native to the land.

commitment

The word corresponds to the Hebrew word *hesed*, which translations render by means of expressions such as steadfast love or loving-kindness or goodness. The Old Testament uses this word to refer to an extraordinary act of generosity, allegiance, or grace whereby someone pledges himself or herself to someone else when there is no prior relationship between them and therefore no reason why the person should do so. Thus in Joshua 2, Rahab appropriately speaks of her protection of the Israelite spies as an act of commitment. It can also refer to a similar extraordinary act that takes place when there is a relationship between people but one party has let the other party down and therefore has no right to expect any faithfulness from the other. If the party that has been let down continues being faithful, she or he is showing this kind of commitment. In their response to Rahab, the Israelite spies declare that they will relate to her in this way. In the New Testament, the special word for love, *agapē,* is equivalent to *hesed.*

composition
This is the Hebrew word commonly translated "psalm." It comes from the Hebrew word for music, so it seems to refer to a musical composition.

covenant
The Hebrew word *berit* covers covenants, treaties, and contracts, but these are all ways in which people make a formal commitment about something, and I have used the word *covenant* for all three. Where you have a legal system to which people can appeal, contracts assume a system for resolving disputes and administering justice that can be used if people do not keep their commitments. In contrast, a covenantal relationship does not presuppose an enforceable legal framework of that kind, but a covenant does involve some formal procedure that confirms the seriousness of the solemn commitment one party makes to another. Thus the Old Testament often speaks of *sealing* a covenant, literally of *cutting* it (the background lies in the kind of formal procedure described in Genesis 15 and Jeremiah 34:18–20, though such an actual procedure would hardly be required every time someone made a covenantal commitment). People make covenants sometimes *to* other people and sometimes *with* other people. The former implies something more one-sided; the latter, something more mutual.

cry, cry out
In describing people's response when oppressed by others, the Old Testament often uses a word used to describe Abel's blood crying out to God, the outcry of the people of Sodom under their oppression, the Israelites' crying out in **Egypt**, and the outcry of people who are unfairly treated within Israel in later centuries. It denotes an urgent cry that presses God for **deliverance**, a cry that God can be relied on to hear even when people deserve the experience that is assailing them.

David's story
The introductions to a number of psalms refer to incidents in David's life, which is told in 1 and 2 Samuel. Looking at the account of these

incidents commonly produces two results. One can see points at which it is possible to imagine David praying at this point in the way the psalm does. But one can also see other elements in the psalm that do not fit. Psalm 51 provides a good example. The possible implication is that the references in the introductions do not imply that David actually prayed the psalm at this point but rather that it is illuminating to consider the psalm and the story alongside each other because there is this overlap.

decision, see authority

deliver, deliverer, deliverance
In the Old Testament, modern translations often use the words *save*, *savior*, and *salvation*, but these terms give a misleading impression. In Christian usage, these words commonly refer to our personal relationship with God and to the enjoyment of heaven. The Old Testament does speak of our personal relationship with God, but it does not use this group of words in that connection. They refer rather to God's practical intervention to get Israel or the individual out of a mess of some kind, such as false accusations by individuals within the community or invasion by enemies.

Egypt, Egyptians
Egypt was the major regional power to the south of **Canaan** and the country where Jacob's family found refuge, where they ended up as serfs, and from which the Israelites then needed to escape. In Moses' time Egypt controlled Canaan; in subsequent centuries it was sometimes a threat to Israel, sometimes a potential ally.

Ephraim
After the reign of David and Solomon, the nation of **Israel** split into two. Most of the twelve Israelite clans set up an independent state in the north, separate from **Judah** and Jerusalem and from the line of David. Because it was the bigger of the two states, politically it kept the name Israel, which is confusing because Israel is still the name of the people of God as a whole. In the prophets, it is sometimes difficult to tell whether "Israel" refers to the people of God or just to the northern

state. But sometimes the state is referred to by the name of Ephraim as one of its dominant clans, so I use this term to refer to that northern state to try to reduce the confusion.

exile

At the end of the seventh century **Babylon** became the major power in **Judah**'s world, but Judah was inclined to rebel against its authority. As part of a successful campaign to get Judah to submit properly to its authority, in 597 and in 587 BC the Babylonians transported many people from Jerusalem to Babylon. They made a special point of transporting people in leadership positions, such as members of the royal family and the court, priests, and prophets (Ezekiel was one of them). These people were thus compelled to live in Babylonia for the next fifty years or so. Through the same period, people back in Judah were also under Babylonian authority. Though they were not physically in exile, they were living in the exile as a period of time.

faithful, faithfulness

In English Bibles these Hebrew words (*saddiq*, *sedaqah*) are usually translated "righteous/righteousness," but they point to a particular slant on what we might mean by righteousness. They suggest doing the right thing by the people with whom one is in a relationship, the members of one's community. Thus they are nearer "faithful/faithfulness" than "righteous/righteousness."

faithless, faithlessness

Words for sin that suggests the opposite of **faithful/faithfulness**, they suggest an attitude to God and to other people that expresses a contempt for what right relationships deserve.

Greece

In 336 BC, Greek forces under Alexander the Great took control of the **Persian** Empire, but after Alexander's death in 333 his empire split up. The largest part, to the north and east of Palestine, was ruled by one of his generals, Seleucus, and his successors. **Judah** was under its control for much of the next two centuries, though it was at the extreme south-western border of this empire and sometimes came under the control of the Ptolemaic Empire in **Egypt** (ruled by successors of another of Alexander's officers).

inscription

The word *inscription* is included in the introductions to some psalms, possibly an indication that the psalm was inscribed in clay, like **Babylonian** psalms, possibly to give permanent expression to the prayer (see the story of Hezekiah's prayer in Isaiah 38).

instruction

Like *inscription* the word *instruction* is also sometimes included in the introduction to a psalm, perhaps indicating that the psalm is designated as a model for prayer or praise.

Israel

Originally, Israel was the new name God gave Abraham's grandson, Jacob. Jacob's twelve sons were then forefathers of the twelve clans that comprise the people Israel. In the time of Saul and David these twelve clans became more of a political entity. So Israel was both the people of God and a nation or state like other nations or states. After Solomon's day, this state split into two separate states, **Ephraim** and **Judah**. Because Ephraim was the larger by far, it often continued to be referred to as Israel. So if one is thinking of the people of God, Judah is part of Israel. If one is thinking politically, Judah is not part of Israel. Once Ephraim has gone out of existence, then for practical purposes Judah *is* Israel, as the people of God.

Jeduthun

One of the leaders of the music in temple worship appointed by David, according to 1 Chronicles 16 and 25; his descendants continued to have this role, and the psalms' references may be to these Jeduthites. "On Jeduthun" perhaps signifies a way of singing associated with him or them.

Judah

One of the twelve sons of Jacob, then the clan that traces its ancestry to him, then the dominant clan in the southern of the two states after the time of Solomon. Later, as a **Persian** province or colony, it was known as Yehud.

leader

This term in the introductions to Psalms likely denotes a worship leader (see the comment on Asaph in Psalm 50).

Master, Masters

The word *baal* is an ordinary Hebrew word for a master, lord, or owner, but the word is also used to describe a **Canaanite** god. It thus parallels the word *Lord* as used to describe Yahweh. Further, in effect, *Master* can be a proper name, like *Lord*. To make the difference clear, the Old Testament generally uses *Master* for a foreign god and *Lord* for the real God, Yahweh. Like other ancient peoples, the Canaanites acknowledged a number of gods, and strictly the Master was simply one of them, though he was one of the most prominent. In addition, a title such as "The Master of Peor" suggests that the Master was believed to be manifest and known in different ways and different places. The Old Testament uses the plural *Masters* to refer to Canaanite gods in general.

name

The name of someone stands for the person; thus God's name stands for God. The Old Testament talks of the temple as a place where God's name dwells. It's one of the ways it handles the paradox involved in speaking of the temple as a place where God lives. It knows this is a nonsense: how could a building contain the God who could not be contained by the entire heavens? Yet Israel knows that God does in some sense dwell in the temple. They know that they can talk with God when they go there; they are aware that they can talk with God anywhere, but there is a special guarantee of this in the temple. They know that they can make offerings there and that God is there to receive them. One way they try to square the circle in speaking of God's presence in the temple is to speak of God's name being present, because the name sums up the person. Uttering the name of someone brings home his or her reality; it's almost as if the person is there. When you say someone's name, there is a sense in which you conjure up the person. When people murmur "Jesus, Jesus" in their prayers, it brings home the reality of Jesus' presence. Likewise, when Israel proclaimed the name **Yahweh** in worship, it brought home the reality of Yahweh's presence.

parallelism

Lines in the psalms (and in much Old Testament poetry) are usually self-contained and divide into two halves, with about three important

233

words in each half. Parallelism refers to the way the second half of a line usually restates, augments, completes, clarifies, or contrasts with the first half. It wouldn't be surprising if this practice linked with people using the psalms antiphonally, perhaps with the leader saying the first half and the congregation responding with the second half.

peace

The Hebrew word *shalom* can suggest peace after there has been conflict, but it often points to a richer notion, to the idea of fullness of life. The KJV sometimes translates it "welfare," and modern translations use words such as "well-being" or "prosperity." It suggests that everything is going well for you.

Persia, Persians

The third Middle Eastern superpower. Under the leadership of Cyrus the Great, Persia took control of the **Babylonian** empire in 539 BC. Isaiah 40–55 sees Yahweh's hand in raising up Cyrus as the means of restoring **Judah** after the **exile**. Judah and surrounding peoples such as Samaria, Ammon, and Ashdod became Persian provinces or colonies. The Persians stayed in power for two centuries until defeated by **Greece**.

Philistia, Philistines

A people who came from across the Mediterranean to settle in **Canaan** at the same time as the Israelites were establishing themselves in Canaan, so that the two peoples formed an accidental pincer movement on the existent inhabitants of the country and became each other's rivals for control of the area.

Qorahites

One of the temple choirs, according to 2 Chronicles 20:19. The Qorahite psalms (e.g., Psalms 42–49) presumably formed part of their repertoire.

Rise

The Hebrew *selah* often comes at the end of lines in psalms, and sometimes in the middle. It means something like "rise," but we do not know what sense attaches to the word there. Were people to stand, or did the tune rise, or what? My favorite theory is that it was what David said when he broke a string—which fits the fact that we cannot see a pattern in the word's occurrence.

sackcloth
Sack does not suggest something uncomfortable; it refers to the humble cloth from which ordinary people's garments were made. It stands in contrast to impressive clothes or the kind of clothes in which important people would appear in public.

Sheol
The most frequent of the Hebrew names for the place where we go when we die. In the New Testament it is called Hades. It is not a place of punishment or suffering but simply a resting place for everyone, a kind of nonphysical analogue to the tomb as the resting place for our bodies.

Torah
The word *torah* means teaching, and in Psalms and elsewhere it can have that general meaning, but it is also the Hebrew word for the first five books of the Bible. It is then commonly translated as if it means Law, but this title gives a misleading impression. Genesis is nothing like law, and even Exodus to Deuteronomy are not legalistic books. The word "teaching" gives a clearer impression of the nature of the Torah.

Well-being, see peace

Yahweh
In most English Bibles, the word "LORD" often comes in all capitals, as sometimes does the word "GOD" in similar format. These represent the name of God, Yahweh. In later Old Testament times, Israelites stopped using the name Yahweh and started to refer to Yahweh as "the Lord." There may be two reasons. They wanted other people to recognize that Yahweh was the one true God, but this strange, foreign-sounding name could give the impression that Yahweh was just Israel's tribal god, and "the Lord" was a term anyone could recognize. In addition, they did not want to fall foul of the warning in the Ten Commandments about misusing Yahweh's name. Translations into other languages then followed

suit in substituting an expression such as "the Lord" for the name Yahweh. The downsides are that it obscures the fact that God wanted to be known by name, that often the text refers to Yahweh and not some other (so-called) god or lord, and that it gives the impression that God is much more "lordly" and patriarchal than actually God is. (The form "Jehovah" is not a real word but a mixture of the consonants of Yahweh and the vowels of the word for "Lord," to remind people in reading Scripture that they should say "the Lord," not the actual name.)

Yahweh Armies

This title for God usually appears in English Bibles as "the LORD of Hosts," but it is a more puzzling expression than that translation implies. The word for LORD is actually the name of God, **Yahweh**, and the word for Hosts is the regular Hebrew word for armies; it is the word that appears on the back of an Israeli military truck. So more literally the expression means "Yahweh [of] Armies," which is just as odd in Hebrew as "Goldingay of Armies" would be. In general terms its likely implication is clear: it suggests that Yahweh is the embodiment of or controller of all war-making power, in heaven or on earth.

Zion

An alternative name for Jerusalem. Whereas *Jerusalem* is a more political or geographical term, *Zion* is a more religious or theological one (ironically, given the modern meaning of *Zionist*). Zion stands for the place **Yahweh** dwells among his people and the place they meet with Yahweh.

CPSIA information can be obtained at www.ICGtesting.com
Printed in the USA
BVOW08s1041220813

329228BV00007B/123/P

9 780664 233839